Ruppert's Practical Classic Bangerpedia 1980 - 1990

James Ruppert

FORESIGHT PUBLICATIONS

ISBN: 978-1-9160522-9-1

RUPPERT'S BANGERPEDIA 1980 - 1990

BANGERDEDICATION

To everyone who drives on the
1980s motoring margins, or aspires to.

EXCUSES EXCUSES

The Publisher and Author cannot guarantee the pin point accuracy of every single stat in this Bangerpedia, so can't be responsible for any decisions the reader makes based on the information contained inside.
Any questions?
By all means email the Bangernomics organisation for friendly free advice.
james@bangernomics.com

WHAT'S IN THE BANGERPEDIA?

THANKS VERY MUCH

Dee & Olivia
(their names are above the title after all)

Cheers to the enthusiast Bangernomicists who donated their fine '80s Bangers for the covers.

Fiat 126 - Nick Deacon
Talbot Rancho - Clive Nelson
Volkswagen Santana - Neville Armstrong
Volkswagen Golf Mark 2 - R.D.Ruppert FRCS

Miami Vice Admiral David Milloy
for photographic assistance

All the writers and sub editors I have worked with over the years, on various publications including Parker's Price Guide, Used Car Buyer, Car Week, Car, Practical Classics, Classic Cars, Fast Ford, 911 and Porsche World, Golf Xtreme, Mini World, Mini Magazine, The Independent, The Times, The Evening Standard, Performance Car, Autocar, Free Car Mag, Bangernomics Mag and loads I've forgotten.

READ THIS FIRST

Let's start where we always do with the recurring mantra that becomes more true by the day: 'They don't sell Bangers anymore.' I believe that actually stopped in 2010 at the very latest. That's why we are going back in time with every Bangerpedia that arrives, simply because we can. I'll get to the whys and wherefores shortly.

More accurately we should now be saying that: 'They don't maintain Bangers anymore.' The new 'they' is not car manufacturers, but car owners. Once upon a time it was us that kept older cars, referred to as Bangers, going. Prolonging their useful lives by finding parts in scrapyards, teasing them through the MoT and generally doing the ethical and responsible thing by keeping them on the road. Fewer are bothering with Bangernomics, except that things are about to change. At the time of typing this there is a ban on the sale of brand new diesel and petrol vehicles from 2030. That means enthusiasts like us are starting to look backwards, so maybe Bangerpedias will come in handy.

Back in the day Bangers were cars that were fixable, a bit tired with the odd dent and not remotely exotic. In most cases these cars had become old, unfashionable and consequently cheap. The trouble is we are now looking at models that are many decades old. Read the subtitle, 'Practical Classics'. That's an admission that most cars, whatever they are, now qualify as historically significant. Maybe I called it 'PC' to be a bit snooty to a publication that has shamelessly pilfered and recycled for their own gain, Bangernomics, but I couldn't possibly comment. Anyway, a usable and ideally mostly fixable Banger from decades ago is a dream, but now almost an impossibility to source and buy. That seems to render all Bangerpedias from now on pretty pointless despite what I've said about 2030.

At least I know why you are here because you've very kindly paid for the book, but what on earth am I doing? Great question. I will admit that from now on Bangerpedias are of limited practical use. Any buying advice is going to be largely pointless. The vehicles covered will either be restored or scrap, unless we are lucky enough to find a decently preserved daily runner belonging to an old aged pensioner who could not afford, or even want anything more contemporary.

The truth is then, outside of a very lucky 'Barn' discovery the chances of actually finding some of the Bangers featured in these pages is now becoming rather difficult. I don't like to depress myself by going on the websites to find out, 'how many rotten clssics are left' but for the purposes of this introduction I had to in order to prove how futile compiling a Bangerpedia has become.

For instance and just a few pages ahead, I have rashly given The original Honda Jazz (identified as a 3GM) five Slogs. That means you should go out and buy one and revel in the brilliantness of it. Except that for most of its life there have been only a handful in circulation. Indeed, the numbers have been bolstered by personal imports from Japan. The Internet tells me there are three of them and 13 on SORN which may mean they are being saved, or quite likely 'slammed' for the purposes of automotive fashion.

Let's look at Talbot Tagoras, (one was on the cover briefly, before the Santana), none are on the road and just seven are on SORN. It is also incredible that the utterly unloved Alfa Romeo 6 exists. There are two of them on the road and five in lock ups, under a tarpaulin, on a drive, or heaven knows where. The thing is that enthusiasts will always go that extra mile to save an Alfa Romeo and quite right too.

So where am I going with all this? Dunno, you will have to wait, because what you have here is some time travelling to the 1980s. It is a place that I personally know well. The decade in which I bought and sold cars on a professional basis. This was also the era when I first started writing about what I could see going on around me in the motor trade for magazines and newspapers. I took the era for granted and did not appreciate what an amazing time it was to be in the market for a new car, with the knock on effect being that here was the first decent generation of Bangers to go and buy used in the late '80s and early '90s.

In many ways the 1980s is when vehicle quality

improved across the board. Every manufacturer had to raise their game and it was no longer as easy to get away with a sub standard product. Having said that there were still plenty of 1970s hangovers mainly built by British car companies. That's why I thought it was worth including some models that finished in 1980, whereas I'll leave some others for the '70s Bangerpedia.

I did feel compelled to include the outdated but still charming British Leyland offerings including the MGB GT and roadster which became a collector's item, whereas the Triumph Dolly, certainly didn't. What came next was interesting as the British car industry began to turn Japanese in order to survive. That's how we got the Triumph Acclaim and Rovers became Rondas.

Japan was now in the European market with a vengeance. It only took them a decade to build up to becoming full blown official operations that they owned and no longer relying on independent importers. 1984 is when Datsun became Nissan and Colt turned into Mitsubishi. I have tried to reflect that in the listings and I'm sure I've put Datsuns where Nissans are and quite possibly vice versa. The simple truth is that building Japanese cars in Britain was very big news, not least because it meant the supply of Bangers increased and were better built than ever.

There are some overlaps with the 1990s Bangerpedia. However, many of cars have been re-rated, the pictures may have changed and some of the opinions. As ever there are plenty of vehicles which will never be Bangers short of an economic and societal breakdown. That means Astons, Lamborghinis, Ferraris and the high end Porsches are always outside of the remit. I have sneaked a Bristol into the mix because dear reader that's what they became and for the reasons stated in the entry. Luxobarges always depreciate and become affordable once there is no company account to subsidies their running costs. I have tried to fix mistakes and a couple that should have been in the '90s Bangerpedia because production had not quite finished are certainly in these pages. If I have left anything out from the '80s then rest assured it certainly will be in the '70s edition which will probably take another two years to put together.

What we have here are all classic cars. Anything that survives from that era almost has to be, however marginal or disliked it is. These are not Bangers, whatever the market is like at the time of reading this, but these will be vehicles that have appreciated and worth more than the few quid we might have paid for some of these in the '90s and 2000s. That brings us to the question we now have to ask again,'So what's the point of this Bangerpedia?'

It's a sort of reference book. In an age when your phone can tell you something about every car from the '80s and deliver multiple images here is something a little more relaxed. I believe I'm identifying what were Bangers and could have bought ten years after they were made, for less than you would imagine. This isn't a searchable online database (although it is as a pdf), a physical book that you can refer to, argue with, even reminisce with and keep in the smallest room on the house.

Yet again, if I have missed anything, by all means let me know, I might care and possibly include it in future, with a credit to you. This does have my name and my angle on the whole encyclopedia format suggesting what is and isn't a Banger. If you don't like it go and write your own. There is a lot for anoraks to argue about, so be my guest.

Like previous Bangerpedias, this was a difficult bit of literature to assemble. I tried to use printed sources, you know books and magazines, as I have a lot of that real stuff on shelves. Car trade specification guides from Glass's and CAP. Also old books, magazines, brochures, those wonderful motor show guides and the odd website. Incredibly that did not necessarily unravel the mystery of what the literage of random '80s boot areas were with the seats up and folded. That is becoming more difficult hence the odd cu ft for relief.

The stats have little to do with what actual buyers need to know, because they won't be buying it as a Banger. These are now classic cars and the dimensions in the Bangerpedia might help when it comes to parking it in the garage. Otherwise and increasingly I will have to include some fairly random facts and figures to fill the space. As ever the Bangerpedia is really me just doing what I feel like when it is the early hours of the morning. It is my often sarcastic musings that keep me doing the Bangerpedia. This remains the only reference material for what counted as a Banger at the time based on what I know.

Bangerpedias remain imperfect and data expert Keith WR Jones is probably considering some sort of restraining order to stop me doing any more and he may well be correct.

When it comes to illustrations I have stuck with the black and white images with a touch of retro art effect which went down well enough to act as a recognition guide of sorts. The pictures are either sourced from my own extensive collection, or original manufacturer press pictures and brochures. I have not obsessed about getting rear views of estates, but some I have manually fiddled to make them look even more arty. There are a minimal amount of 'what to look fors'. We are now in ancient history and I will happily mention well known head gasket, bore wear and suspension nonsense, but really at this point everything will be rotten. There will be exceptions, but that's the bodywork on Reliants, Lotuses and anything stored in a dehumidified environment. Maybe one of those prized MGB Limited Editions.

I'm sure you have got the message that this is my Bangerpedia. My rules and mistakes. I hope the Practical Classics Bangerpedia proves to a bit useful rather than being a definitive guide to all the vehicles produced between 1980 to 1990. Mostly though I think it will just start arguments between classic car clever dicks. Provided they have bought a copy of the Bangerpedia I don't mind. I do feel the need to restate that I accept no responsibility for any decision you make based on the contents of this book.

Incidentally, there will be a 1970s Bangerpedia, provisionally titled, Crisis Classics, because of course that was a decade of trouble, when there was fuel rationing and everyone was on strike, mostly at British Leyland, Chrysler, Vauxhall and Ford. NEWS FLASH: No there won't be a '70s

Bangerpedia, just yet. That's because the worlds needs a Modern one to cope with the 2030 diesel/petrol ban deadline. So we've stopped the presses on the old and started the research on the 2010-2025 new/banger car time line. Just so you know, this publication will not contain electricity vehicles. Hybrids with caveats, but no battery appliances.

With all that in mind, always remember that buying any used car, whether or not you have a Bangerpedia stuffed up your jumper, is largely a matter of luck as well as judgement. That's why remind used car buyers to always beware of Slog the Dog. He is not to be relied upon when it comes to rating old cars either.

James Ruppert...

...Wrote this Bangerpedia at various points in 2024 although work began years earlier. '24 the end of an era for me in the mainstream motoring media, but still living it large with a couple of old cars in Bangerfolkshire, The Great Banger Isles. Below is a typical German heavy 1980s forecourt. It was Warwick Motors near Chiswick in West London. Great days and great cars. Most likely this is now the site of some badly designed, overpriced rabbit hutch flats.

WARWIC
E726 VK
E619 FLH

Bangerpedia Decoded

1980 - 1990 are the build years although sometimes there is a disparity between the on sale, or launch, production and registration years. Overall I have triangulated the data to arrive at the best possible beginning and end dates based on the available facts. Depending on models I have included some that were made up to 1990 and ignored some others, because of space and over tiredness, or I just thought, I'll cover those in the next Bangerpedia.

Engines: Engine sizes for petrol and a D means diesel. I have taken to when there is just the one or a couple of engines to listing the full cc **MPG**: Best to worst official combined figures **BHP**: From time to time I might have squeezed in the old fashioned brake horse power. **Gearbox:** Man/Auto where possible the number of ratios **Boot:** Litres for where relevant seats up and folded where known, sometimes cu/ft more amusement or when the conversion to litres seems all wrong. **Seats**: Number of, sometimes 2+2 when if it seems obvious, or not enough room this is deleted. **Doors:** Number of, unless it was so obvious, I've deleted for space. **Towing:** Maximum braked in kg **Top Speed**: Fastest and Slowest, not always the turbo-nutter one **0-60:** Best and worst in Seconds, it could actually be 0-62 because of kph element, but thought that the 60 is neater unless indicated otherwise. **Weight**: Kerb unladen in kgs ideally the lightest and heaviest in the model range. **Turning**: The circle the banger will turn in metres. **Price:** Just for one section (Yank Tanks) I have decided to include the price when put on sale. A nice idea for future Bangerpedias perhaps.

Then there is the rating system. This involves Slog the Bangernomic Dog who has been on this journey for some time. It used to be beware of the dog, but in the interests of clarity it has to be the more Slogs the better. Readers would associate it with a star system anyway.

Just the one Slog means you should definitely avoid. That seems obvious. This is probably a triple whammy of potential unreliability, compromised fixability and the overall expense of doing so. Actually very few one stars considering this is decades ago which might need revisiting in the future.

Two Slogs is a fairly questionable Banger. Quite likely to have an average reputation for not breaking down. It might have some added element of overall averageness, be it in the practicality, driving or repair departments. There are some surprising two stars, but actually that is being generous in some. Actually this is now the 1980s and some vehicle parts are becoming very hard to find.

Three Slogs is most Bangers. It averages out as being good value for money, easy to own, does what it originally said in the manufacturers brochure. This is the default rating. Every Banger starts with a three and the whole team work up or down from there.

Four Slogs is jolly good going for any Banger. If you've got any standards then this is the one to aim for, even though as we know buying a Banger is not a precise science. You end up with what you can afford or what is available. If it is a four star Banger then great. This will do a job with some style. Quite often I should have made it a five, but wasn't thinking straight. Overall it is 80s tastic.

Five Slogs is the Classic Banger Gold standard. These are going to be the real legends which are unarguably brilliant Bangers. Most of these are going to be Japanese, but they will have a genuine reputation for being very good indeed at being a Banger. Considering.

No Slogs? I think they all score at least one. I might have given one Banger a 6 Slog rating in the last one, but I think I have been pretty sensible this time.

Anyway, here they are. Bangers or more accurately Classics grouped together according to their dimensions and/or their claimed abilities and attributes. Plus a short introduction about what you are going to look at, so you can skip that and make your own mind up about that group of motors.

Cover stars at rest, thanks to Nick, Neville and Clive.

Mini Bangers - Town Centre AVs

The Mini was still there or thereabouts, despite the arrival of the Metro and rather more sophisticated offerings from the Far East.

Even so a basic mini City was effectively the obvious second/spare car for town duties. However, there were changes coming to the miniverse. Actually this was the point at which British Leyland/Rover went into mad marketing mode. Premium pricing the old thing, adding stripes and daft names to make the most of the nostalgia, finally making a profit of them.

Despite the hype, the Metro was no more special than many of the older Euro rivals. This was comfortable, but seemed to date very quickly. The Metro even became a proper supermini when more doors were added, but it never worked its way into the small car owner's heart like the original Issigonis one.

Fiat finally recovered their small car mojo (as the charmingly agricultural 126s continued) with the arrival of the fabulous Panda. In many ways this was the biggest leap forward for tots since the mini itself. Technically nothing special it was the design and execution, courtesy of Giugiaro that made it stand out from the rest. Adding four wheel drive only made it more useful and it remains all the SUV most civilians will ever need.

Japan always had Kei car culture, but officially it never made sense to bring over boat loads when there were the voluntary import restrictions in place. The Honda Jazz proved just how good these could be. The Colt Mirage was a sophisticated thing while the Suzuki SC was loadsa high revving fun.

By contrast. Most of the Euroboxes seemed just a trifle dull (that would be the Talbot Samba and related Pug 104), or outdated, like the mini and the Fiat 127. Classy efforts worked in small numbers, see further the Lancia Y10, or cheap and cheerful Zastavas.

The truth was that the small car market had to grow to survive. Mini cars made mini, if any profits, hence the mini marketing push. Things would change and get bigger.

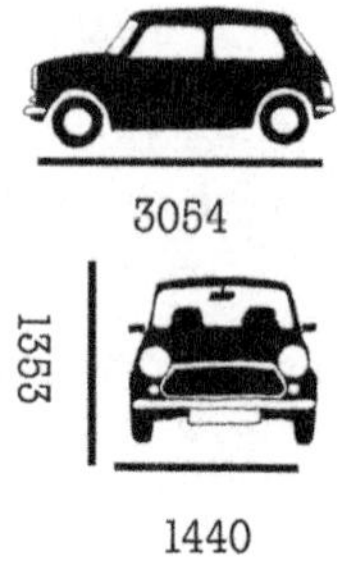

Austin Mini 1980 - 1990

Outclassed in City terms, but no one did practicality and parkability better. Curse of the special editions, but good used value and bonus of the 1098cc A series sometimes. Cheap, obviously rusty but easy to fix, blown head gaskets, collapsed suspension, rattly timing chain. '80s street furniture. **Engines:** 998 •1098 **MPG**: 34-37 **BHP**: 41-45 **MPH**: 75-82 **Turning**: 8.9 **Gearbox:** Man **Boot:** 120 **Seats**: 4

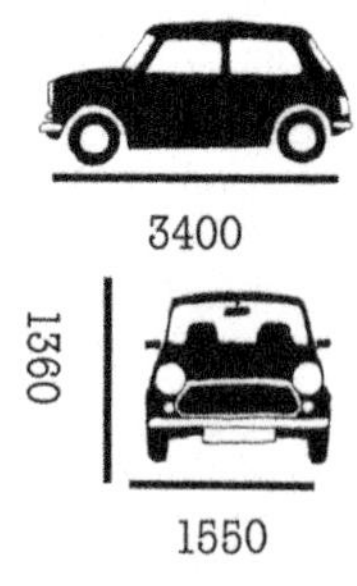

Austin Metro 3 Door 1980 - 1990

Hatchbacked mini and only marginally more convenient, just another shopping 'box. Until it needed fixing Hydragas delivered a great ride and excellent handling. Fancy Vanden Plas pointless except it had 72 instead of 63bhp along with the trimmings. Autoboxes common enough for OAP adopters. Rust and worn out A Series Plus. **Engines:** 998 •1275 **MPG**: 40.1-49.1 **BHP**: 43-58 **MPH**: 80-90 **Turning**: 10.71 **Gearbox:** Man/auto **Boot:** 230/960 **Seats**: 4

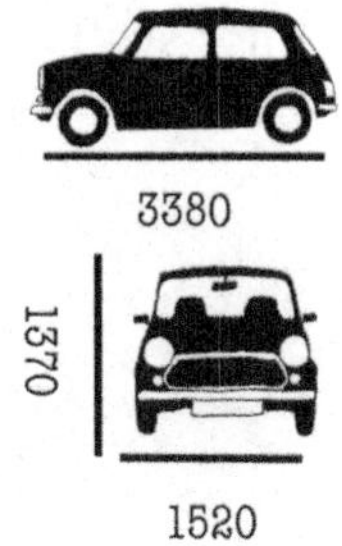

Citroen LNA 1983 - 1985

Scratch the surface, behind the extra bits of plastic trim is a Pug 104 +Talbot Samba, otherwise a cute bob tailed shopper with little to go wrong. Air cooled basic at home (Snail engine) in the GB had the 1.1 T series engine, but it never really caught on in UK when the Visa was still around. Spiritually a 2CV with less doors. **Engine:** 1124cc

MPG: 50.4 **BHP**: 50 **Gearbox:** Man **Boot:** 214 **Seats**: 4

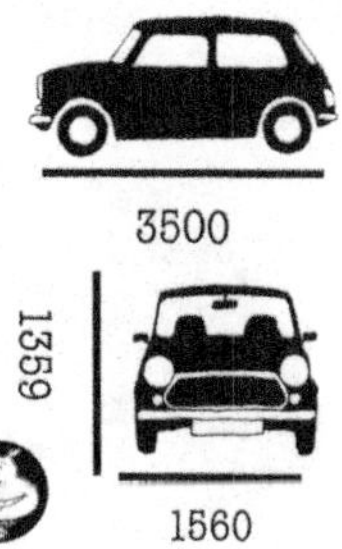

Citroen AX 3 Door 1987 - 1997

3 Door is the very definition of a lightweight hatch, folded cardboard construction means some spectacular mpg figures. Endless special editions, Pug 106 related, but better use of space, comfortable, rear legroom marginal. Small petrols get smoky and oil leaky with age. Easily dented and damaged. 1.4 very nippy and easy enough to look after.

Engines: 1.0 • 1.1 • 1.3 • 1.4 • 1.4D **MPG**: 41.2

Turning: 10.2m **Gearbox:** Man **Boot:** 273/668 **Seats**: 4

Fiat 126 1977 - 1987

Proper ultra basic Italian peasant propulsion. Big in the home market and in the UK a spare shopper with a terrible ride and a raucous soundtrack. That didn't matter when it delivered maximum miles to the gallon. Rust wiped out most before the air cooled bucket of bolts would give up. Lots of oil leaks and gearbox not the strongest. Deserved cover star.

Engine: 594/652cc **MPG**: 47 **BHP**: 24 **Turning**: 9.3m
Gearbox: 4spd **Boot:** 110 **Seats**: 4 **Doors:** 3

Fiat 126 BIS 1987 - 1992

Bigger than a mini? Frantically noisy 2 cylinder with a rock hard ride and barely enough room for two. Shoddily Polski put together and not a lot going for it but quirky charm. Mostly a rust bucket these days, not much electrical to go wrong, engine has a finite life, so big miles without a rebuild spell trouble. Lots of oil leaks and gearbox not the strongest.

Engine: 704 **MPG**: 50.4 **BHP**: 26 **Turning**: 9.3m
Gearbox: 4spd **Boot:** 110 **Seats**: 4 **Doors:** 3

Fiat Panda 1980 - 2002

Brilliant Basic Box delivered in the City. Mark 2 in 1986 with Lancia Y10 suspension & overhead cam FIRE engines. Charming, but often in a badly finished, falling apart sort of way. 1000 is pick of the engine bunch, CVT might not work anymore and the 4×4 is rare and elsewhere in this Bangerpedia. Rust, gear selection, bore wear blue smoke.
Engines: 769•903•999cc **MPG**: 40.9-48.6 **Gearbox:** 4-5spd **Turning:** 9.2 **Boot:** 269 **Seats**: 4 **Doors:** 3

Fiat 127 1971 - 1983

Still going strong into the '80s with fashionably big headlamps and added plastic trim. One of the very best of the original Euroboxes now showing its age upgrading from pushrod to overhead cam engines improved matters and it was always lots of fun to drive, especially GT. Rust, gear selection, bore wear blue smoke are most of the possible killers. **Engines:** 903• 1049• 1301 **BHP**: 40-75 **MPG**:33.6 **Gearbox:** 4/5 spd **MPH**: 78-91 **Boot:** 360 **Seats**: 4 **Doors:** 3

Lancia Y10 1985 - 1991

Upmarket Italian box which was reassuringly quirky. The teeny Turbo was a hoot, but many buyers went for the 1.05 litre Touring then the 999cc FIRE. Most spelt trouble of course, but there were special editions, extra sound deadening and suspension upgrades in '89. CVT Selectronic worth avoiding. '90 Series 2 available in UK for 5 minutes.
Engines: 1.0 • 1.05 • 1.1 • 1.3 **MPG**: 34 - 52 **Gearbox:** 5spd
Turning: 9.8 **Weight:** 720 **Boot:** 195 **Seats**: 4 **Doors:** 3

Honda Jazz 1984 - 1985

A massive foot longer than a mini, Austin Rover already had the Japanese City name, hence the Jazz. Incredible build quality and an amazing three valve per cylinder, stratified charge combustion chambers caused unfashionably low emissions. Import restrictions meant more money in flogging Civics. Short-lived but best mini of the decade.
Engines: 1231cc **MPG**: 43.5 **MPH**: 91.5 **Gearbox:** 5spd
Boot: 205 **Weight:** 635-735 **Seats**: 5 **Doors:** 3

Mazda 121 1988 - 1991

One of the car makers realising that a high roofline boosted space inside a stumpy City car shape. Incredibly there was a Suntop version with an electric sunroof. A couple of engines and a five speed gearbox so it was a lively thing that could do the business out of the City. Mazda build quality always good news, lasted as long as the bodywork did.

Engines: 1139 • 1324cc **BHP**: 65 **MPG**:42 **Gearbox:** 5spd **Boot:**190 **Weight:** 755 **Seats**: 4 **Doors:** 3

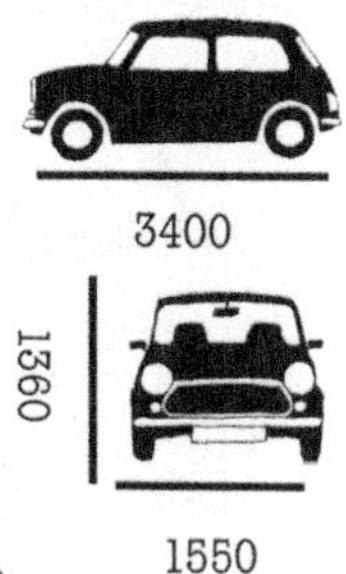

MG Metro 1982 - 1990

An odd way to bring back a dead badge, but there was form for this. Sticking the 1275cc A Plus in tuned form, up to 72bhp, like the Vanden Plas. It did have red seatbelts unlike the VDP, alloy wheels and decals down the flanks. Steel wheels from '87. Hydragas leaks, head gasket grief.

Engines: 1275cc **BHP**: 72 **MPH**: 100 **MPG**: 42 **0-60:** 12.2 **Gearbox:** 4spd **Boot:** 230/960 **Seats**: 4 **Doors:** 3

Colt Mirage 1978 - 1984

It's a Mitsubishi but badged Colt over here. State of the art Euro box, but from Japan and a milestone for Mitzi being their first front driver. Two engines and the bigger 1.4 had a unique 8-speed two stick, speed or economy option. Makes a Metro seem Prehistoric, well built and unlikely to break down. Just another rot victim.

Engines: 1244 • 1410cc **MPH**: 92 **MPG**: 33
Gearbox: 8spd/auto **Boot:** n/a **Turning**: 9.8 **Seats**: 4

Peugeot 104 Z 1974 - 1988

Is it a coupe' (called that in the early years), or a two door non-hatch? It's still a mini so let's stick with that. That 20cm off the wheelbase certainly made it more of a City car. Uprated interior and distinctive headlamps, 'hot' ZS with 66 bhp 1.1. Premium priced over the years and slight upgrades as it got the Samba dashboard in 1983.

Engines: 1124 • 1360cc **MPG**:36 **MPH**: 101 **Gearbox:** 4spd
Boot: 155 **Turning:** 9.4 **Seats**: 4 **Doors:** 2

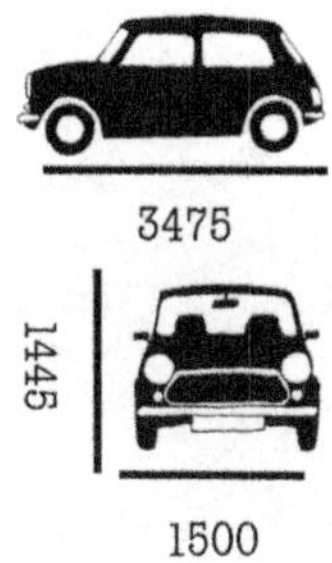

SEAT Marbella 1988 - 1995

Spanish Panda, just a very old fashioned holiday rental. Crude with back to basics appeal, loadsa special eds, GLX had rear wash/wipe and cloth trim, so utter luxury. Shabby paint, sun bleached plastic, oil leaks, snapped clutch cable, worn suspension, wheel bearings. Rough and neglected because it isn't a Fiat. **Engines:** 843 • 903 **Turning:**9.6 **MPG**: 42-44 **MPH**: 78-83 **Gearbox:** Man **Boot:** 269 **Seats**: 4

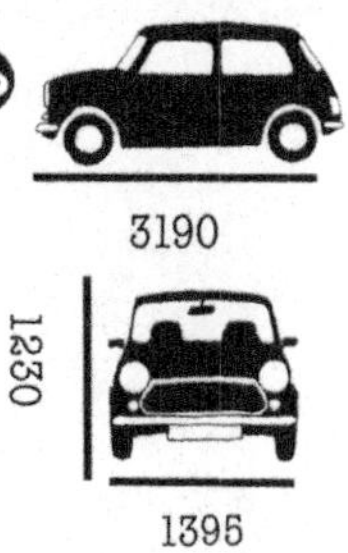

Suzuki SC100 1979 - 1982

Japanese mini, similar size but engine at the other end. Weighed just 630kg and pushed along by an eager little engine driving the rear wheels.. It has been compared to a titchy 911 with handling that can be just as exciting. GX model only in UK, Europe got a slightly different Cervo version. 1980 new switchgear. **Engines:** 970cc **BHP**: 49 **Turning: MPG**: 41.9 **MPH**: 76 **Gearbox:** Man **Boot:** n/a **Doors:** 2 **Seats**: 4

Talbot Samba 1982 - 1986

Three door Peugeot 104, but a tad longer so there is more room in the back. No chrome trim, but a decent big engine and five speed gearbox like the Z coupe was most fun. Otherwise same range of units from Europe and very useful hatchback door. Deserved to do much better, but it died along with the Talbot badge.

Engines: 954/1124/1360cc **Turning:**9.8 **MPG**: 45 **MPH**: 91
Gearbox: Man 4-5spd **Boot:** 236/950 **Seats**: 4

Volvo 66 1975 - 1980

Daf 66 becomes the Volvo 66, a two door saloon and also smallish estate/protohatch, sadly the coupe died. Still had Renault power and that fantastic rubber band related (constantly variable) Variomatic transmission to make driving simple and slightly boring. Volvo patent big safe rubber bumpers and matt black trim for this half brick..

Engines: 1108/1289cc **Turning:** n/a **MPG:**35 **MPH:** 81
Gearbox: CVT auto **Boot:** 290 **Doors:** 2/3 **Seats:** 4

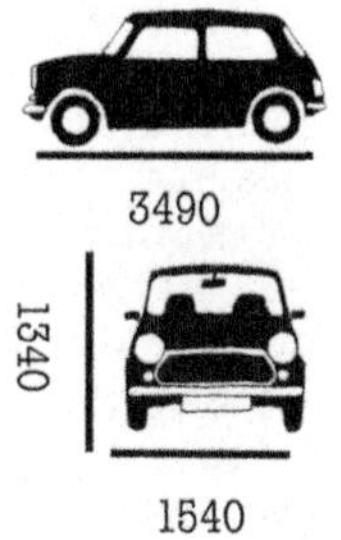

Zastava Yugo 45 •55 •65 1983 - 1991

A fairly grim and built to a price sort of thing when brand new. Back of the lot used orphan, or a one private owner example rotting in the drive. Neglected and a problem to get parts for, retro Eastern Bloc cool now, otherwise marginal with the few survivors having everything wrong with them.

Engines: 903 • 1.3 **BHP**: 45•65 **MPG**: 38 - 45

Gearbox: 4spd **Weight:** 750 **Boot:** 170/750 **Seats**: 4

Super Banger Shoppers - Running Errands

Welcome to the golden age of the supermini. This is when they matured, some grew up and even grew extra doors and became such a vital part of everyone's motoring lives eventually as Bangers.

It was the French and Italians who started all the hatchery and in the '80s they kept on going. The Renault 5 was always perfectly formed so there wasn't much that needed updating, but the Super Cinque when it arrived was what everyone needed. Just as significant and certainly more fun to drive was the Peugeot 205. Not only the GTi, as they were all light and practical models.

Fiat really got their act together with the Uno which was a remarkably attractive, practical and fun to drive model. Very much an Italian version of the Golf in a more stylish package. A certain amount of flimsiness, but it looked so good and you could pack it full of people and shopping.

When it came to more doors it gave the Metro more of an angle in the small family market. For the Fiesta it came very late indeed, but the three door was always the bread and butter model, then updated a few times it just got better, a more solid performer which wouldn't let buyers down.

Japan was now supplying some incredibly impressive hatchback cars, many specifically tuned to European tastes. The Nissan Micra is a case in point which went on to become a driving school fixture. The Toyota was a similar unbreakable tot, which would last forever. Arguably the most sophisticated and comfy of the lot was the Honda Civic which for me has had the highest of positive used car buyer feedback. Plus there was the high tech Subaru Justy with a useful ingredient: four wheel drive, which was to become a defining feature of so many '80s models.

Apologies for some real British oddities which didn't necessarily have the full compliment of wheels. It is a bit of stretch to call any Reliant a supermini, but why not? The long forgotten Kitten might work for some, but this marque was still an intrinsic part of car culture in this country. Never bought by fools to replace their horses...

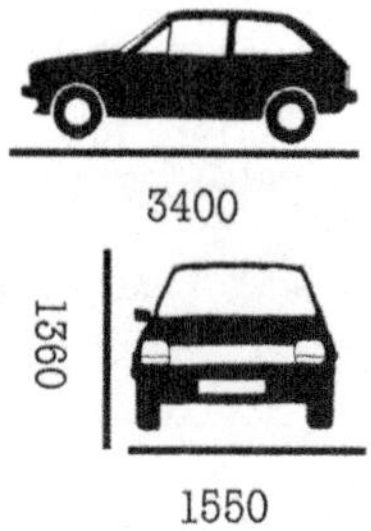

Austin Metro 1985 - 1990

Finally gets the five doors it needed to be competitive and replace the old 1100/1300. Wider suspension subframes, along with a new dashboard design. Lost Austin Badge in 1987, but it didn't say Rover either. Plenty of issues to keep you busy beyond oil leaks, shot suspension and engine unreliability. Not a very super mini at the time.

Engines: 998/1275cc **MPG**: 39-42 **Gearbox:** 4spd/3spd Auto **Boot:** 230/960 **MPH:** 93 **Turning**: 9.8 **Doors:** 3/5

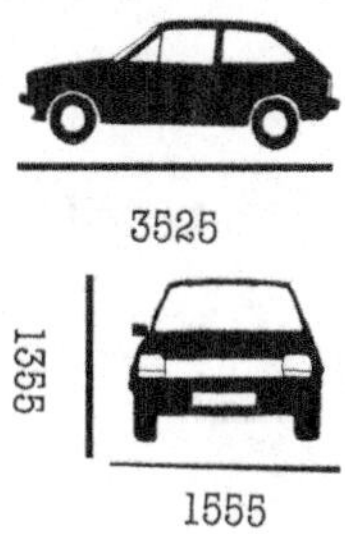

Citroen AX 1987 - 1997

Extra doors boosted practicality, still ultra economical. Endless special editions, Pug 106 related, but slightly better use of space, comfortable enough in front, rear legroom marginal. Small petrols get smoky and oil leaky with age. Easily dented and damaged. 1.4 very nippy, overall easy enough to look after.

Engines: 1.0 • 1.3 • 1.4 • 1.4D **MPG**: 45 **Gearbox:** 4-5spd **Boot:** 273/1170 **Turning**: 9.2 **Doors:** 5 **Weight:** 805

Citroen Visa 1979 - 1989

It looked like a weird old Citroen alright, hence the cylinder selector for wipers and lights, but now getting Pug powerplants to keep them moving economically forwards and there was a colossal amount of engines to choose from. Visa II in 1981 cleaned up the nose and rear end. Diesel 1769cc from 1984. Engines will smoke and rattle.

Engines: 652 •952•1.2• 1.4•1.6•1.8D **MPG**: 33-42
Gearbox: Man **Boot:** 300 **Seats**: 5 **Turning**: 9.5

Daihatsu Domino 1983 - 1989

This was a properly tiny thing with half a normal engine, a two cylinder 617cc thing which got an extra pot and became 846cc with the added bonus of a five speed gearbox. Quite fun to drive, but very tight inside if there were more than a couple of bodies. Engines, despite screaming in over revved pain, very difficult to kill.

Engines: 617 •846cc **MPG**: 44-52 **Gearbox:** 4-5spd
Boot: n/a **Seats**: 4 **Turning**: n/a **Doors:** 3/5

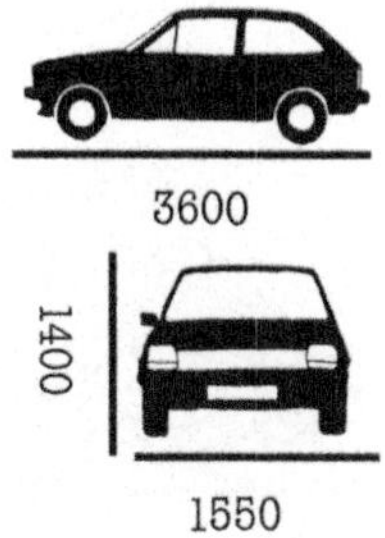

Daihatsu Charade 1981 - 1987

Satisfyingly complicated overhead camshaft engine available as a petrol and diesel, highly unusual at the time, plus there was a turbo with impressive 64 and 46bhp outputs. GTi gets to over 103mph, so quite a lot of talents. Combined with excellent build quality and engineering, one of the best shoppers of that era.

Engines: 993 • 993D **MPG**: 40-45 **Gearbox:** 4 spd **Boot:** 128 **Seats**: 4 **Turning**:9.2 **Doors:** 3/5 **Weight:** 685

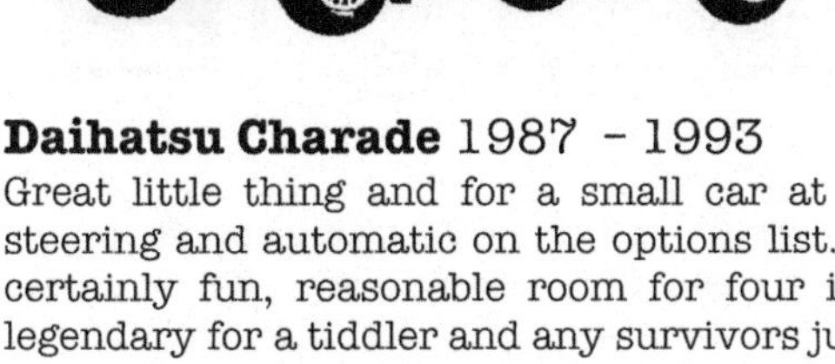

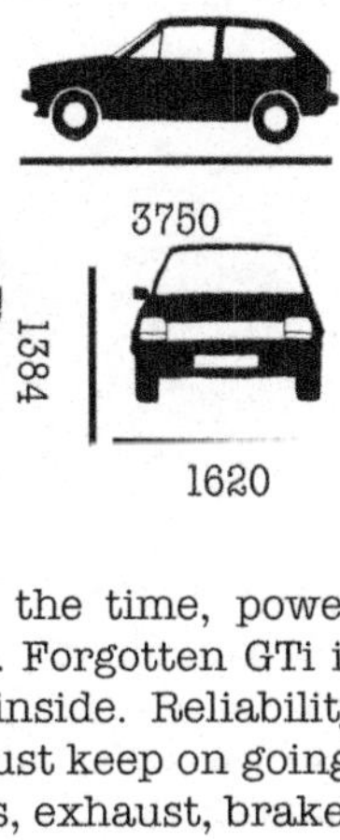

Daihatsu Charade 1987 - 1993

Great little thing and for a small car at the time, power steering and automatic on the options list. Forgotten GTi is certainly fun, reasonable room for four inside. Reliability legendary for a tiddler and any survivors just keep on going. Parts will always be the issue and it is tyres, exhaust, brakes and suspension that are worn out.

Engines: 1.0 • 1.3 **MPG**: 47.9-58.9 **Gearbox:** 5spd/2spd Auto **Boot:** 152/384 **Seats**: 4 **Doors:** 5 **Weight:** 720

Fiat Uno 1983 - 1995

Wonderfully exuberant small family hatch that is great to drive and massively practical. Superb inside, good seats and very easy to live with excellent economy from the tiny engines inc diesel. There always were ownership issues, oil leaks, clattery tappets, gearbox bearings, short clutch life, CVT pricey to fix, weak electricals and leaky driveshafts.

Engines: 903 • 999 • 1.1 • 1.2 • 1.3 • 1.7d **BHP:** 45-118
MPG: 36-51 **Gearbox:** Man/CVT **Boot:** 248/968 **Doors:** 3/5

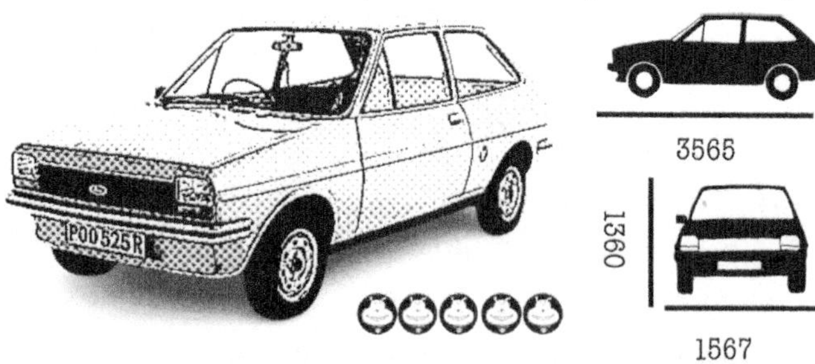

Ford Fiesta 1976 - 1983

Fiesta enters the '80s as one of the best superminis for the people. Pretty, practical and reliable, with three engine options and plenty of special editions like the Quartz, Carnival and Finesse. Noisy transmission bearings, worn radius arm bearings, carburettors probably replaced by now. Bodged clutch replacements and smoking rattly engines.

Engines: 1.0 • 1.2 • 1.3 **BHP:** 44-69 **MPG**: 29-47
Gearbox: 4spd **Turning**: 9.3 **Boot:** 255/1000 **Seats**: 4

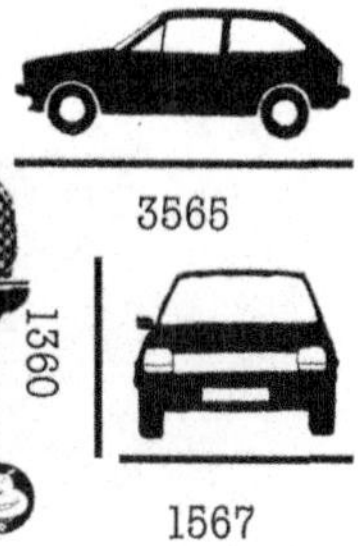

Ford Fiesta 1983 - 1989

Fiesta facelift meant a tidied-up interior, a new dashboard and a 1.6 litre diesel engine. A five-speed manual gearbox, high-security Chubb locks and an option for an automatic gearbox were all now on the useful extras list. From 1986 new CVH 1.3 and 1.4 units. Rare CVT on the 1.1. Wear and tear especially the small engines puffing blue smoke.
Engines: 1.0 • 1.1 • 1.3 • 1.4 • 1.6D **MPG**: 36-50
Gearbox: Man/Auto **Turning**: 9.3/9.8 **Boot:** 311/1093

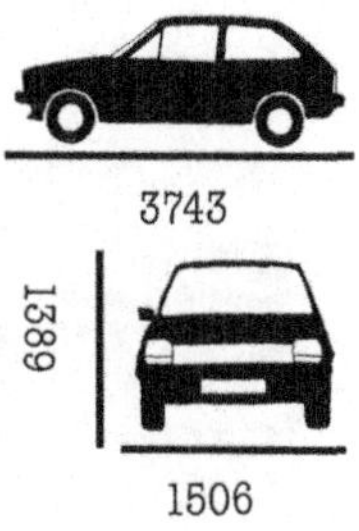

Ford Fiesta 1989 - 1997

Fiesta grows up with a five door version. Bigger than before and became available with ABS. Despite all those fancy Quartz special editions and well equipped Ghias this remains one of the toughest and best superminis ever. Still has oil leaks, heads gaskets, coolant leaks, shot gearbox mountings and clutch adjusters. Classic lived on alongside Mk 4.
Engines: 1.0 • 1.1 • 1.3 • 1.4 • 1.6 1.8D **BHP:** 45-110
MPG: 38.7-53.3 **Gearbox:** Man/Auto **Boot:** 311/1093

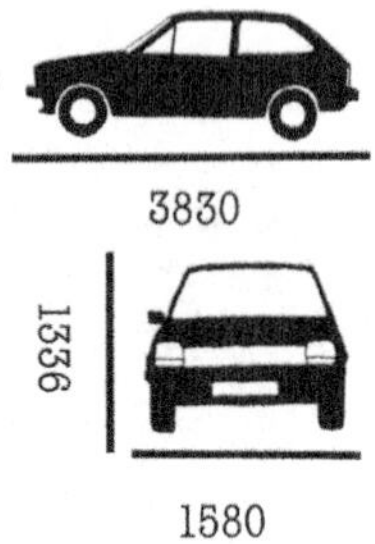

Honda Civic 1980 - 1983

Second Generation Civic, bigger than before but only the three door for the UK. Decent overhead cam 1.3 and 1.5 engines with useful 5 speed gearbox and a three speed auto. The Ballade saloon available as a Triumph Acclaim. Comfortable and quite sophisticated compared to all the other shoppers. Ultra durable mechanicals.

Engines: 1.4 • 1.5 **BHP**: 59-64 **MPG**: 34-47 **Turning**: 9.6
Gearbox: Man/Auto **Boot:** 188 **Seats**: 4 **Doors:** 3

Honda Civic 1983 - 1987

Still just a hatch and now in the mini Aerodeck era, but plus a five door model. From 1984 low emission 12 valve engines. Plus added sportiness with the 100bhp GT here to do the shopping faster from 1985. Superb mechanicals would help these run on for decades. Owners adored them quite rightly.

Engines: 1.4 • 1.5 **BHP**:75-110 **MPG**:32-35 **Turning**:10.4
Gearbox: Man/Auto **Boot:** 187 **Seats**: 4 **Doors:** 3/5

Honda Civic 1987 - 1991

Great cars, arguably best looking of the Aerodeck era. Which did come as four wheel drive and estates, but not always available in the UK. 16 valve over head cam engines, double cams on the 1.6. Mechanicals will go on forever, just more difficult and expensive to fix than an Escort. Nothing looks cooler or goes better for longer. Proper supermini legend.

Engines: 1.3 • 1.6 **MPG**: 38.2-42.8 **Gearbox:** 5spd
Weight: 835-1025 **Boot:** 250 **Seats**: 4 **Doors:** 3/5

Mitsubishi Colt 1983 - 1988

Using the Lancer saloon as a basis with new engines and a useful 5spd gearbox. In 1986 slight restyle with a new interior plus a diesel engine that no one was very bothered about. Solid and sensible just not very stylish, but most importantly reliable. Rust and neglect, brakes and exhaust get it before engine does.

Engines: 1.2 • 1.5 • 1.8D **MPG**: 33.9-47.1 **Gearbox:** 5spd
Boot: 315 **Turning:** 10.3 **Seats**: 4 **Doors:** 3/5

Mitsubishi Colt 1988 - 1992

Refined version of the previous model. In '92 it was refined and restyled. There's a load of engines from the shopping 1.3, mid range 1.5 and hot-ish 1.6 and GTi 1.8. Blimey there were updates every five minutes. There was a clever automatic gearbox. The only model you remember is the sporty Mirage. Rust and neglect, brakes and exhaust.

Engines: 1.3 • 1.6 **BHP:** 69-123 **MPG**: 39.2-42.8
Gearbox: 5spd/3spd Auto **Boot:** 240/830 **Seats**: 4 **Doors:** 3

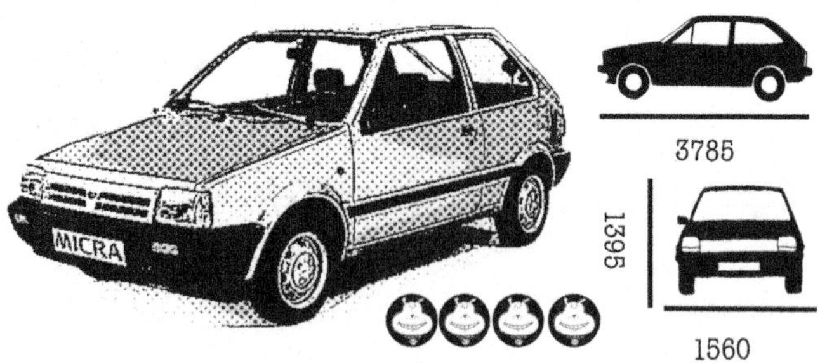

Datsun/Nissan Micra 1982 - 1992

Rumour is that this is a folded paper ITAL design like a Japanese Polo and just as good. Badged March (Japan) and other fancy things, but in the UK it was the best of the new minis and taught a generation to drive. Rattly timing chains. Rusty bodywork and suspension obviously. Mass airflow sensors and starting issues. Mostly extinct.

Engines: 1.0 • 1.2 **MPG**: 38.5-47.5 **BHP**: 50-60 **Turning:** 9.2
Gearbox: 4-5spd **Boot:** 203 **Seats**: 5 **Doors:** 3/5

Peugeot 205 1983 - 1996

One of those supermini legends, very light, even flimsy at times, but practical, economic and easy to get along with. 1988 TU petrols and new dashboard only model revisions of note. Small petrol and big diesels are the ones to last a life time. Well known for oil leaks, smokey engines, noisy cams and blowing head gaskets. Still great to drive.

Engines: 1.1 • 1.4 • 1.8D **MPG**: 35.7-57.9 **Gearbox:** 4-5spd **Boot:** 216/1200 **Turning:** 11 **Seats**: 4 **Doors:** 3/5

Reliant Rialto 1981 - 1998

Replaced the Robin for a few years in order to put some distance between the recalled and troublesome old model and it came as a saloon, estate and panel van. Sat on a galvanised chassis. Styling by International Automotive Design with headlights from the Austin Metro. Some interesting '80s incarnations like the SE.

Engines: 848cc **Speed**: 80 **0-62:** 16.0 **MPG**: 43.6 **Weight**: 436 **Gearbox:** Man 4 speed **Payload:** 344kg

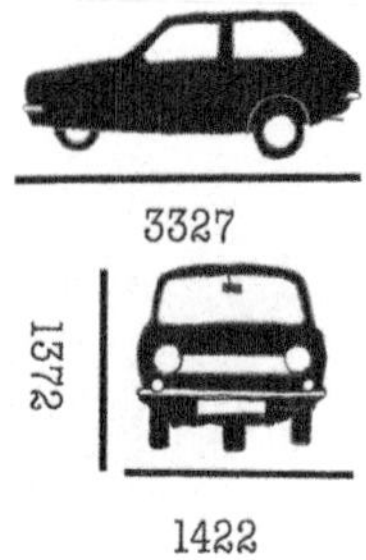

Reliant Robin 1973 - 1982

Replaced the Regal and the opening rear window was a glass hatch that allowed access to the useful boot. Came with a bigger 850cc engine and SU carburettors from 1975. Safer than early three wheel efforts as it actually has an anti-roll bar. Available as a Standard, Super, Estate and Van.

Engines: 848cc **Speed**: 78 **0-60:** 13.9 **MPG**: 43.6
Weight: 450 **Gearbox:** Man **Boot:** 30 cu feet

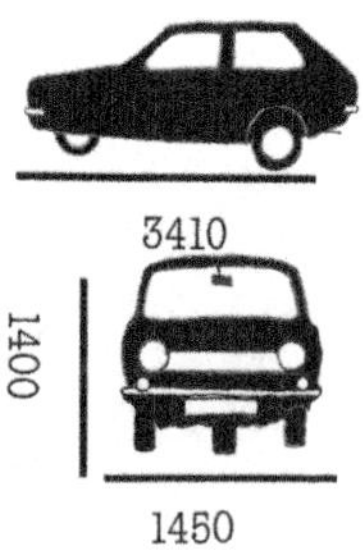

Reliant Robin 1989 - 1999

Return of the Robin II with a new fiberglass body attached to a galvanised chassis, 'cool' single central windscreen wiper and a rather useful rear hatchback. Distinguished by its Fiesta frontage. There was a final 50 of these with a commemorative plaque on the dash. Basically for winter resting motorcyclists, change my mind...

Engines: 848cc **Speed**: 78 **0-60:** 13.9 **MPG**: 43.6
Weight: 450 **Gearbox:** 4spd **Boot:** 30 cu feet

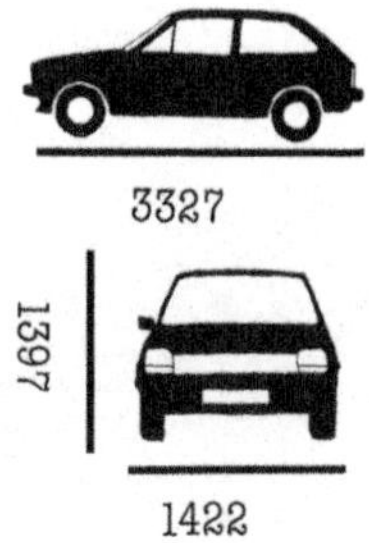

Reliant Kitten 1975 - 1982

A Robin with a very useful extra wheel. Same 848cc engine, otherwise identical from the rear with side opening door and wash/wipe. Longer gearstick as engine further forward. Amazing turning circle of rack and pinion steering was 25 feet in old money. Available as a van from 1977 and estate, from 1975 too. More comfy/sharper DL model.

Engine: 848cc **Speed**: 80 **MPG**: 60 **Boot:** 43 cu feet van

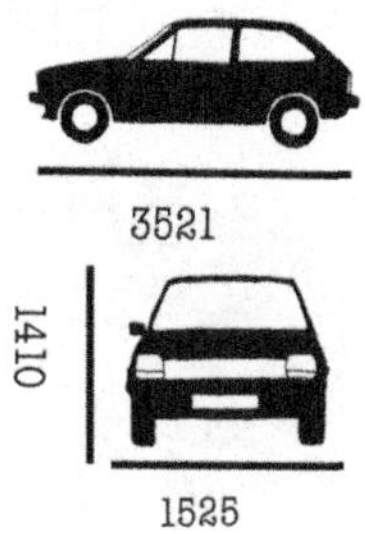

Renault 5 1972 - 1984

Well established and barely needed changing as Europe's best little box entered the '80s with automatic gearbox and a wide range of trim levels with the TL and GTL being the favourites, whilst the basic ones stayed in France. Great to drive and easy to own head gaskets, gearbox bearings, oil leaks, as well as average build quality, then called rusty...

Engines: 800 • 850 • 1.0 • 1.1 • 1.3 • 1.4 **MPG**: 47

Turning: 9.75 **Gearbox:** 4-5spd/3spd Auto **Boot:** 270/900

Renault 5 1984 - 1996

The Super Cinq saw the engines becoming transverse like all the other boxes and some bigger ones being fitted. Inside a big hooded dashboard and outside the styling was smoothed off. Better as a budget buy and the 1.4 best all rounder. Build average, electrics, head gaskets, gearbox bearings, oil leaks and like everything from this era, rust.

Engines: 1.0 • 1.1 • 1.3 • 1.4 • 1.7 • 1.6D **MPG**: 41-51.6
Turning: 10.25 **BHP**: 47-90 **Boot:** 270/900 **Doors:** 3/5

SEAT Ibiza 1985 - 1992

Sharp '80s styling which was inevitably by ITAL Design, the Porsche involvement was real, but mostly marketing, despite nice handling and the Fiat 903cc unit barely alive. Revised in '89. Looks good, otherwise average supermini with a sluggish diesel and the mid range 1.2 probably the best. Oil leaks, worn front suspension and beaten panels.

Engines: 903 • 1.2 • 1.5 • 1.7D **MPG**: 39.8- 42 **Gearbox:** 5spd
Boot: 320 **Weight**: 900 **Turning**: 10.1 **Seats**: 5 **Doors:** 3/5

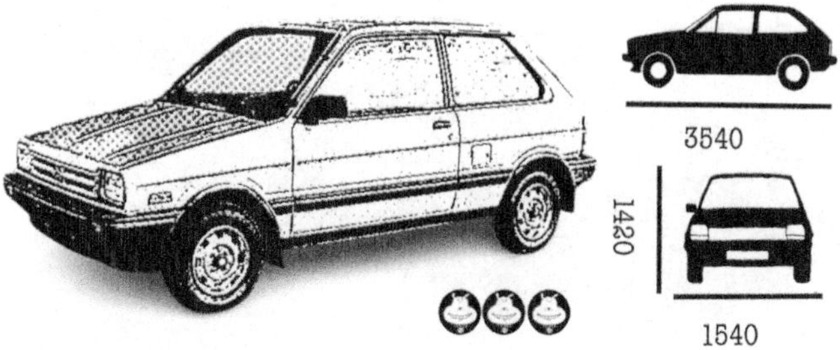

Subaru Justy 1986 - 1989

Proper '80s oddity that had a purpose in Japan and was just a costly micro 4×4 that no one knew they needed. Pushed along by a frantic three cylinder and a reasonably complicated electronic stepless automatic transmission that made a Range Rover seem ancient. Usually run into the ground when brakes and suspension need fixing.

Engines: 1189cc **MPG**: 34.8 **Gearbox:** 5spd/Auto
Boot: 158/1000 **MPH**: 96 **Seats**: 4 **Doors:** 3/5

Subaru Justy 1989 - 1996

More reliable than a contemporary Range Rover on a damp Wednesday night. Certainly part time 4×4 and stepless automatic transmission blew buyers minds. Three cylinder makes a racket, decent amount of room inside, who knows the intended target market. Cost a lot new, when used it is brakes and suspension which failed first.

Engines: 997 • 1.2 **MPG**: 39.8 **Gearbox:** 5spd/3spd Auto
Boot: 198 **Weight**: 750 **Doors:** 3/5

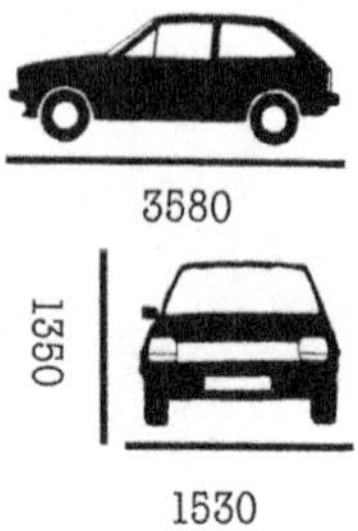

Suzuki Swift SA310 1984 - 1986

The original Swift supermini which had a distinctive three cylinder thrum, but the 5 speed gearbox helped even out the revs. There was a quintessential '80s specification GL which had a groovy digital dashboard. Lost the washing machine model number for the Swift badge after a year. Cracked cylinder heads could also bring it to a halt.
Engine: 993cc **MPH:** 85 **BHP**: 50 **MPG**: 49 **Gearbox:** 5spd **Weight:** 675 **Boot:** 250 **Doors:** 3

Suzuki Swift 1985 - 1991

Proper back to basics Japanese boxes with nothing going for them apart from reliability and fuel economy. What more do you want? Split fold rear seats standard. 1.0 and 1.3 engines plus a fun filled GTi. Running costs are reasonable enough. So simply wear and tear and how many have survived abuse/neglect? **Engines:** 1.0 • 1.3 **BHP:**50-101 **MPG**: 51.4 **Gearbox:** 5spd **Boot:** 249/579

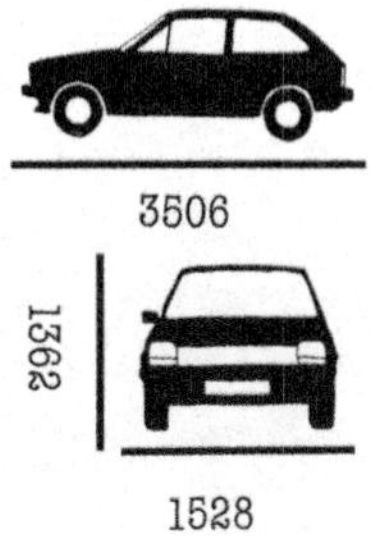

Talbot Sunbeam 1977 - 1981

Previously a Chrysler. Here is what happens when you take three inches out of the old Avenger, combine that with engines out of that saloon and an Imp unit for 928cc. The result was an excellent Eurobox with a glass tailgate that struck a chord with buyers who can drag their shopping over the loading lip. 1981 new front end. Avoid Imp engines.

Engines: 928cc • 1.3 • 1.6 **MPH**: 95 **MPG**: 37 **Gearbox:** 4spd
Boot: 420 **Doors:** 3

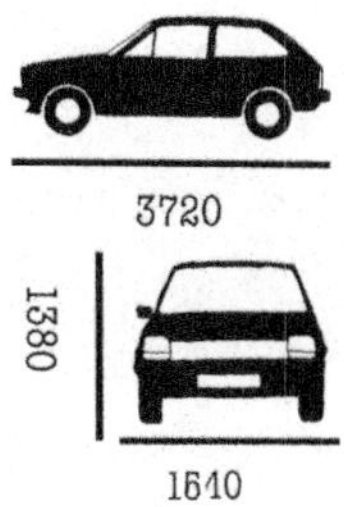

Toyota Starlet 1978 - 1984

This looked like a Eurobox on top. But it was still an old fashioned rear wheel drive set up with dull but reliable overhead valve engines. From 1982 the 1290cc was available and the five speed gearboxes made progress sweeter. The really sensible buy compared to so many of the flimsy Euro rivals. They never wore out.

Engines: 1.0 • 1.2 • 1.3 **MPG**: 32-36 **Gearbox:** 4/5spd
Turning: 9.8 **Boot:** 190/630 **Weight:** 735-785 **Doors:** 3/5

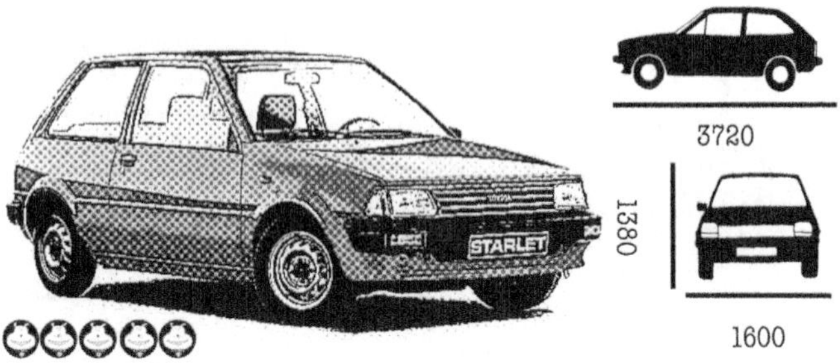

Toyota Starlet 1984 - 1990

Finally gets front drive and transverse engine the restricted import rules were beginning to bite, a pared down range. Decent 1.0 litre 12 valve and the 5spd gearbox meant economy and less stressful progress. Easy to drive/own, mostly utterly reliable. Simply brakes, exhaust and other consumables might cause an issue when well used.

Engines: 999cc **MPG**:32 **Gearbox:** 5spd **Boot:** 190/331
Weight: 736 **Turning:** n/a **Seats**: 4 **Doors:** 3/5

Vauxhall Nova 1983 - 1993

Boxy basic hatch, and a saloon with 2/4 doors which was a people's favourite being practical, easy to fix, despite the noise and overall coarseness. Dull but very worthy with well proven engines. Oil leaks, noisy cams and worn gearbox linkage amongst other high mile/abuse ailments. Amazing choice in the Vauxhall showroom back in the day.

Engines: 1.0 • 1.2 • 1.3 • 1.4 • 1.6 **MPG**: 38.3-56.1
Gearbox: 4/5spd **Boot:** 225 **Turning**: 9.4 **Doors:** 2/3/4/5

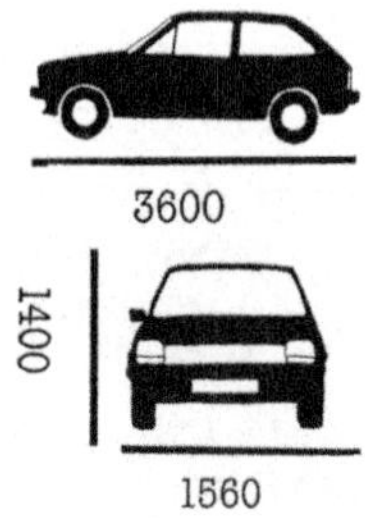

Volkswagen Polo 1975 - 1981

Simply a shrunken Golf in an equally stylish and simple hatchback body pulled along by new single cam engines and four speed gearboxes. Nice to drive. Pretty basic just N and L trim originally and bullet proof. Blown head gaskets, broken starters, leaking brake cylinders. Other bodystyle options.

Engines: 895cc • 1.1 **MPG**: 37 **BHP:** 40-60 **Gearbox:** 4spd **Weight**: 685 **Boot:** 285/900 **Turning:** 9.6

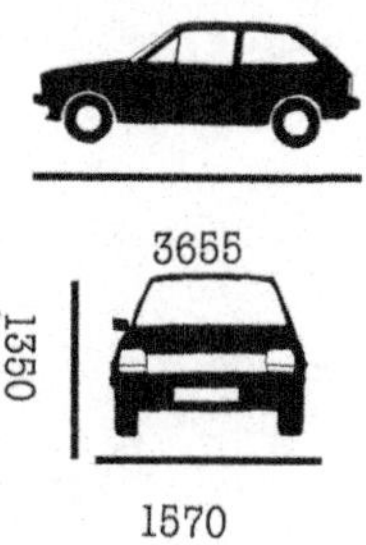

Volkswagen Polo 1981 - 1994

Brilliant Bread Van estate is distinctive and more practical, but you could now get the original Polo in Coupe format see elsewhere. Hydraulic tappet engines from 1985 and the 1.1 Formel E economy model with an overdrive fourth gear lasted a year. Bullet proof, blown head gaskets, broken starters, leaking brake cylinders.

Engines: 895cc • 1.1 • 1.3 **MPG**: 32 **Gearbox:**4/spd **Weight**:685 **Boot:** 240/915 **Turning:** 9.6

Volkswagen Derby 1977 - 1981

Pointless Bangerpedia entry no:1 is the saloonisation of the humble Polo for markets that liked to have a boot at the back. All dimensions and wheelbase as the hatch, but that big old boot adds an old fashioned foot to the overall length. Pretty basic and bullet proof, blown head gaskets, broken starters, leaking brake cylinders can bring it to a halt.

Engines: 1.0 • 1.1 • 1.3 **MPG**:44 **Gearbox:** 4-5spd
Weight: 700 **Boot:** 515 **Turning:** 9.6

Volkswagen Classic 1981 - 1992

Pointless Bangerpedia Entry No 2. But for the purposes of completeness the other tiny and not unattractive, but oddly forgettable saloon. As the Polo in spec and dimensions apart from that booty overhang. Bullet proof, but the issues on well used examples always were: blown head gaskets, broken starters, leaking brake cylinders.

Engines: 895cc • 1.1 • 1.3 **MPG**: 32 **Gearbox:**4/5spd
Weight:1064 **Boot:** 521 **Turning:** 9.6

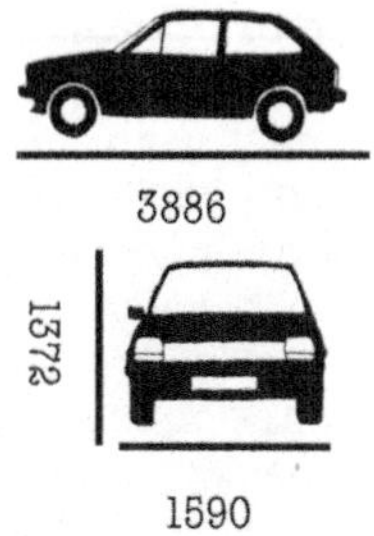

Zastava Yugo 311 • 511 • 513 1971 - 1990

In a previous life this was a Fiat 128 saloon. Ancient tech with coarse mechanicals of course. Rarely cherished, mostly endured because it was cheap and cheerless. Not a great deal to say about these, although technically in circulation for decades, now extinct. Being rough and basic has its advantages, smoke, oil leaks and rust are a given.

Engines: 1.1 • 1.3 **MPG:** 38.2 **Gearbox:** 4spdAuto
Boot: 325/1010 **Seats**: 5 **Doors:** 3/5

EuroBangerBox - Commute Shop Repeat

Here is the most important category for manufacturers and eventually Banger buyers. Family cars for the people and now in the '80s the vast majority are Eurobox hatches. Yes most of the best family cars are now VW Golfs, variations on that theme, or carbon copies.

This is the cross over point where the brilliant original Golf is replaced by the beefed up Mark 2 which was even better and more practical. Crucially VW did not forget about the marketplaces that loved an old fashioned boot. For the used car buyer considering a Jetta gave them more choice and they cost less than the regular hatched choice.

Whatever Volkswagen could do, their equally big, but not quite as creative rivals could copy and usually offer for less. The Ford Escort had always been the go-to family car. Adding a hatch was only going to make it even better. Ditto the Vauxhall Astra which was a decent entry into the market and a Euro (Opel) designed improvement over the Chevette. The Fiat Tipo was an interesting and useful addition to the market.

British Leyland had to raise their game as the competition became even more intense, so despite the Allegro lingering on for a couple of years the only way to improve matters was to turn Japanese. In came the Triumph Acclaim and Rover 200 that if you scratched the surface, were Hondas. As a short term fix it worked and the second generation 200 was something of a revelation as Honda quality came to UK car factories..

Old school Japanese trail blazers-were still around. the legacy Datsuns, Cherrys and Sunnys were still doing what they always had been since the '70s, starting first time. Also, Mazda 323s kept on going and evolving.

Interesting to see the odd really ancient family vehicles, some able to traverse a field with sheep and eggs on board, not only survive but also outlive the '80s. The Citroen 2CV and Renault's version, the 4, were certainly a chic choice, but they were also good value. Basically these were brand new Bangers.

Alfa Romeo 33 1983 - 1995

Grown up Alfasud with 1.3 and 1.5 power, less sporty than before really just a boring family hatch, but a big seller. Revamped in '89 with 1.7 engine option galvanised body, revised rear suspension, all had power steering and fuel injection. Fragile Alcantara trim and comfy Recaros. Engines need looking after. **Engines:** 1.3 • 1.5 • 1.7.
MPG: 35.8-36.7 **Gearbox:** 5spd **Boot:** 350 **Weight**: 910

Alfa Romeo Alfasud 1972 - 1983

Something of a legend when it comes to performance and intent, but in reality a basic (4spd, rubber mats), rust prone package for the masses because not everyone had a TI. Three-door Giardinetta effectively a mini estate, so hatchback from 1981 brought real practicality. These were the very definition of rust bucket.
Engines: 1.3 • 1.4 • 1.5 **BHP**: 63 • 70 • 83 **MPH**: 94-106 **MPG**:37-40 **Gearbox:** 4-5spd **Boot:** 400 **Doors:** 3/5

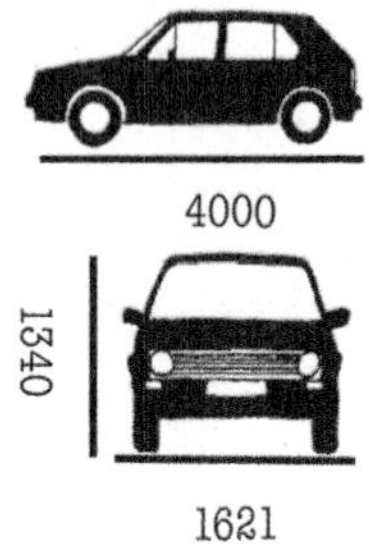

Alfa Romeo Arna 1984 - 1986

Something of an Alfa aberration, essentially Alfa flat fours inserted into a Nissan Cherry body. Unloved, unwanted and not very well built. Shortlived with 1.2 and also 1.4 power in '85, then 1.5 TI as the hot hatch version. However, no specification changes and it disappeared without leaving a trace. Shockingly underwhelming and fragile.

Engines: 1.2•1.4•1.5 **BHP:** 62•85•94 **MPG**:27-37 **MPH:**96- 109 **Gearbox:** 5spd **Boot:** 250 **Seats**: 5 **Doors:** 3/5

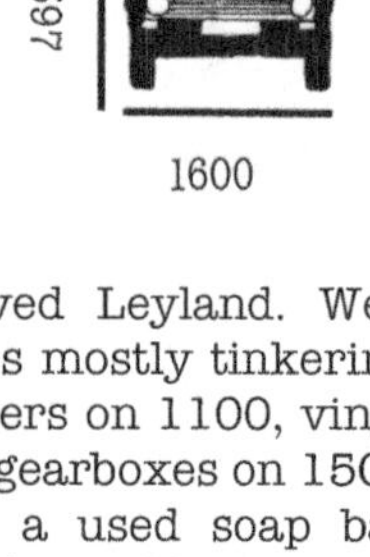

Austin Allegro 1973 - 1983

Last Mark 3 gasp for the most unloved Leyland. Well publicised build quality glitches. Upgrades mostly tinkering at the rusty edges, black grille and bumpers on 1100, vinyl roof and black trim on the 1300, 5 speed gearboxes on 1500 and 1750 Equipe special edition. Just a used soap bar shaped bundle of mechanical and bodywork trouble.

Engines: 1.1•1.3•1.5•1.7 **BHP:** 45-80 **MPG**:27-38 **MPH:** 80-96 **Gearbox:** 4-5spd/4spd Auto **Boot:** 455

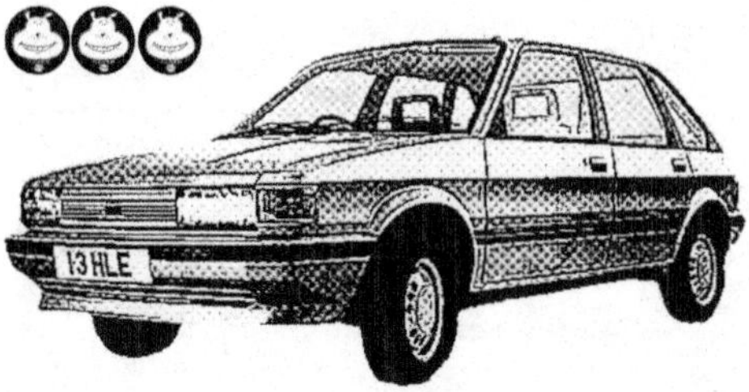

4001

1419

1687

Austin Maestro 1983- 1994

Underwhelmingly modest effort which did most things OK with a decent amount of interior space. Gets Montego engine upgrades in '84 with 1.6 and 2.0 units. Diesel delivered fairly spectacular 50mpg+ but only available in the van until the '90s arrived. Austin badge dropped in '87. Water leaks, oil and coolant leaks, least of your worries.

Engines: 1.3 • 1.6 • 2.0 **MPG**: 38 **MPH**:97- 115
Turning: 10.21 **Gearbox:** 4-5spd/3spd Auto **Boot:** 300

3780

1600

1481

Citroen 2CV 1949 - 1990

Still alive and with a decade ahead of it mostly as some form of special edition. Disc braked standard version from '81 called Special with round headlamps, otherwise, two tone Charleston in '81, Beachcomber and Dolly in '83, Bamboo in '87. Major oil leaks, ignition coils and starters all go pop.

Engines: 602cc **MPG**: 36 **MPH**: 71 **Gearbox:** 4spd
Boot: 220 **Weight:** 560 **Turning:** 10.8 **Seats**: 4 **Doors:** 4

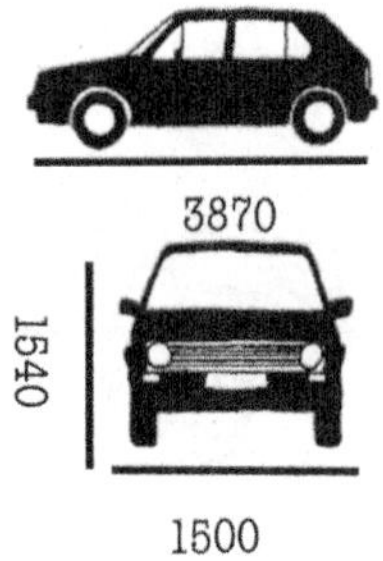

Citroen Dyane 6 1968 - 1985

Hatched 2CV, lacking some of the charm at the time, but on reflection more of the same peasant appeal which made it halfway through the decade. Got an illuminated choke and new windscreen wiper switch in 1981 and that was it. Like the 2CV would rot, otherwise it is major oil leaks and failure of components like starters and ignition coils.

Engines: 602cc **MPG**: 46 **MPH**: 75 **Gearbox:** 4spd
Boot: 343 **Weight:** 610 **Turning:** 10.8 **Seats**: 4 **Doors:** 5

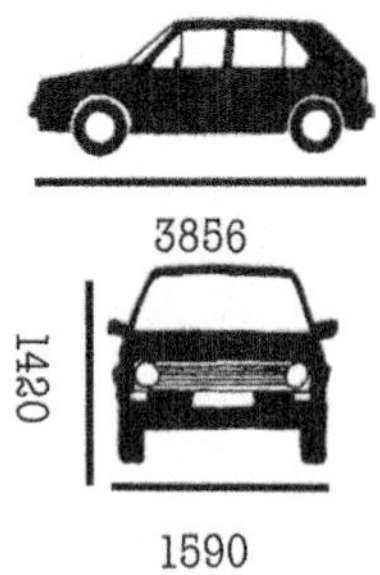

Fiat 128 1969 - 1981

Ultra traditional three box saloon from the late '60s, yet advanced for the time with overhead cam engine and front wheel drive. Great to drive and practical, some sources suggest it was available until 1984 as imports. Certainly some knocking around unsold at the back of the lot.

Engine: 1.3 **MPG**: 35 **Gearbox:** 4spd **Boot:** 370
Weight: 805-850 **Turning**: 9.8 **Seats**: 4 **Doors:** 4

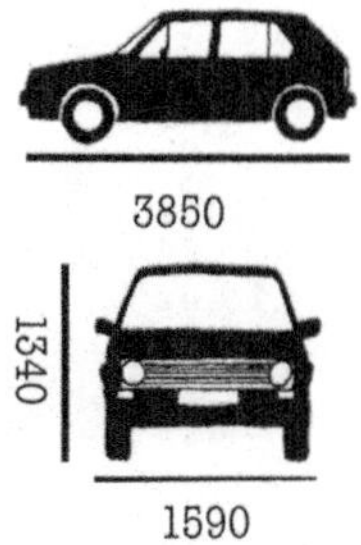

Fiat Strada 1978 - 1988

Looked interesting when launched but had a terrible reputation for letting owners down. Given a serious spruce up in 1983 with a less challenging front end and better fascia with electric windows and better seat trim on all but the basic 1100. Fast TC ones now available. Rust was the big killer along with terrible overall build quality.

Engines: 1.2 • 1.4 • 1.5 • 1.6 **MPG**: 31-38 **Gearbox:** 4-5spd **Boot:** 370/1250 **Turning:** 10.3 **Seats**: 5 **Doors:** 3/5

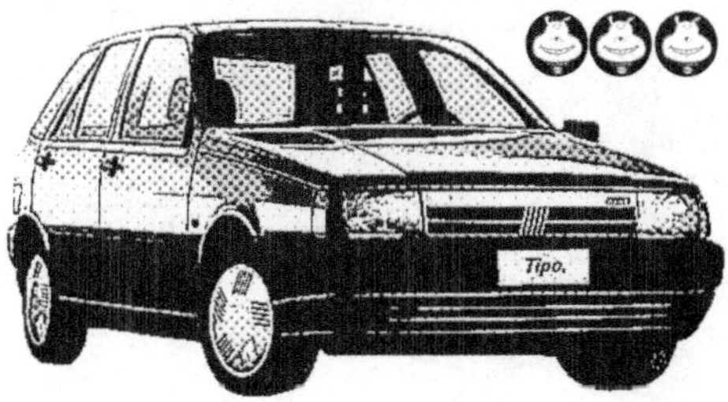

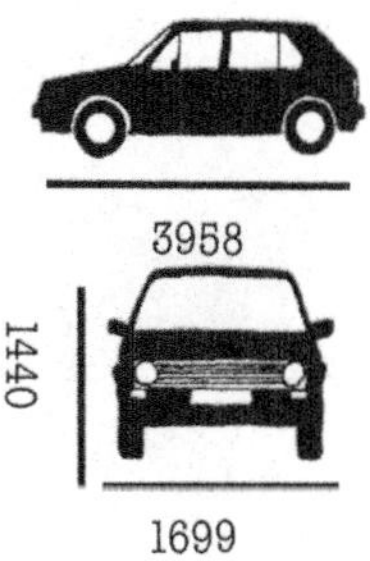

Fiat Tipo 1988 - 1995

One of the best of the '80s alt-Golf hatches that was spacious and fun to drive. Galvanised bodywork at least killed off the rust gremlins for a while. Made a lot more sense than a flakey Strada. When buying it is the usual Fiat flimsiness, so electrical issues, smokey diesels, oil and coolant leaks. Cambelt change if and when you can buy one.

Engines: 1.4 • 1.6 • 1.8 • 2.0 • 1.7D • 1.9D **MPG**: 29.3-46.1 **Gearbox:** 5spd/CVT **Boot:** 350/710 **Seats**: 5 **Doors:** 3/5

Ford Escort 1980 - 1986

Escort switches to front wheel drive to join the modern world along with MacPherson struts keeping it all off the ground. Instant bestseller and huge range of model derivatives, basic models become Populars in 1986, otherwise L, GL and Ghias plus countless special editions. Most run into the ground, but always a cheap fix.

Engines: 1.3 • 1.4 • 1.6 • 1.8D **MPG**:29-49
Gearbox: 5spd/3spd Auto **Boot:** 306 **Seats**: 5 **Doors:** 3/4/5

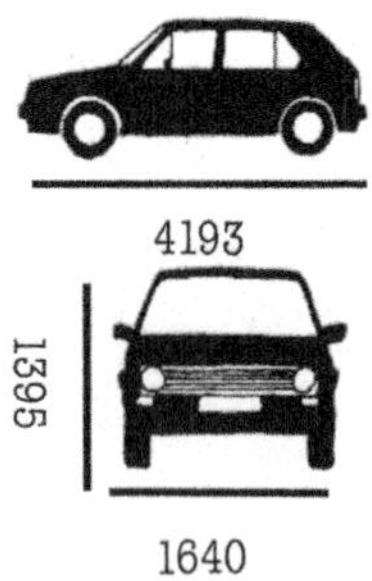

Ford Orion 1983 - 1996

Demand for boots continued and the Orion was the Escort answer. Exactly the same as hatch, just some different trims. Facelifted Orion II in 1986 was just that different bonnet and polycarbonate bumpers. Inside a new dashboard and Granada stalks. After that just minor updates and more bits of plastic. Private owners really looked after them.

Engines: 1.3 • 1.6 • 1.8D **MPG**:29-49 **Turning:** 9.8
Gearbox: 5spd/3spdAuto **Boot:** 451 **Seats**: 5 **Doors:** 4

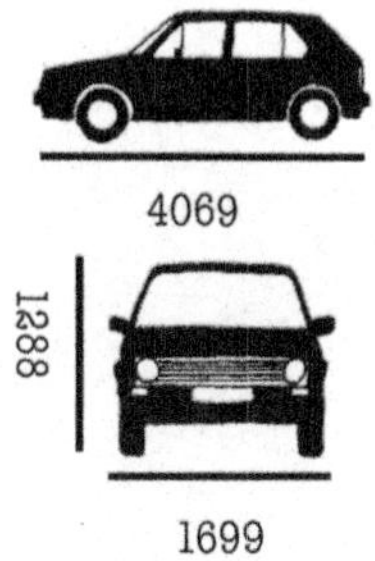

Ford Escort 1986 - 1990

More of the same successful hatchback package and Ford sensibly did not mess about with their winning formula. Escort II got a sloping gum shield bonnet and polycarbonate bumpers. Inside a new dashboard and Granada stalks. After that just minor updates and more bits of plastic. Everyone was happy with a car that went on delivering, despite rot.

Engines: 1.3 • 1.4 • 1.6 • 1.8D **MPG**:29-49
Gearbox: 5spd/3spdAuto **Boot:** 306 **Seats**: 5 **Doors:** 3/4/5

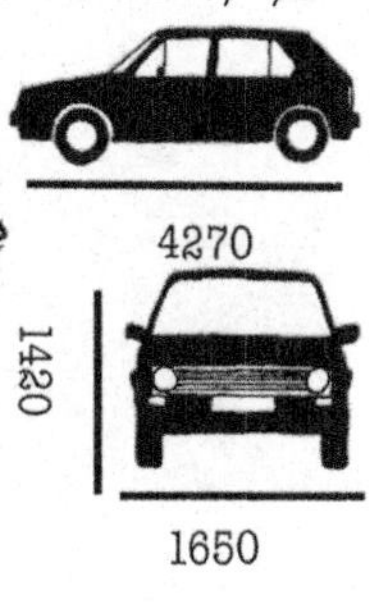

FSO Polonez 1978 - 1991

How to make the original utterly unexceptional Fiat rebadged product even worser, just stick a big hatch body on top. Had a radio cassette. Still terrible to drive. Unpleasantly distracting especially when re-designated as LE with fiberglass extensions. Engine went from 1.5 to 1.6 in 1989. The Poles made over a million. State sponsored sales...

Engines: 1.6 **MPG**:40 **Gearbox:** 4/5spd **Weight**: 1274
Boot: 425/800 **Seats**: 5 **Doors:** 5

FSO 125p 1968 - 1991

A Lada built slightly closer to it's Italian homeland. There isn't very much to say about what is a 1960s Fiat which was actually not half badly built, just very basic. Most problems like all used cars came with the subsequent owners who didn't give them very much love. A very ancient owning and driving experience. Above mine: plasters on the indicators.
Engines: 1.3 • 1.5 **MPG**:29-31 **Gearbox:** 4spd **Weight**: 960 **Boot:** 385 **Seats**: 5 **Doors:** 4

Honda Ballade 1986 - 1989

Civic saloons for the Brits and built in Blighty right next to those posh 200 Series Rovers. Did have some unique parts though like the 1.5 engine available with carburettors or a 12 valve injected version. Very durable and noisy cams plus smoke means its never been cared for. Underrated and only loses a Slog because not Nippon sourced.
Engines: 1.5 **MPG**: 33.5 **Gearbox:** 5spd/Auto **Boot:** 430 **Weight:** 850 **Seats**: 5 **Doors:** 4

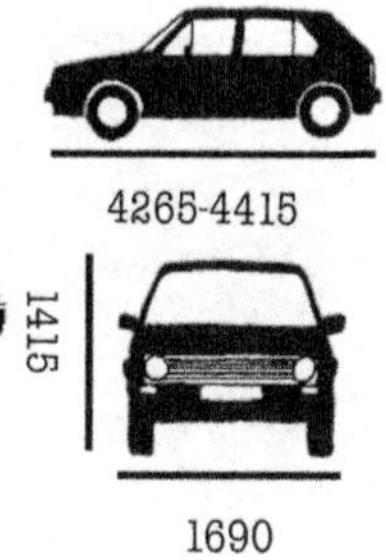

Honda Concerto 1989 - 1991

Upscaled and like the Rover 200 equivalent designed for Brits and Europhiles and as before badge engineered and made in GB, used only Honda engines, so this where the clever money went, especially as power steering was standard. No real issues all, rust is probably more of an issue which can kill it. Mechanicals remain the most durable and only need the most basic servicing.

Engines: 1.4 • 1.5 • 1.6 **BHP:** 89-110 **MPG**:36
Gearbox: 5 spd/Auto **Boot:** 370 **Seats**: 5 **Doors:** 4

Hyundai Pony X2 1982 - 1990

Body by Ital Design and all the mechanicals from Mitsubishi, so what could go wrong? Nothing, these are ultra-reliable, otherwise unremarkable to drive, dated, but usefully spacious. Decent equipment levels plus value pricing and it would last forever whether you wanted it to or not.

Engines: 1238 • 1439 • 1468 **MPG**:34 **Gearbox:** 4spd
Boot: 300 **Turning**:9.6 **Seats**: 5 **Doors:** 3/4/5

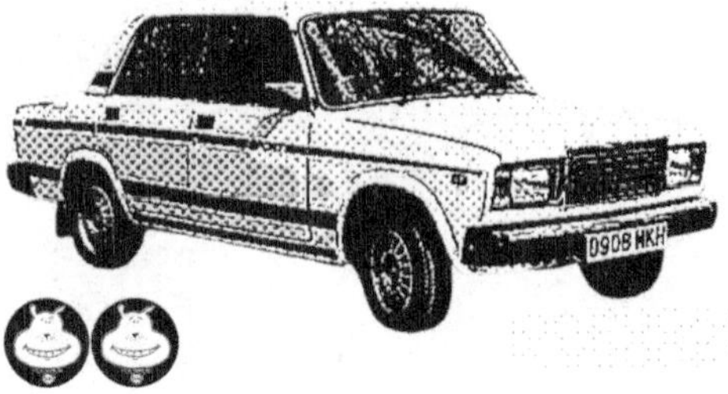

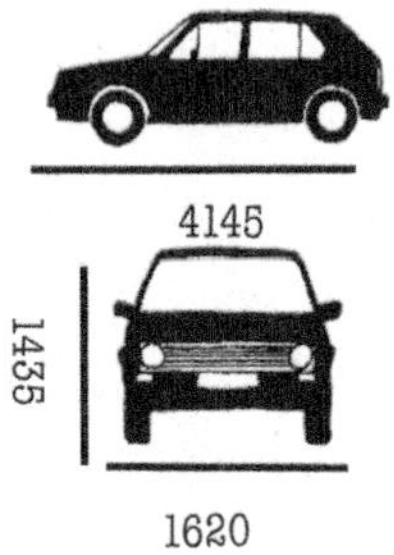

Lada Riva 1970 - 1996

Instead of just being an engine size it was called the Riva from 1984. Cheap and cheerless old Fiat three box saloon and there's also an estate on offer too which were all shockingly popular on account of its dirtcheapness. Not much to recommend it, especially a few neglectful owners down the line. Noisy diff, knocking big ends.

Engines: 1.3 • 1.5 • 1.6 **MPG**: 29.7-31.5 **Gearbox:** 4spd
Boot: 385 **Weight**: 1057 **Seats**: 5 **Doors:** 4

Lada Samara 1984 - 1996

This is properly USSR Russian so it is pretty dreadful. Ugly, coarse and shoddy. Terrible new, much worse, used. Has lots of low level easily added, insignificant kit like radio cassettes, sunroofs and coach lines. 5 door hatch from 1988, plus some more grey plastic fascia material and seat trim. Usually on its last remoulds when up for sale. Don't bother.

Engines: 1.1 • 1.3 • 1.5 **MPG**: 36.1-39.8 **Gearbox:** 4spd
Boot: 330/940 **Weight**: 930 **Seats**: 5 **Doors:** 3/5

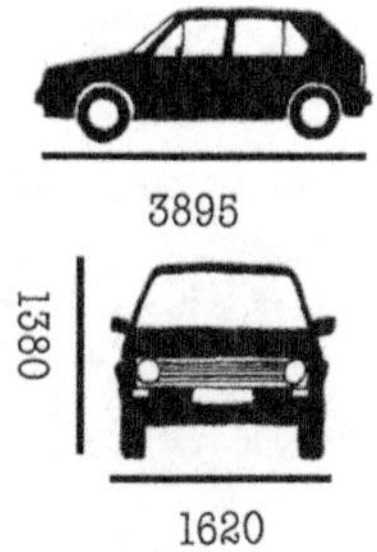

Lancia Delta 1979 - 1994

Boxy '70s hatch which is best known for being a rallying winning blistered arched legend. It also was fine at shopping., but indifferently built. Averagely capable 1300, whilst 1600 has a bit more zing. Hard to find a cooking non Inter model anymore. If you get lucky then it will be rusty, with smokey tired mechanicals and collapsing trim.

Engines: 1.3 • 1.6 • 2.0 **MPG**: 35.3 **Gearbox:** 5spd
Boot: 260/940 **Seats**: 5 **Doors:** 5

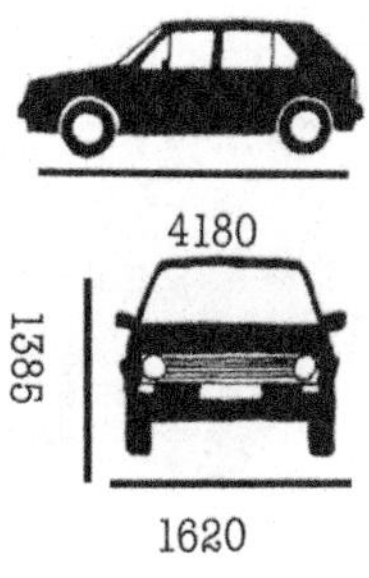

Lancia Prisma 1983 - 1990

Three Box Delta which just confused buyers most went for the practical hatch, making this very rare so ultra instant Banger. Indifferently built if not as flakey as '70s Lancias. Averagely capable 1300, whilst 1600 has a bit more zing. Hard to find a cooking model anymore which will be rusty, with smokey tired mechanicals and collapsing trim.

Engines: 1.3 • 1.6 **BHP**: 77 • 104 **MPH**: 101 • 111 **MPG**: 35.3
Gearbox: 5spd **Boot:** 450/740 **Seats**: 4 **Doors:** 4

Mazda 323 1981 - 1985

Mazza's first excursion down the front wheel drive route which combined with some brand new overhead camshaft engines to make a great hatch. Came with four speed gearbox originally and the 1.5 got a 5 speed from 1983, which was also the year for a bit of minor tidying up around the grille area. Obviously utterly reliable.

Engines: 1.0 • 1.3 • 1.5 **MPG**:37 **Gearbox:** 4spd/5spd/Auto **Boot:** 300 **Weight**: 815-920-**Seats**: 4 **Doors:** 3/5

Mazda 323 1985 - 1987

Spot the difference, the all new body does not look very different. Not very much happened over the two year interim lifecycle. There was a fuel injected 1.6 engine which as hardly a hot hatch, that would be the Turbo Rally with 4×4 running gear which would get to 60mph in under 8 seconds. The simpler ones won't ever breakdown.

Engines: 1.0 • 1.3 • 1.5 • 1.6 **MPG**:29-37
Gearbox: 4spd/5spd /Auto **Boot:** 315 **Doors:** 3/5

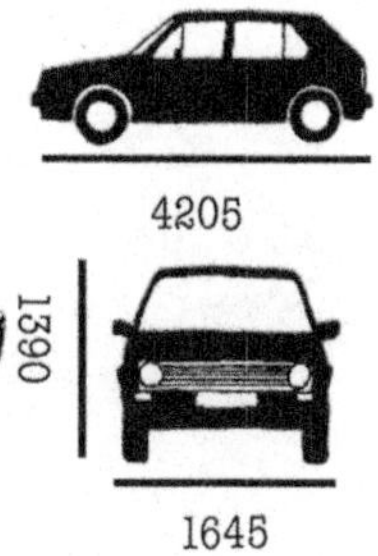

Mazda 323 1987 - 1989

Another two year stop gap model with a facelift that meant a lower bonnet, new front bumpers with ducts in them, Halogen lights side stripes and mud flaps on the LUX model. Technically the small engine is all you need and all but the entry level models have power steering. Lasts forever.

Engines: 1.3•1.5•1.6 **BHP**: 67•74•85 **MPG**: 30-40 **Gearbox:** 4spd/5spd /Auto **Boot:** 315 **Doors:** 3/5

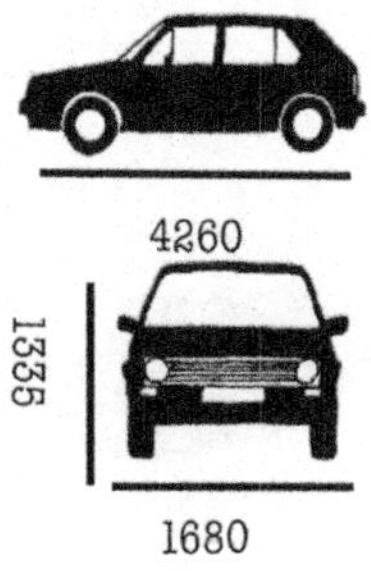

Mazda 323 1989 - 1994

There are several styles and it's the 5 door fastback which we all know and love especially with pop up headlamps. Executive specification a popular choice. Injected engines from 1991, modded suspension and an optional automatic with the 1.6 engine. Overall incredibly reliable and hard to fault unless neglected + servicing skipped.

Engines: 1.3 • 1.6 • 1.8 **MPG**: 33.8-38.3 **Gearbox:** 5spd/Auto **Boot:** 309 **Seats**: 5 **Doors:** 3/4/5

Mitsubishi/Colt Tredia 1982 - 1985

No, me neither. The completely forgotten about Tredia, mainly because it fell between an imagined gap that existed between the Lancer and Galant. A solid three box shape with a couple of standard power units plus a 1.6 turbo that was fancied up with alloys some stripes and sports seats. Not surprisingly dropped after three years.

Engines: 1.4 • 1.6 **MPG**: 37 **Gearbox:** Man **Boot:** n/a
Weight: 890-930 **Seats**: 4 **Doors:** 4

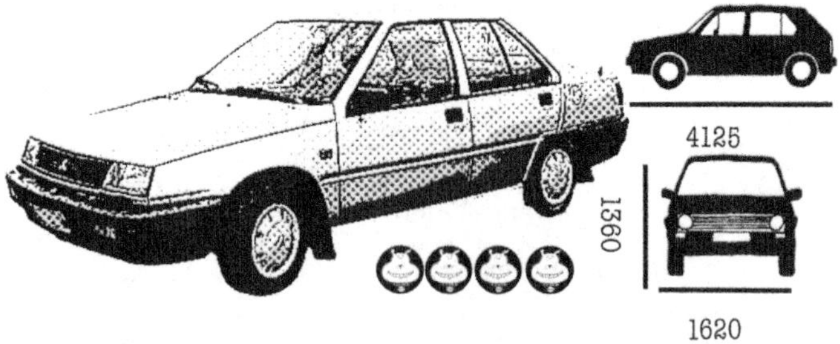

Mitsubishi Lancer 1984 - 1989

Here is a bigger version of the Colt hatch also available in saloon and estate formats with the same 1.2 and 1.5 overhead camshaft engines. The 1.5 came with a 5spd gearbox, but significantly there was also a 1.8 diesel across the range. Petrol 'economy' deletes everything useful, electric windows, mirrors, central locking, power steering.

Engines: 1.2 • 1.5 • 1.8D **MPG**: 28-47 **Gearbox:** 5spd
Boot: n/a **Weight**: 965 **Doors:** 4/5

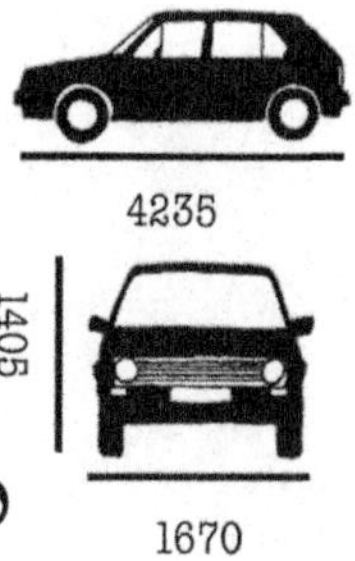

Mitsubishi Lancer 1989 - 1991

Not a great deal to write home about, just a very reliable and dull collection of saloons and hatches. Longer wheelbase saloons, so more rear legroom. Top of the range GTis and also four wheel drive versions. Hard to kill but the nation still bought cheap to fix Escorts. Ones that are left will simply be overtired and need exhausts + alternators.

Engines: 1.3 • 1.5 • 1.8D **MPG**: 32.7-47 **Gearbox:** 5spd/Auto
Boot: 337 **Weight**: 975 **Seats**: 5 **Doors:** 5

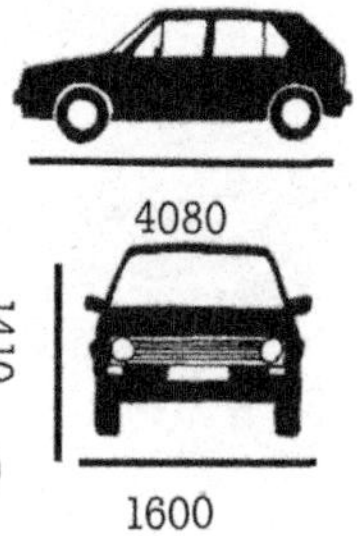

Datsun Violet 1977 - 1981

Legendary old Datsun that made it into the '80s in good health. Always great value and although the performance SSS had a few fans it was all the cooking J models which took the sales glory. Old age means oil leaks, chirping camshaft and collapsing trim like all the other dustbin Datsuns from that era.

Engines: 1.4 • 1.6 **MPG**: 29-**BHP**: 63 • 81 **Gearbox:** 4spd
Boot: n/a **Weight:** 891-945 **Seats**: 4 **Doors:** 4

Datsun Cherry 1978 - 1982

Here's the N10 model which continued on from where the previous Cherry left off and underneath that new body there is the original wheelbase and strut suspension metalwork. There was a bit of excitement in the '80s when the old engines were replaced in 1981 by overhead cam ones. Popular workhorse, which rarely broke down but rusted.

Engines: 1.0 • 1.2 • 1.3 **BHP**: 44-69 **MPG**: 35 **Gearbox:** 4spd **Boot:** 310 **Seats**: 4 **Doors:** 2/4

Nissan Cherry GTI Europe 1983 - 1984

Worth a mention as the first Japanese car to be built in Europe, otherwise see the Alfa Arna for the grim details. At least here they tried to sex it up a bit as a GTi. The bodies were posted to Alfa who did their installation magic, but no one was very convinced. Interesting but a BITZA which never worked, is overlooked and not even rated. Two Slogs.

Engine: 1.5 **BHP**: 94 **MPH**:109 **0-60:** 9.2 **MPG**:29-34.5 **Gearbox:** 5spd **Boot:** 310 **Seats**: 4 **Doors:** 3

Nissan Cherry 1983 - 1986

Last blast for the old Cherry, now just a hatchback with loads of engines plus a new 1488cc unit attached to a three speed automatic gearbox or a turbo. Magnificently reliable in basic form, not a joy to drive, but oh so easy to own. Almost 1.5m built and obviously the only thing that KO'd them was rot. Not around for very long at all.

Engines: 1.0 • 1.2 • 1.3 • 1.5 **MPG**: 36-39-42
Gearbox: 5spd/Auto **Boot:** 310 Weight: 820- **Doors:** 3/5

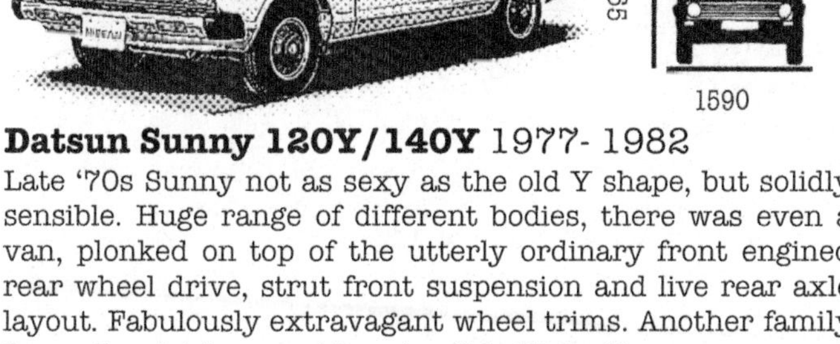

Datsun Sunny 120Y/140Y 1977- 1982

Late '70s Sunny not as sexy as the old Y shape, but solidly sensible. Huge range of different bodies, there was even a van, plonked on top of the utterly ordinary front engined rear wheel drive, strut front suspension and live rear axle layout. Fabulously extravagant wheel trims. Another family favourite which proved how terrible BL had become.

Engines: 1.2 • 1.4 **MPG**: 28-35 **Gearbox:** 4spd/3spd Auto
Boot: 310 **Weight:** 810 **Seats**: 4 **Doors:** 2/4

Datsun/Nissan Sunny 1982 - 1986

Sunny goes rather square and also up to date with a transverse engine driving the front wheels. Not only that, there were strut suspension up front and trailing arms at the rear. It also got the Cherry engines and this was a recipe for yet more utter reliability over the next four years which is all the buyers wanted.

Engines: 1.3 • 1.5 **MPG**:36-42 **Gearbox:** 5spd/Auto **Boot:**n/a **Turning:** 10 **Seats**: 4 **Doors:** 2/4

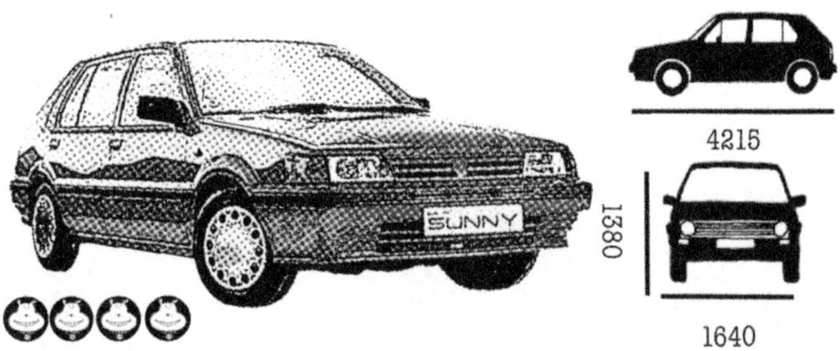

Nissan Sunny 1986 - 1991

Legendary old lag that made it into the '90s in good health with rounded bodywork. Engine uprates in the '80s when in '89 a new 12 valve 1.4 with 83bhp, revamped 1.6 went up to 94bhp. Diesel power courtesy of the 1.7 with 53bhp delivering 40mpg overall. Old age means oil leaks, chirping camshaft and collapsing trim.

Engines: 1.3 • 1.4 • 1.6 • 1.7D **MPG**: 38-40
Gearbox: 5spd/Auto **Boot:** 409 **Seats**: 4 **Doors:** 4/5

Opel Kadett 1979 - 1984

This is the last new Opel to come the UK market and the point at which it effectively merged with the Griffin. This was roomy, great to drive and had new overhead cam 1.3 and 1.6 engines. Rust and those camshafts failing were the issues, otherwise a proper rival to the market leading Golf. Dropped from the price lists in 1982.

Engines: 1.0 • 1.3 • 1.6 • 1.8 **MPG**: 33-35 **Gearbox:** 4-5spd **Boot:** 490/1360 **Turning:** 10.5 **Seats**: 4 **Doors:** 4/5

Peugeot 305 1977 - 1988

Handsome Pininfarina style combined with some perky engines and also economical ones, in particular the 1.9 diesel delivered a very useful circa 40mpg. Facelift in '83, with a swept back-nose, lots more engine options and the extra perky 105bhp 1580cc XU engine from the 205GTI. Obviously they all rusted away, but were OK while it lasted.

Engines: 1.3 • 1.5 • 1.6 • 2.0 • 1.9D **MPG**: 30-40
Gearbox: 4-5spd **Boot:** 464 **Seats**: 5 **Doors:** 4

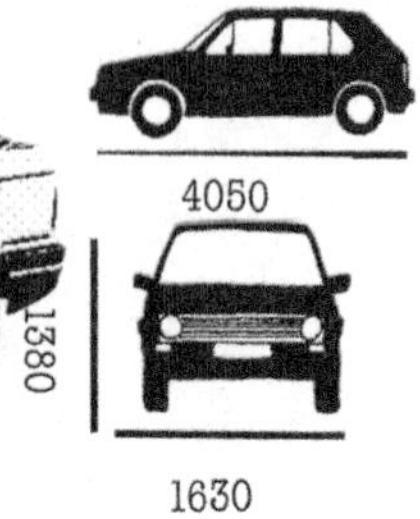

Peugeot 309 1987 - 1993

Brit designed hatch was always a spacious and practical proposition which got on with the job. Small petrol struggles, 1.6 petrol is perfect and 1.8 diesel goes on forever delivering almost 50mpg. Neglected and underrated so has oil and coolant leaks, blown gaskets and smoky clattery diesels which make a racket as the body falls apart.

Engines: 1.2 • 1.3 • 1.4 • 1.5 • 1.6D • 1.9D **MPG**: 34.7-48.2
Gearbox: 4-5spd **Boot:** 295/615 **Seats**: 5 **Doors:** 3/5

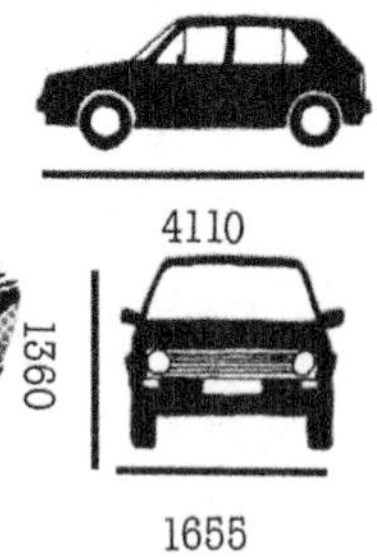

Proton Mpi 1989 - 1996

A Mitsubishi Lancer without the personality, 4WD or wings. Deathly dull but reliable of course. Very dated and plasticky, the 1.5 engine is less hard work than 1.3, SE has pointless electric windows and a bodykit. GLS has power steering and a sunroof plus a radio, which is all you need. They eventually disintegrate with overwork and under servicing.

Engines: 1.3 • 1.5 **MPG**: 33.6-38.1 **Gearbox:** 5spd
Boot: 400 **Weight**: 980 **Seats**: 5 **Doors:** 4/5

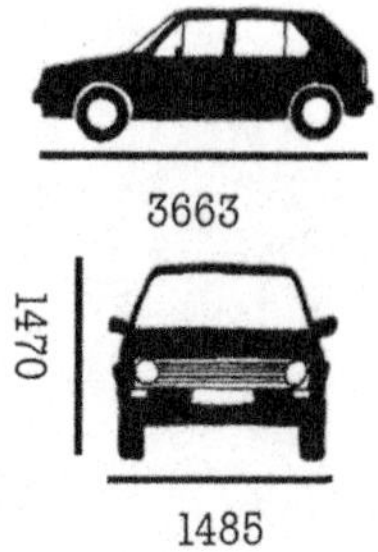

Renault 4 1961 - 1992

Legacy model with 8m editions, bought on price rather than as a retro thing. The 1.1 GTL was the ten year run out model which was able to keep up with modern traffic whilst making you deaf. Essentially the thinking Francophiles 2CV. Charming, even when disintegrating. Body rots away of course and the engine not entirely happy with unleaded fuel.

Engines: 1108 **MPG**: 45 **Gearbox:** 4spd **Boot:** 295/1175
Weight: 600 **Turning**: 10.1 **Seats**: 5 **Doors:** 3/5

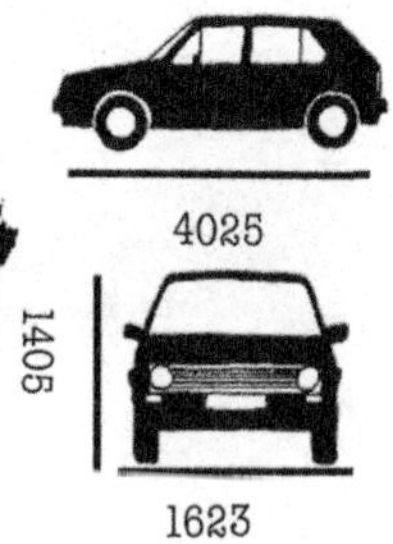

Renault 14 1976 - 1982

Here was another crack at making a Gallic Golf and beneath the Pompidou Centre displayed puffy body is the inverted engine and running gear from the Pug 104 and Citroen Visa. Turned out to be something of a French Allegro. Certainly not easy to work on which condemned many to an early scrapyard appointment. Nice to drive though.

Engines: 1218 • 1360cc **MPG**: 29 - 38 **BHP**: 58-60
Gearbox: 4spd **Boot:** 374 **Seats**: 4 **Doors:** 5

Renault 9 1982 - 1989

One of those remarkably ordinary Car of the Years, sold over a million though. Also one of those World Cars, badged as the Renault Alliance in America. Turbo was dangerously laggy. Otherwise dull and efficient way to get around. Facelifted in '86 with the 11s twin headlights, while the 1.7-litre TXE was also added with '80s Atari style dashboard display.

Engines: 1.1 • 1.3 • 1.4 • 1.7 • 1.6D **MPG**:32-41 **Weight:** 885 - 890 **Gearbox:** 5spd **Boot:** 402 **Seats**: 4 **Doors:** 4

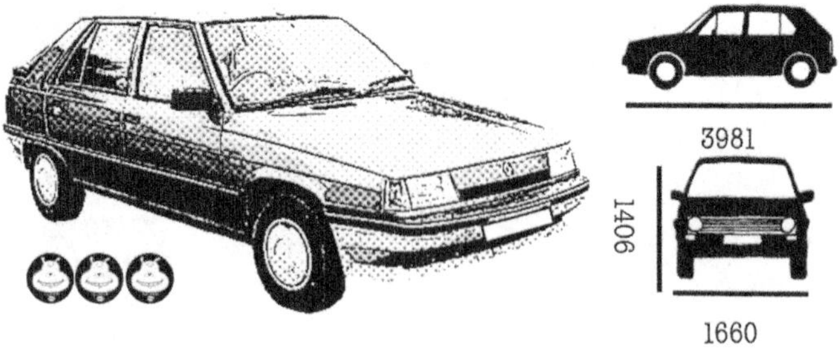

Renault 11 1983 - 1989

If the 9 was the truly dull taxi spec one, the 11 had a degree of sexy practicality with its glass hatch and funky four headlamps up front. The TXE had the first voice synthesizer in Europe to talk at you (pre Maestro) as well as the Atari dash. Parts are impossible while rust and perished window seals are the least of your problems.

Engines: 1.1 • 1.3 • 1.4 • 1.7 • 1.6D **MPG**: 32-41 **Weight**: 898 **Gearbox:** 5spd/Auto **Boot:** 337 **Seats**: 4 **Doors:** 5

Renault 19 1988 - 1996

Decent family hatches and saloon (Chamade) that got much better as the '90s progressed. One claim to fame is that it's the last Renault to have a number instead of a name. Not one of Giugiaro's best, dull but comfy. The gear linkage can be weak, oil leaks, rough running and electricals.

Engines: 1.4 • 1.8 • 1.9D **MPG**: 35.3-46.1 **Kerb:** 948
Gearbox: 5spd/Auto **Boot:** 386-1310 **Seats**: 5 **Doors:** 3/4/5

Rover 213/216 1984 - 1989

This is the Ronda turning point, it's a Britified Jap. initially available with Honda 1342cc engine, four specs standard, S, SE and Vanden Plas. 1985 Austin Rover S series 1598cc with a carburettor and EFI. Honda gearbox helped smooth progress, well built and reputation for reliability perfect for the OAP 'Mrs Bookay' demographic. Rustification kills 'em.

Engines: 1.4 • 1.6 **MPG**: 32.3 **Gearbox:** 5spd/3spd Auto
Boot: 431 **Weight:** 870-889 **Turning:** 9.5m **Seats**: 4

Rover 200 1989 - 1996

Honda Concerto with a classy Rover twist which was a big hit with tough Peugeot diesels and smooth Japanese 1.6. SLis had power steering and is pick of the range. Felt modern at the time and got snazzy chrome grilles and side impact bars in '93. Rover engines can leak oil and sound cammy, Pug diesels get smoky and clattery.

Engines: 1.4 • 1.6 • 1.8 • 1.8D **MPG**: 32.3.-48.9 **Gearbox:** 5spd/Auto **Boot:** 300/610 **Seats**: 5 **Doors:** 3/5

SEAT Malaga 1985 - 1992

A Fiat Strada with a boot glued on is one description which also came with a 1.2 Italian petrol engine whilst much was made of the Porsche connection with the 1.5. The 1.7 diesel effectively replaced it in the UK. Not a lot to recommend it when it comes to being interesting. Sharp '80s styling, awful confused dashboard and a dull drive. Smoky worn engines.

Engines: 1.2 • 1.5 • 1.7D **MPG**: 34-42 **Weight**: 940 **Gearbox:** 5spd **Boot:** 515 **Seats**: 5

Skoda Estelle 1977 - 1992

More of the same old tech based on the ancient 1964 1000MB with a restyle, the fuel tank moved to the rear and the radiator to the front. Estelle monicker only for the UK and II in 1984 with wider track, uprated brakes, plastic grille and rectangular headlamps. Always a handful despite uprated 120s and 130s, essentially a cheapey value Eastie.

Engines: 1046cc • 1289cc **MPG**: 30 **Gearbox:** 4spd/5spd **Boot:** 400 **Turning:** 11 **Seats**: 4 **Doors:** 4

Skoda Favorit 1988 - 1995

Czech new era that got better once the Volkswagen Group became involved. The Germans upped the quality, revised the suspension, interior and tweaked engines. Properly basic but from '94 alloys, removable rear seat and rear wash/wipe. L and LX marginal spec ones. Oily engines that get smoky, sticky gearboxes and poor electrical earths.

Engines: 1.3 • 1.6 • 1.9D **MPG**: 39.3-41.3 **Gearbox:** 4-5spd **Weight:** 894 **Boot:** 251/1038 **Seats**: 5 **Doors:** 5

Subaru 1600/1800 1980 - 1989

Like most Subarus a bizarre offering at the time when most people didn't think they needed four wheel drive, but there were various front/rear wheel drive options too, plus turbos, saloons, estates, hatchbacks and coupes. Baffling really, but mostly didn't break down and if they did when ancient and worn out most were tossed away. Mostly Farmer's Shopper.

Engines: 1595 • 1781cc **MPG**: 25-30 **Gearbox:** 5spd/Auto **Weight**: 860 - 1126 **Boot:** n/a **Seats**: 4 **Doors:** 3/4/5

Talbot Horizon 1977 - 1985

Good looking Chrysler box based on the Simca 1100, slack steering and indifferent gear change not impressive, but still Euro Car of the Year. Talbot from '79, focus on economy from '81 1.2 and 1.5 with 5spd 'box, Peugeot XUD 1.9 diesel from '82. Slimmed down range in '85 then Pug 309 arrived.

Engines: 1.2 • 1.3 • 1.5 • 1.6 • 1.9D **MPG**: 36-39 **Gearbox:** 4-5spd **Weight**: 960-994 **Boot:** 313 **Seats**: 4 **Doors:** 3/4

Toyota Corolla 1979 - 1987

Rear wheel wheel drive Corollas power into the '80s as a saloon, hatchback and estate version used the small old push rod engine. A million seller by '83 the estate/coupe soldiered on in the original RWD format. The simplest of Corollas and mechanically indestructible, the body was another matter of course.

Engines: 1.3 • 1.6 **MPG**: 30-35 **BHP:** 60-113
Gearbox: 5spd/Auto **Boot:** n/a **Turning:** 9.4 **Seats**: 4

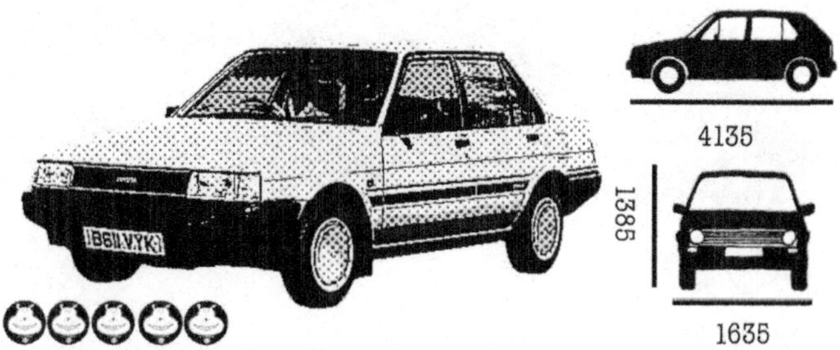

Toyota Corolla 1983 - 1987

Rightly concerned about remaining reliable the front wheel drive system had to be bulletproof. McPherson strut suspension all round. Quite high tech 2A engine designed to be more economical in '85 the multi-valve, three per cylinder delivered more mpg. Better spec, split/fold rear seats, central locking and electric windows.

Engines: 1290 • 1295cc **BHP:** 74-81 **MPG**: 30-36
Gearbox: 5spd/Auto **Boot:** 504-530 **Seats**: 4 **Doors:** 3/4

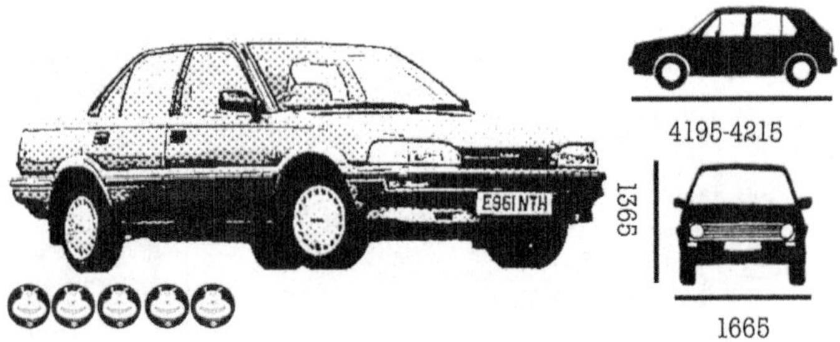

Toyota Corolla 1987 - 1992

6th generation brought lots of bodywork options, but the lift/ hatchbacks and saloons are the meat & two veg here. Actually a good car to own and drive and not the deadly dull thing history might have you believe. Power steering standard in 1990 which is fairly classy, unlike later incarnations. Driven into the ground, yet still survive.

Engines: 1.3 • 1.6 **MPG**: 32-40 **Gearbox:** 5spd/Auto
Boot: 419 **Seats**: 5 **Doors:** 3/5

Toyota Tercel 1982 - 1985

Corolla related, it had the same wheelbase and the front wheels did the work. Struts at the front and trailing arm suspension at the rear. Very reliable, economical and able to plod on for several lifetimes. Actually OK to drive. L20 by designation mostly overlooked and forgotten it was groundbreakingly ordinary.

Engine: 1.3 **MPG**: 42.6 **BHP**: 65 **Gearbox:** 5spd
Boot: 263/736 **Weight**: 895 **Seats**: 4 **Doors:** 3/5

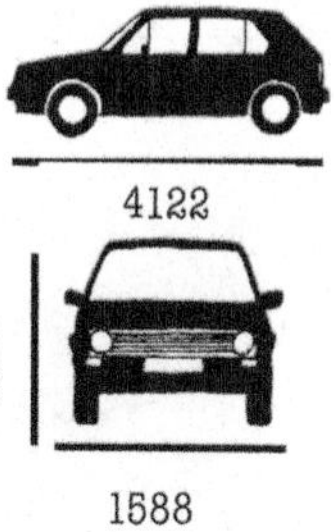

Triumph Dolomite 1300 • 1500 1976 - 1980

Here just to prove that these dated, sit up and beg saloons just made it into the '80s. As every other manufacturer went FWD, Triumph decided on a return to retro RWD. Basically charming, the HL had the posh Brit trimmings (wood cappings) and looked a bit like a Sprint. Averagely unreliable with blowing head gaskets and fragile gearboxes.

Engines: 1.3 • 1.5 **BHP:** 58-71 **MPG**:23-35
Gearbox: 4spd/Auto **Boot:** n/a **Weight:** 943-951

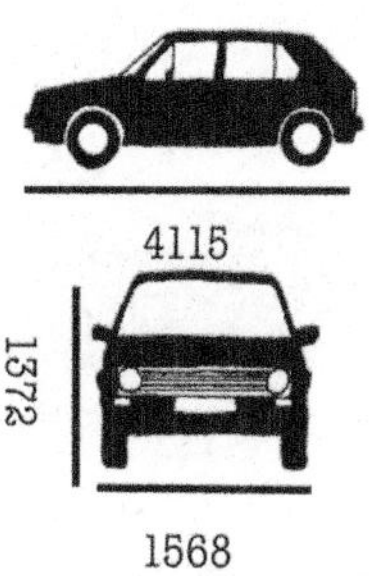

Triumph Dolomite 1850 • Sprint 1976 - 1980

Here we are at peak Dolly, the 1850HL was the top of the range and with the 'world's first' 16 valve head added it became a proper Touring car legend. Except that in real life the Sprint was an unreliable old dog that became a Banger pretty sharpish. Dated and impractical old things in the brave new 'hot hatch' decade, literally deader than Disco.

Engines: 1854 • 1998cc **BHP:** 91-127 **MPG**:23-30 **Gearbox:** 4spd/Overdrive/Auto **MPH**: 103-115 **0-60:** 10.9-8.7

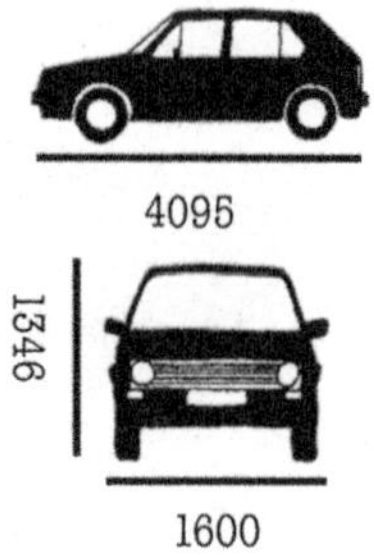

Triumph Acclaim 1981 - 1984

Triumph suddenly turned Japanese as part of a plan to save British Leyland. It sort of worked, taking a Honda Ballade and adding Brit Badges, but not the bodge build element. Powered by a Honda-designed 1.4-litre engine, it was fitted with twin-carbs. All the specs: L, the HL and HLS, plus the top of the range CD (chrome bumpers, headlight washers).
Engines: 1335cc **MPG**: 32 **Gearbox:** 5spd/3spd Auto
Boot: 430 **Seats**: 5 **Doors:** 4

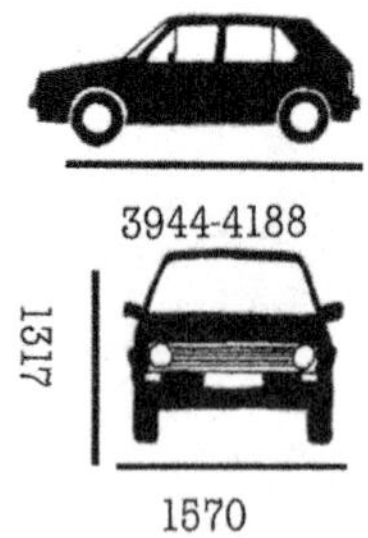

Vauxhall Chevette 1975 - 1984

Luton's last design gasp on top of General Motors 'T World Car' platform, but sawing 11 inches off the back end, fitting a hatch and the old Viva engine. Tidy on the road, however rear drive seemed old hat by the '80s and arrival of the Astra meant loads of special editions to compensate, which at least delivered more standard kit.
Engines: 1256cc **BHP**: 57 **MPG**:35-40 **Gearbox:** 4spd
Weight: 846 **Boot:** 396 **Seats**: 4 **Doors:** 2/3/4/5

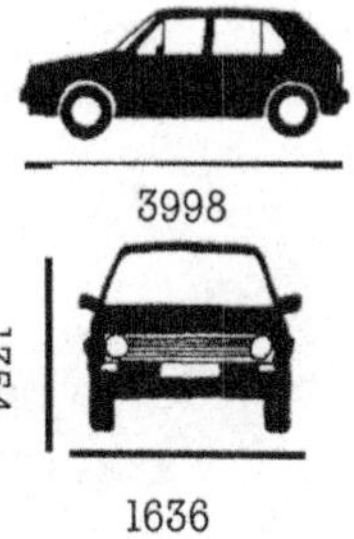

Vauxhall Astra 1980 - 1984

Original squarial one, Griffin badged Opel Kadett. Original high spec German built GLs, 1300S 75bhp engine. 1300E 60bhp from 1981 along with 1.2-litre overhead valve models, then the L and SR, followed by a pokey 90bhp 1.6-litre in 1982. Very popular, practical and good to drive with decent diesel options, plus the really hot SR ones.

Engines: 1.3 • 1.6 • 1.6D • 1.8D **BHP**: 60-90 **MPG**: 33-41.3 **Boot:** 490/1360 **Gearbox:** 4spd/5spd **Turning:** 10.5

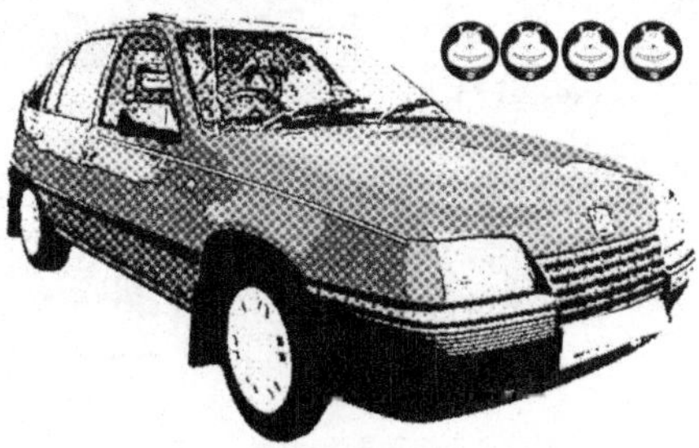

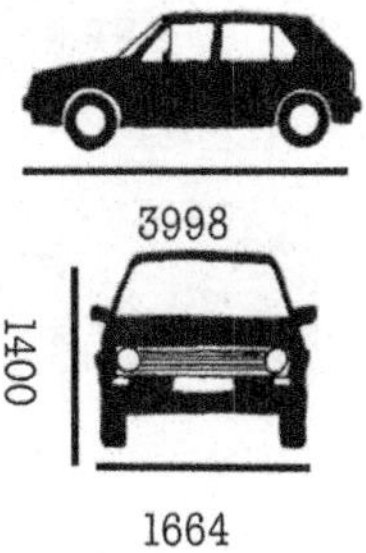

Vauxhall Astra 1984 - 1991

Arguably better than a contemporary Escort, new blobby aero styling and it gets car of the year. Belmont saloon from '86. Great range of engines and the slogging diesel delivered amazing economy for the low level rep. A popular company and family motor which was cheap to fix and easy to look after. Worn, brakes, suspension and smoking diesels.

Engines: 1.2 • 1.3 • 1.4 • 1.6 • 1.8 • 2.0 • 1.6D • 1.7D **MPG**: 34-48 **Gearbox:** Man/Auto **Boot:** 360/720 **Seats**: 5 **Doors:** 3/4/5

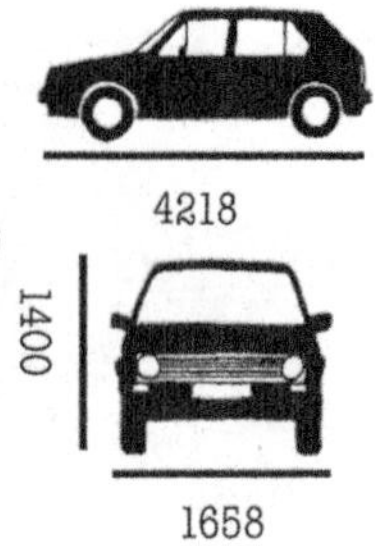

Vauxhall Belmont 1986 - 1991

Booted Astra very much more of the same and quite right too, dated but reliable. 16 valve engine a lot more lively, but the dreary 8v 1.4 will get you there and the grim 1.7D without using much fuel at all. Offensively boring to some, but perfect for the undemanding working class garden centre runs. Might have: worn engines, clutch/suspension.
Engines: 1.4 • 1.6 • 1.8 • 2.0 • 1.7D **MPG**: 34.1-49.1 **Gearbox:** Man/Auto **Boot:** 360/1200 **Seats**: 5 **Doors:** 3/4/5

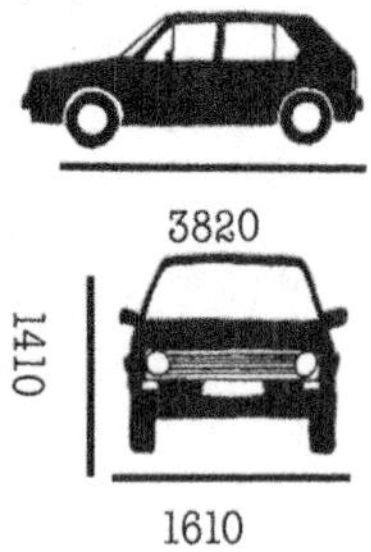

Volkswagen Golf 1974 - 1983

Many might argue the bestest Golf of all time, heavyish to drive without power steering, especially GTI but solid as a rock. Avoid the tiniest petrols, automatics good, diesel delivers a solid mpg return. Mean specifications, aim for GL. Can have oil leaks, blown head gaskets, smoky diesels, snapped clutch cable. Mostly neglect, overall tough as nuts.
Engines: 1.0 • 1.3 • 1.6 • 1.8 • 1.6D **MPG**: 35.1-54.2
Gearbox: 4-5spd/Auto **Weight:** 750-810 **Boot:** 370 **Seats**: 4

Volkswagen Golf 1984 - 1992

This is what this section is all about the model that changed everything. Golfication meant neat practical hatch, with transverse petrol and diesel variants. Changed everything automotively forever. Also the GTI... Can have oil leaks, blown head gaskets, smoky diesels, snapped clutch cable. Mostly neglect, overall tough as nuts.

Engines: 1.0 • 1.3 • 1.6 • 1.8 • 1.6D **BHP:** 49-109 **MPG**: 33-48
Gearbox: 4-5spd/Auto **Weight:** 725-1245 **Boot:** 380-1247

Volkswagen Jetta 1981 - 1984

Almost a foot longer than a Golf, so a bit heavier, but it does a have great big secure boot that's a third larger, but mostly it is 100% more dull than the hatch. Limited showroom appeal, but always big value as a used buy. Can have oil leaks, blown head gaskets, smoky diesels, snapped clutch cable. Tough as the big old boot.

Engines: 1.0 • 1.3 • 1.5 • 1.6 **MPG**: 26-36 **Weight**: 825-890
Gearbox: 4-5spd/Auto **Boot:** 377 **Seats**: 4 **Doors:** 4

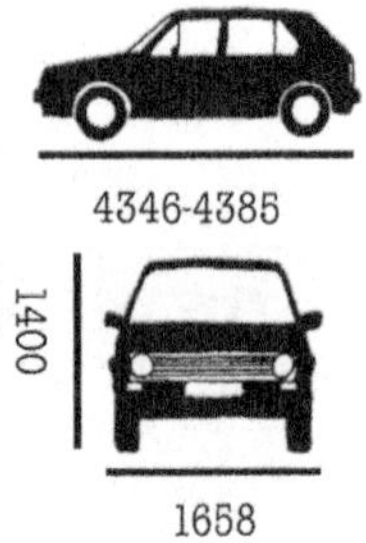

Volkswagen Jetta 1984 - 1992

Changing the name doesn't change what it is, a booted Golf of course. Main attraction always was that its cheaper than the equivalent Golf, and actually these were better built and felt more solid. Major safety features didn't arrive until the '90s, but it was all about being a value Banger. Succumbs to smoking diesel, clattery petrols and general wornoutness.

Engines: 1.6•1.8•2.0•1.9D **MPG**: 34.1-55.3 **Weight**; 1045
Gearbox: 4-5spd/Auto **Boot:** 527 **Seats**: 5 **Doors:** 4

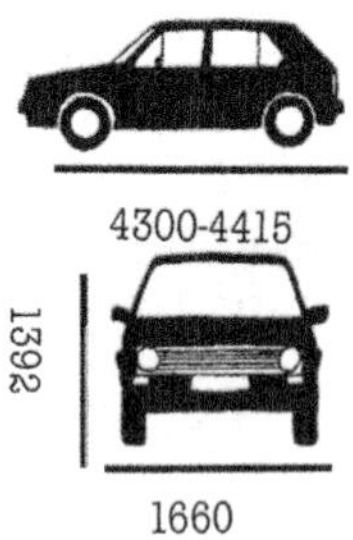

Volvo 340/360 1976 - 1991

DAF origins, but 340 is the 1.4/1.7 and 360 the 2.0. Beloved of their mostly elderly owners who appreciate the van size carrying capacity and don't mind Renault power. There's a huge number of what to look fors from the cracked manifold to the CVT transmission playing up, water pump and much more. Unremarkably solid though.

Engines: 1.4•1.7•2.0 **MPG**: 32.2-43.6 **Weight** 1091
Gearbox: 5spd Man/Auto **Boot:** 1800 **Doors**: 3/4/5

Zastava Yugo Sana 1989 - 1993

Another Eastern blocker trying to come to terms with the current decade. This is a reheated Fiat Tipo underneath with an OK ItalDesign body on top. Fairly terrible as a package despite the Tipo ingredients, so not good drive or great to own, built down to a price, but had a rear wash/wipe and a rev counter, as if that mattered. Grim as they come and go.

Engines: 1.4 **BHP**: 70 **MPG**:43 **Gearbox:** 4-5spd
Boot: 410/1280 **Weight**:873 **Seats**: 5 **Doors:** 5

Banger Fleet Favourites

The rump of the Banger market has always been the retired business models. At this point there is something of a transition from saloons to hatches, although the three boxers remained popular and existed alongside the liftbacks.

Undoubtedly the biggest news was the retirement of the Cortina and it's replacement by the Sierra. I can confirm that it did not go especially smoothly. Essentially all that happened was a body transplant and that certainly seemed like the clever thing to do. It wouldn't upset the fleet managers, but unfortunately the Jelly Mould shape did. Great news for Banger buyers who could avoid an old rusty Dustbin Cortina and get a new fangled Jelly Sierra for less.

That meant the fleet car wars were roundly won by the Vauxhall Cavalier. The Mark 2 and then the 3 at the end of the decade sealed it for Luton, while Ford played catch up, although the Sapphire did well enough as everyone got used to the redesigned Sierra.

Everything else on the market was either a novelty or going out of fashion. British Leyland persisted with the Marina and for some reason reckoned that with some matt black paint/plastic and a name change, no one would notice the Ital was a rehash. The Montego was dated, but would do a job without embarrassment.

Incredibly the Maxi limped into the, 80s whilst the big hatch format didn't exactly save Talbot, although the old Chrysler Alpine was a valiant effort, but the Solara suggested that all was lost.

Datsun became Nissan and with the new Bluebird things changed. Japan came to Britain and changed car production forever. In the background the Hyundai Stellar made its debut and delivered electric windows to the ordinary car buyer, but there was no hint yet that they would be the future.

For those that wanted reliability with added dullness, the Volkswagen Passat was always reliably there. Otherwise the Honda Accord was comfortably sophisticated even if the badge signified boring.

Alfa Romeo Giuletta 1977 - 1985

Nowt to do with the '54 original, based on the Alfetta, so it's front engine transaxle gearbox with a wedgy, high tail body on top. In '79 it got the 1779cc engine taller final drive ratio, and a Super 2.0 in '81. Impact bumpers and side rubbing strips on '82, then in 1983 deep front spoiler, headlight wash/wipe from 1.8, 2.0 gets electric front windows.

Engines: 1.6•1.8•2.0 **BHP**: 108-128 **MPH**: 109-115 **0-60:** 12.2-9.6 **Gearbox:** 5spd **Boot:** 350 **Seats**: 5 **Doors:** 4

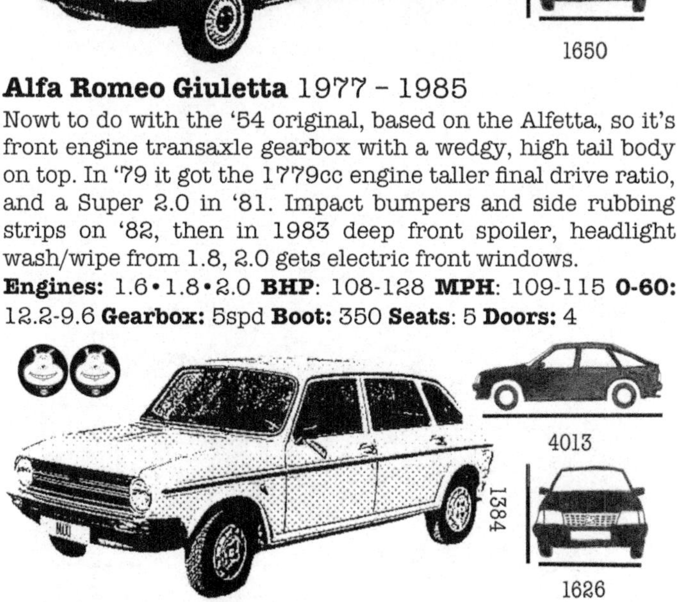

Austin Maxi 1969 - 1981

beyond its expiry date and just the one 1748cc version of the E series engine. Impossible to make this surviving BMC relic any more appealing. They tried in 1980 when it became the Maxi 2 with new bumpers, wheel trims and interior bobbins that brightened things up but could not rescue the reputation that remained: badly built big hatch.

Engine: 1750 **BHP:** 71 **MPH**: 101 **MPG**:28 **Gearbox:** Terrible 5spd **Boot:** big/double bed **Seats**: 5 **Doors:** 5

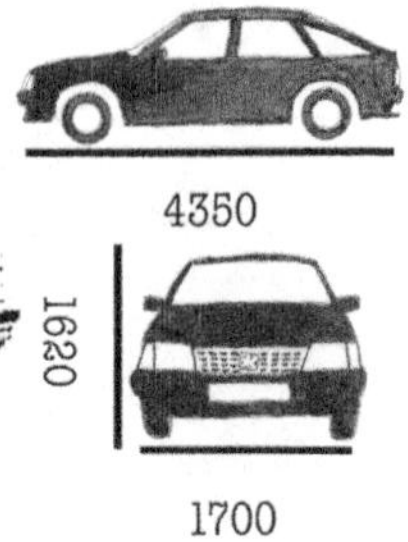

Austin Montego 1983 - 1990

The model that killed Austin Rover and was outdated on arrival, despite solid state dashboard that talked at you. All the Alphabet BL engines on offer. By 1988 Austin had gone, but never badged as a Rover. 1989 facelift and diesel. Blown head gasket, noisy gearbox and most became terminally scruffy with most of the trim going missing or gaffer taped.
Engines: 1.3 • 1.6 • 2.0 • 2.0D **MPG**: 30.5-55.6 **Gearbox:** 5spd **Boot:** 520 **Weight**:950-1106 **Seats**: 4-5 **Doors:** 4

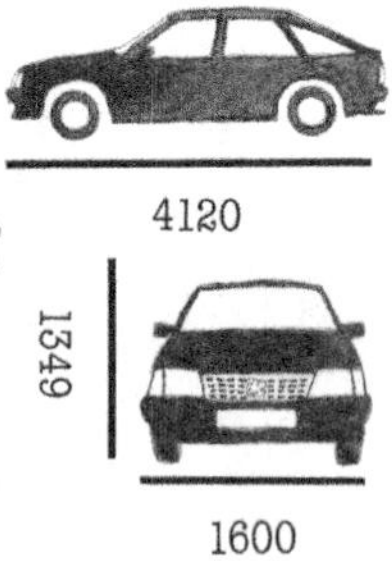

Citroen GSA 1970 - 1985

PSA Group prepared the popular GS for a new decade by calling it the GSA fitting wraparound plastic bumpers, a tailgate and a new 1.3 flat four engine in 1979, but the same bonkers interior. Four disc brakes and CX like self leveling oleo-pneumatic suspension. Would deteriorate down the ownership chain with increasingly bewildered keepers.
Engine: 1299cc **BHP**: 65 **MPH**:99 **MPG**: 30 **Gearbox:** 4-5spd Auto **Boot:** 433 **Weight**: 900 **Seats**: 4/5 **Doors:** 5

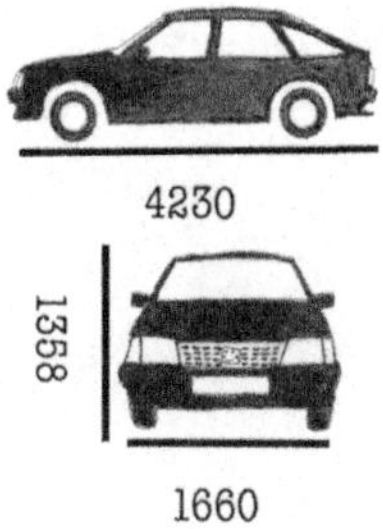

Citroen BX 1982 - 1994

Great Gandini shape. 1.4 base, E, RE, 1.6, RS and TRS. Diesel 19RD in 1984. 19 GT with a 1.9-litre petrol engine. New 1.7-litre diesels arrived in late 1985. Range refresh in '86, clear indicators, new fascia with conventional controls. Plenty to go wrong, suspension and steering, camshaft wear, snapped clutch cables, general electric upsets.

Engines: 1.4 • 1.6 • 1.9 • 1.7D • 1.9D **MPG**: 33.8-48.2
Gearbox: 5spd/Auto **Boot:** 444/1455 **Seats**: 4/5 **Doors:** 5

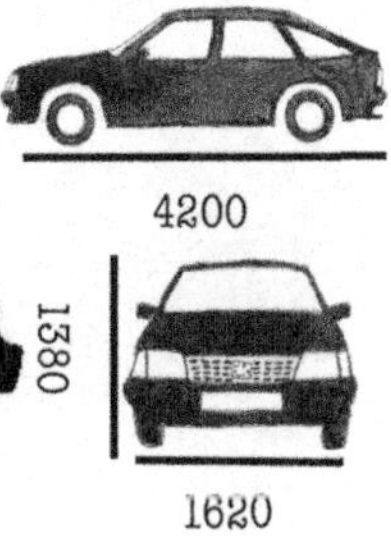

Daihatsu Charmant 1983 - 1987

Generic Far Eastern three box saloon which was based on an old Corolla, which is of course the best reason for buying and then minicabbing to death. 5 speed gearbox and the option on the 1600GLX of a three speed automatic. Leaking window and sunroof seals, noisy camshafts as the miles build up and the inevitable rot monster arrives.

Engines: 1.3 • 1.6 **BHP**: 64-82 **MPG**: 31-32 **Gearbox:** 5spd/3spd Auto **Weight**:860-895 **Boot:** 256 **Doors:** 4

Fiat 132/Argenta 1972 - 1984

Old '70s school saloon updated and renamed in 1981 with thicker rubber bumpers. New corporate grille with forward slash logo. New interior designed to make it more modern with a ton of useful new warning lights. Not a great to deal recommend the Argie, became cheap quickly. Absence of build quality made for an interesting ownership experience.
Engines: 1.5•1.6•1.9•2.0 **BHP**:98-122 **MPH:**102-106 **MPG**:25 **Gearbox:**5spd/3pdA **Weight**:1140–1210 **Boot:** 399

Fiat Miafiori 1978 - 1984

Replaced the 124 and effectively Fiat's Cortina, the cooking examples were pretty grim. A 131 in most markets but name of the factory in the UK. Added plastic over the years in '82 rectangular headlights, black sills to hide the rust and the saloon survived by the estate for six months. Grim build, bore wear and the inevitable collapse of all the trim.
Engines: 1.4•1.6•2.0 **BHP**: 75-113 **MPH**:96-109 **MPG**:25-27 **Gearbox:** 5spd **Weight**:1060-1080 **Boot:** 399 **Doors:** 4

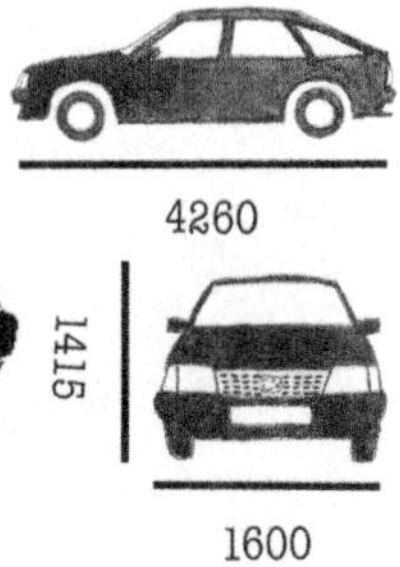

Fiat Regata 1984 - 1990

Nothing more than a three box Strada and as dull as you might expect. Rectangular headlamps and an interior which was unique and comfy bucket seats. 1986, facelift with new doors and some modified body panels. Turbo Diesel in '85. Amusingly early fuel saving stop/start operated with all efficiency you would expect.

Engines: 1.3 • 1.6 • 1.9D **BHP**: 65-101 **MPH**:96-105
MPG: 33-37 **Gearbox:** 4/5spd **Boot:** 513 **Weight**: 867-931

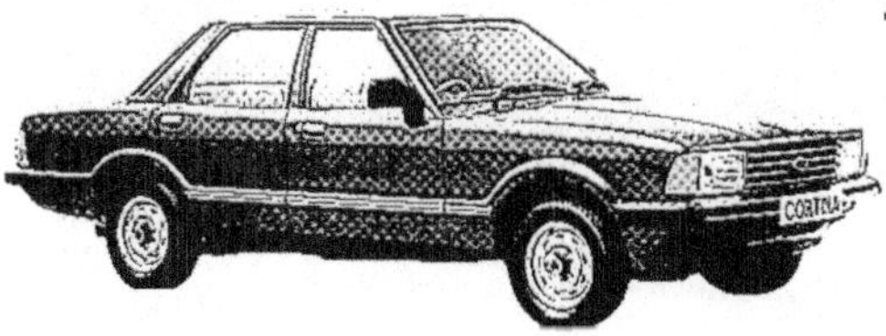

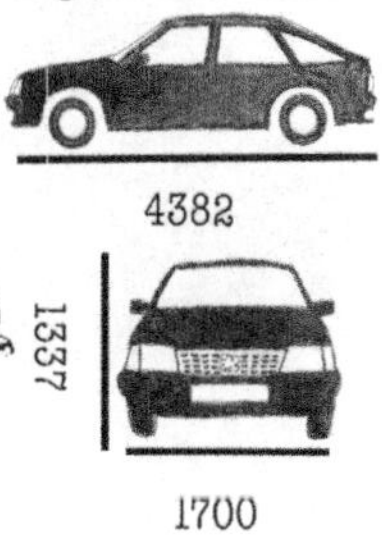

Ford Cortina V 1979 - 1982

Last gasp Dustbin was a pretty decent effort with a wider simpler grille and slightly better rust protection. 2.3-litre V6 incorporated electronic ignition and boosted 116bhp. Crusader run-out model in 1982 was a high spec best seller. Simple front engine, rear drive layout meant wear and tear is all fixable apart from terminal bodywork.

Engines: 1.3•1.6•2.0•2.3 **BHP:** 67-116 **MPG**: 28-31
Gearbox: 5spd/Auto **Boot:** 311 **Weight:** 1035-1128

Ford Sierra 1982 - 1987

Jellymould got off to a slow start then became popular as a hand me down from company fleets to families. It is like working on an old Cortina which makes it one of the better recent period Bangers. Loadsa specs and specials, but ok from the LX upwards for kit. Find a Ghia. Wear and tear which is all fixable apart from terminal bodywork.

Engines: 1.3•1.6•1.8•2.0•2.3•2.9•2.3D **MPG**: 26.1-38.7 **Gearbox:** 5spd/Auto **Boot:** 420 **Seats**: 5 **Doors:** 5

Ford Sierra 1987 - 1992

Mid life refresh with a drop down bonnet, larger headlamps and wrap around indicators, bigger windows and some work at the rear as well as the booted Sapphire. '89 new twin cam 2.0 and five speed gearbox. Can still suffer from blown head gaskets, noisy worn camshafts and blue smoke never mind bodies breaking down to rusty component parts.

Engines: 1.6•1.8•2.0•2.3D **BHP**:74-116 **MPG**: 25-38.7 MPH: 103-118 **Gearbox:** 5spd/Auto **Boot:** 420

Ford Sierra Sapphire 1989 - 1993

Best known for the mad Cossie incarnation, otherwise its a dated rep special and prime Banger with limited appeal. Loadsa specs and specials, but OK from the LX upwards, but you deserve a Ghia. 2.0 which is the best all rounder, diesels are plodders. Wear and tear, worn cams and valve guides which is all fixable apart from terminal bodywork.

Engines: 1.6•1.8•2.0•1.8D **MPG**: 28-38.7 **Gearbox:** 5spd/Auto **Boot:** 413 **Seats**: 5 **Doors:** 4

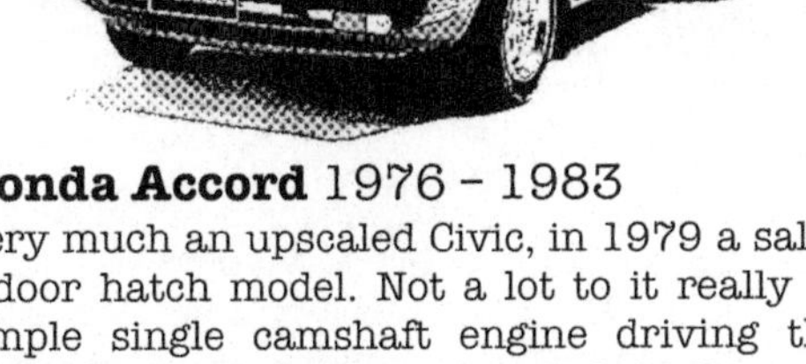

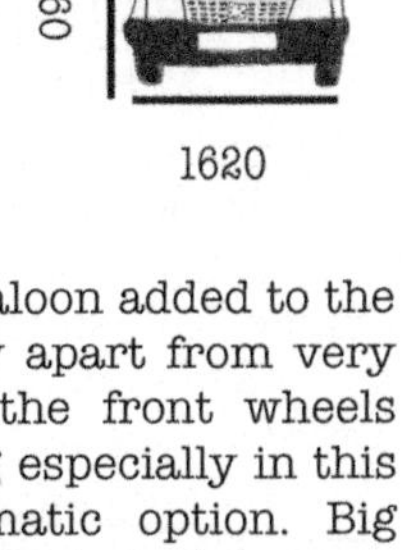

Honda Accord 1976 - 1983

Very much an upscaled Civic, in 1979 a saloon added to the 3-door hatch model. Not a lot to it really apart from very simple single camshaft engine driving the front wheels which was in itself quite forward thinking especially in this conventional marketplace. Plus Hondamatic option. Big appeal is high quality fit and finish and ability to last forever.

Engines: 1599•1602cc **BHP:** 90 **MPG**:36 **MPH**: 90-101 **Gearbox:** 5spd/Auto **Boot:** 452 **Doors:** 3/4

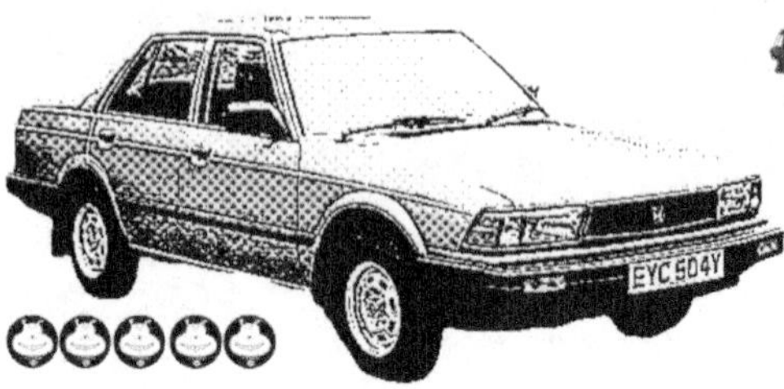

Honda Accord 1983 - 1985

Short term, classy range of unbreakable middle order hatchbacks and saloons that were comfortably dull, but their mechanical simplicity remains at the heart of their appeal. The 1602cc eight valve was soon replaced after a year by a 12 valve 1829cc. Starting to get Japanese levels of spec as the EX had air con and cruise.

Engines: 1.6 • 1602 • 1829cc **BHP**:87-97 **MPG**: 30
Gearbox: 5spd/Auto **Boot:** 425 **Turning**: 10.4 **Seats**: 4/5

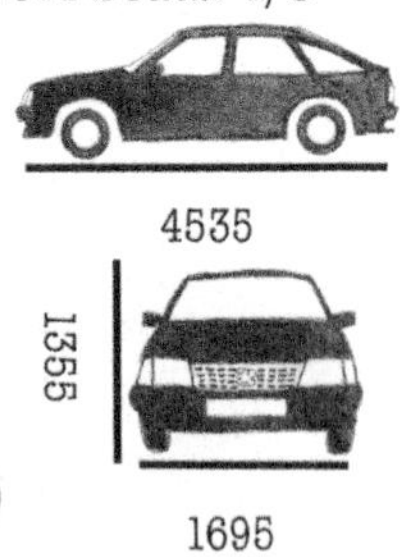

Honda Accord 1985 - 1989

Here is the point at which the Accord became an executive class car, even though we don't Bangercategory it as such. 2.0 engine either with a 12 valve carbs or injection, 106-122bhp and a hairy twin cam 16 valve 16 valve that delivered 137bhp. All came with variable power steering, central locking and electric windows.

Engines: 1955 • 1958cc **BHP**:106-137 **MPH**: 116-121
MPG: 30 **Gearbox:** 5spd/Auto **Boot:** 470 **Weight:**1024

Honda Accord 1989 - 1992

Classy range of unbreakable middle order vehicles that were comfortably dull. Not a great deal to say apart from the obvious, which is the cost of repairing one these days. The uninjected 2.0 is probably worth avoiding, otherwise there is an outside chance of a blown head gasket, worn gearbox and leaky power steering.

Engines: 2.0 • 2.2 **MPG**: 29.1-32.7 **Gearbox:** 5spd/Auto **Boot:** 425 **Turning**: 10.8 **Seats**: 5 **Doors:** 4

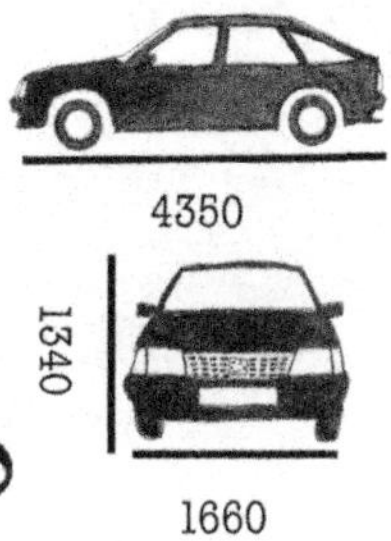

Honda Integra 1986 - 1989

Here is the hatchback Accord that was around for a bit. Oddly stylish with lovely pop up headlamps. Two versions in the UK, a 12 valve 1.5 and a top of the range powered by a 1.6-DOHC 16 valve and 5-speed transmission these were fun to drive and badged as Acuras to make them seem more posh in the States. Obviously a superarity.

Engines: 1.5 • 1.6 **BHP**: 85-125 **MPH**: 104 **MPG**: 32 **Gearbox:** 5spd/Auto **Boot:** 300 **Weight:** 1020: **Doors:** 5

Hyundai Stellar 1984 - 1992

Whatever happened to the Ford Cortina? Well essentially this was better than the original. Built the Dagenham Dustbin under licence, then came up with this which had Mitsubishi mechanicals. Perfect Banger that would last several lifetimes. 1600 GSL had it all, good old fashioned motoring values, that could always be fixed.

Engine: 1.6 **BHP**: 72-74 **MPG:** 33 **Gearbox:** 5spd **Boot:** 433 **Weight:** 1025 **Seats**: 5 **Doors:** 4

Hyundai Sonata 1989 - 1992

Incredibly this model was pitched at the Granada market but priced at Sierra levels. The truth is that it was rather too ambitious. A choice of three four-cylinder engines a 1.8, a 2.0-litre and a 2.4 could not detract from fairly average delivery and it only made sense a couple of owners down the line. Spacious though.

Engines: 1.8 • 2.0 • 2.4 **BHP**: 95-115 **MPH**: 99-111 **MPG:** 25-27 **Gearbox:** 5spd **Boot:** 473 **Weight:** 1225 **Doors:** 4

Mazda Montrose/626 1978 - 1982

Sexy Montrose monicker for the UK just some numbers everywhere else. Wasted on this big metal box of ordinariness sitting on coil springs at the back and struts at the front which was pushed along by single cam engines connected to either a five speed manual or three speed automatic on the 2.0. Tough old thing.

Engines: 1.6 • 1.8 • 2.0 **BHP**: 74-89 **MPH**: 99 **MPG:** 30 **Gearbox:** 5spd/Auto **Boot:** n/a **Weight:** 1060

Mazda 626 1983 - 1987

Now just a number, but an impressive one which added up to the sort of quality and the generous equipment level that the '80s buyer was now demanding in both saloon and hatchback flavours. There was a new 2.0 engine in '84 available in carburettor (102bhp) or injection (120bhp) form. Hard to kill and set the Mazda standard.

Engines: 1.6 • 1.8 • 2.0 **BHP**: 74-120 **MPH**: 99-112 **MPG:** 29-33 **Gearbox:** 5spd/Auto **Boot:** 467 **Weight:** 995-1060

Mazda 626 1987 - 1992

Compared to the European fleet workhorses this was a smart looking high tech thoroughbred with potentially a ton of kit that would shame a Ghia. Smart money bought an Executive instead of a tired Ford, all wheel steering could get you places and into spaces. Mazda build quality came into its own when in hard daily use and beyond as a Taxi.

Engines: 1.8•2.0 **BHP**: 86-146 **MPH**: 109-130 **MPG:** 33 **Gearbox:** 5spd/Auto **Boot:** 467 **Weight:** 1110 **Doors**:4/5

Mitsubishi/Colt Sigma 1976 - 1985

Designed as a top of the range lump and delivered to a bewildered UK marketplace that did appreciate the solidity of the saloon. Interestingly the 1.6 and 2.0 models came from Japan whilst an import restriction dodge saw Aussie built 2.6s in the showroom. Basic but unburstable four cylinder engines with live axle and strut suspension.

Engines: 1.6•2.0•2.6 **BHP**: 86-102 **MPG**: 24-28 **Gearbox:** Man/Auto **Weight:** 1208 **Boot:** n/a **Seats**: 5 **Doors:** 4

Morris Marina 1971 - 1982

The best that BL could do just made it into the '80s as the revised Mark 2 from 1978 with the 1.7 O Series which easily blew a head gasket and needed cam belt attention at 45K, if it ever got there. Had Morry Minor suspension so still needed greased trunnions. Charmingly basic and scraping the barrel BL. Banger of last resort whatever the decade.

Engines: 1.3 • 1.8 • 1.7 **BHP:** 60-83 **MPH**:84-95 **MPG**: 22-28
Gearbox: 4spd **Boot:** 260/640 **Weight**: 880 **Turning:** 10.1

Morris Ital 1982 - 1984

Company car for losers, the one that Italdesign quite rightly denies all knowledge of. Gets the A Plus engine and 12K service intervals. Actually Ital's a BL in house cheapo rectangular headlight and matt black rush job. Automatic 2.0 HLS in '81 and suspension change in '82 with telescopic front dampers across the range and parabolic rear springs.

Engines: 1.3 • 1.7 **BHP:** 61-77 **MPH**:91-97 **MPG**: 22-28
Gearbox: 4spd/A **Boot:**260/640 **Weight**: 950 **Turning:** 10.1

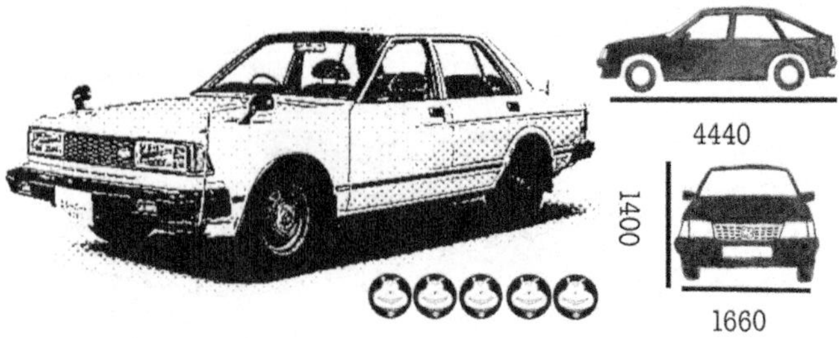

Datsun Bluebird 1980 - 1984

Same old Bluey underneath, on top it is all rather square, not hip, but certainly hard to fault. This 910 series was resolutely rear wheel drive with all the old engines and strut suspension and same wheelbase. Proved very popular in saloon and hatchback formats, the estate is elsewhere, but what you have is the ultimate people's Banger.

Engines: 1.6 • 1.8 • 2.0 **BHP:** 89-104 **MPH:** 106-109 **MPG**:34
Gearbox: 5spd **Weight**: 980-1270 **Boot:** 504 **Doors:** 4/5

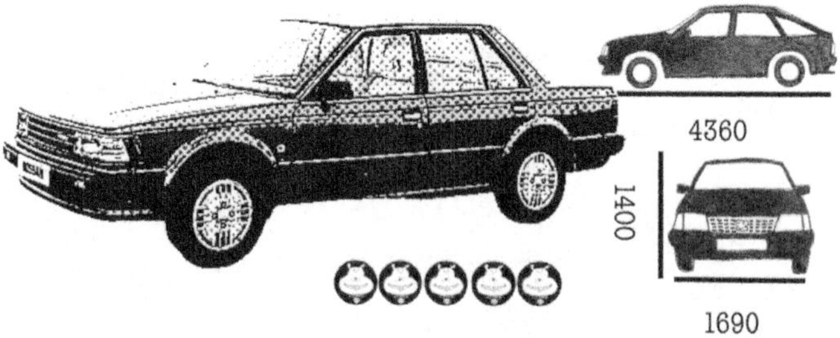

Nissan Bluebird 1984 - 1986

Looks squarely similar, but under the three box is a new age approach which means transverse engines driving the front wheels. Same 1.8 and 2.0 as before with a 5 speed gearbox but there is also a throbbing turbo fitted to the 1.8. Very much the square shape of things to come to the UK. Just as reliable and tough as the RWD ones.

Engines: 1.8 • 2.0 **BHP:** 90-135 **MPH:** 105-108 **MPG**:34
Gearbox: 5spd **Weight**: 1090 **Boot:** 504 **Doors:** 4/5

4480

1390

1650

Nissan Bluebird 1986 - 1990

Unarguably the most important brand new Banger in Bangerpedia History. Built in Blighty (Sunderland). Still a boxy Brit but with a new 1.6 petrol and 2.0 diesel. Extremely well put together, this would become the nation's default taxi for a generation. Also made sense as a solid company fleet mobile. Nothing would be the same after this.

Engines: 1.6 • 1.8 • 2.0 • 2.0D **BHP:** 67-135 **MPH:** 105-108 **MPG**:33-39 **Gearbox:** 5spd **Boot:** 504 **Doors:** 4/5

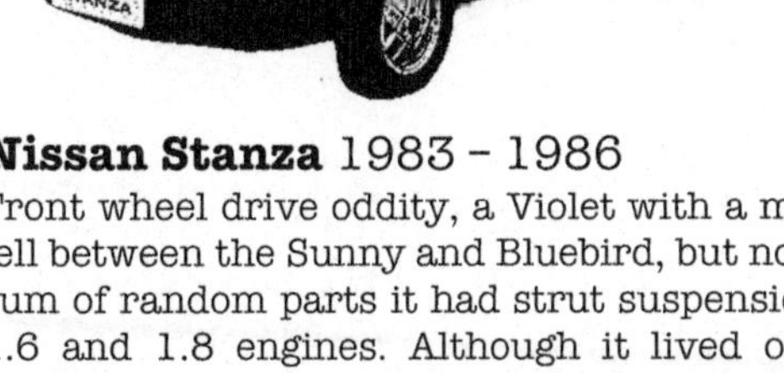

4280

1390

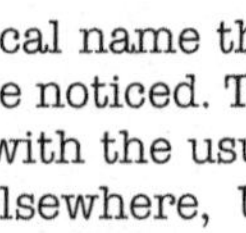

1665

Nissan Stanza 1983 - 1986

Front wheel drive oddity, a Violet with a musical name that fell between the Sunny and Bluebird, but no one noticed. The sum of random parts it had strut suspension with the usual 1.6 and 1.8 engines. Although it lived on elsewhere, UK buyers remained baffled and just bought a Bluebird or Cherry. Survived as a superb back up Banger.

Engines: 1.6 • 1.8 **BHP**: 81-90 **MPG**: 35 **Gearbox:** 5spd/Auto **Weight**: 950 **Boot:** n/a **Seats**: 4 **Doors:** 3/4/5

4330

1380

1670

Opel Ascona 1975 - 1981

Designed for Europe and to fight the Ford Taunus head on, but over here it was the shovel fronted Vauxhall Cavalier. Sold alongside the Griffin badged one as the upmarket version with Rostyle wheels. Came in 1.2, 1.6 and 1.9-litre form. In 1978, the 1.9-litre version was replaced by a 2.0-litre 100bhp version. Overall something of a Quality Banger. **Engines:** 1.2 • 1.6 • 1.9 • 2.0 **BHP**: 74-109 **MPH:**98- 110 **MPG**:31-32 **Weight**: 942-988 **Boot:** 380 **Doors:** 2/4

4490

1460

1690

Peugeot 504 1968 - 1983

Ancient old thing, which looked very dated, but could more than do a solid job. Spacious, practical and proved to be usefully durable. Fuel injected 2.0 litre was impressive and the diesel provided solid, North African Taxi levels of utter dependability. Plenty of oil leaks and some random electrical issues to keep owners occupied. **Engines**: 2.0 • 2.2 • 2.3D **BHP**:69-78 **MPH:** 93-96 **MPG**: 26-37 **Gearbox**: 5spdAuto **Weight:** 1105 **Boot**: 459 **Doors:** 4

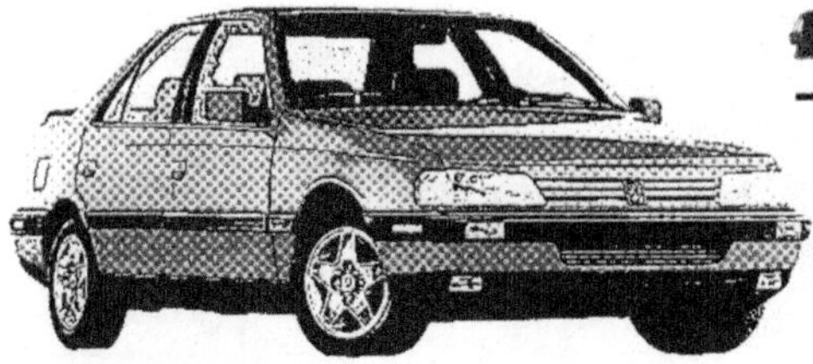

Peugeot 405 1988 – 1996

Full of '80 French style that left Cavaliers and Sierras looking very ordinaire. Nice to drive, comfortable and spacious. Massive range, small petrols struggle but the turbo diesel fabulous for the time. GTX and Executive have all the spec, but the driving fun and durability was all the Banger buyer wanted. Worn suspension, smoky engines mostly.

Engines: 1.4 • 1.6 • 1.8 • 2.0 • 1.9D **MPG**: 30.4-47
Gearbox: 5spd/Auto **Weight**: 934 **Boot:** 470 **Doors:** 4

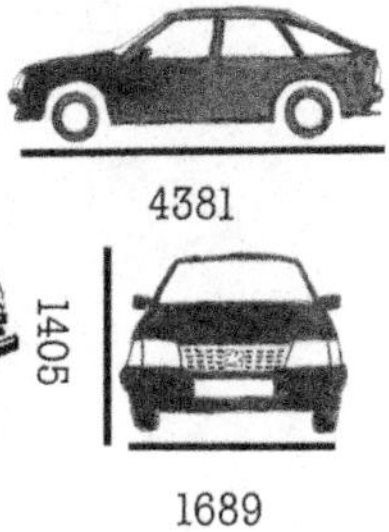

Renault 18 1978 – 1986

In reality an old 12 in a curvy body and a whole bunch of other old engines, but 1980 Diesel 2068cc 65bhp and 1981 Turbo was essentially Fuegoed 1565cc engine that delivered 108bhp, all models revised suspension from the diesel. Mark 2 in '83 new front end and spoilers. Overall a very effective company car that turned into a decent Banger.

Engines: 1.4 • 1.7 • 2.0 • 2.1D **BHP:** 64-125 **MPH**: 97-
MPG: 33-38 **Gearbox:** 5spd **Weight:**900-1046 **Boot:** 396

Renault 21 1986 - 1993

Spacious and smooth riding, not very stylish and a bit flakey when it comes to reliability. Diesels made sense though. Phase 2 in 1989 meant exterior restyle to look like a 25 and the addition of a hatchback which made sense. What finishes them off is dodgy electrics and blown engines. A comfy enough Banger in the real world.

Engines: 1.7 • 2.0 • 1.9D 2.1D **MPG**: 30.9-46.3
Gearbox: 5spd/ Auto **Weight:** 1155 **Boot:** 490 **Doors:** 4/5

Talbot Avenger 1970 - 1981

Badge engineered, previously a Hillman, then Chrysler and long in the tooth Talbot. Ruthlessly conventional with pushrod engines, strut suspension and four speed boxes, but that is what made them prime Bangers in the day. Certainly victims to wear and tear, rot and lack of any care at all. Alt-Cortina and best of all always cheaper than a Dustbin.

Engines: 1.3 • 1.6 **BHP**: 59-69 **MPH**: 89-94 **MPG**: 30.9
Gearbox: 4-5spd/Auto **Weight:** 850-955 **Boot:** 538

Talbot Alpine 1975 - 1985

Previously a Chrysler out of France where it was a Simca, it still looked like the fashionable hatchback, front wheel drive thing. However, indifferently assembled and could be a handful to drive. Always made sense as a great big Banger before rot took a grip and the tappets caused tinnitus. Never really went away, see Solara...

Engines: 1.3•1.5•1.6 **BHP**: 68-88 **MPG**:33.2 **Gearbox:** Man/Auto **Boot:** 283-1387 **Weight:** 1040-1097

Talbot Solara 1982 - 1984

Designed to replace the big Chrysler 180 instead that plonked a three box Alpine body on top that was 75mm longer with a floor pan modified behind the rear seats so the boot is gi-normous and rear legroom a tad leggier. If anything this development made them a bit cheaper and less desirable than a contemporary Alpine.

Engines: 1.3•1.6 **BHP**: 68-88 **MPG**:33.2

Gearbox: 5spd/Auto **Boot:** 452 **Weight:** 1040-1097 **Doors:** 4

Talbot Minx/Rapier 1984 - 1986

And finally the Rootes Group model name treasure chest was raided for one last time as the saloon and hatchback limped on for one more year, this time with 1.6 engine only. Few knew or cared that it existed but Linwood chucked out a fair few of them. Not the pool company car of choice, almost built to be a Banger.

Engines: 1.6 **BHP**: 88 **MPG**:33.2 **Gearbox:** 5spd/Auto
Boot: 283-1387 **Weight:** 1040-1097 **Doors:** 4/5

Toyota Carina 1977 - 1984

Second bestseller to the Corolla, it was revamped in 1980 adding 120mm to the car's length with bigger, more crash-resistant bumpers. In 1981 a five-speed gearbox was standardised and a new 1.8-litre version of the T-series engine offered 95bhp known as the Carina 1.8 GL. Third generation from '84, but same bland Corollability.

Engines: 1.6 • 1.8 **BHP**: 74-83 **MPH**: 93-106 **MPG**:32
Gearbox: 5spd/Auto **Weight:** 940 **Boot:**450

4370

1365

1670

Toyota Carina II 1984 - 1988

Numeral designation for the new front wheel drive model in trad saloon and groovy liftback configurations to broaden the appeal. 1.6 and 2.0 petrol power, diesel customers were stuck with the saloon. Facelift in '85 with boosted petrol power plus Executive spec Liftbacks with electric windows and alloys. Remained reliable to their core.

Engines: 1.6 • 1.8 • 2.0D **BHP**: 86-121 **MPH**: 109-112 **MPG**:31-39 **Gearbox:** 5spd/Auto **Boot:** 346 **Doors:** 4/5

4400

1370

1690

Toyota Carina 1988 - 1992

5th Gen was all new, designed to be more spacious and economical and better to drive on crap UK roads with improved sixteen valve 1.6 and 2.0 engines. Liftback only until the saloon arrived in 1990. A good run up to the Brit built E. In the real Banger world smoky high mile engines, wear and tear for suspension and other consumables.

Engines: 1.6 • 2.0 • 2.0D **BHP**: 105-121 **MPH**: 115-121 **MPG**: 33-40 **Gearbox:** 5spd/Auto **Boot:** 535 **Doors:** 4/5

Vauxhall Cavalier 1975 - 1981

Opel Ascona based, built in Luton just before the '80s this shovel fronted fleet car could do a job on the nation's motorways then service loyally as a family Banger. Just made it into the '80s before the cavalry, or is that the new Cavalier arrived? Hardware was pretty hard, but the bodywork was the usual softy when salt was added.

Engines: 1.3 • 1.6 • 1.9 • 2.0 **BHP**: 74-89 **MPH**: 98-104
MPG:26-32 **Gearbox:** 5spd/Auto **Boot:** 380 **Doors:** 2/4

Vauxhall Cavalier 1981 - 1989

Cavalier out Cortina'd the Sierra and won with it's front wheel drive and saloon or hatch options, running tidily on MacPherson struts up front and torsion beam at the rear engines were constantly updated. Later models were durable although noisy camshafts and hard valve stems, so smoke and drama as the miles built up. A cheap fix at the time.

Engines: 1.3 • 1.6 • 1.8 • 2.0 • 1.6D **BHP**: 59-114 **MPH**: 93-116
MPG:30-38 **Gearbox:** 5spd/Auto **Boot:** 510 **Doors:** 4/5

4432

1400

1706

Vauxhall Cavalier 1988 - 1995

Fleet favourite blossomed in the '80s which filtered down to family duties. Practical, reliable and comfortable plus as the years went on more equipment. CD and Diplomats have it all, SRi has gas shocks and close ratio gearbox. These can be driven 24 hours a day. Oil leaks, ticking camshaft, smoky engine, worn gear linkage and suspension – the watch spots.

Engines: 1.4 • 1.6 • 1.8 • 2.0 • 2.5 • 1.7D **MPG**:30.8-48.9
Gearbox: 5spd/Auto **Boot:** 384 **Seats**: 5 **Doors:** 4/5

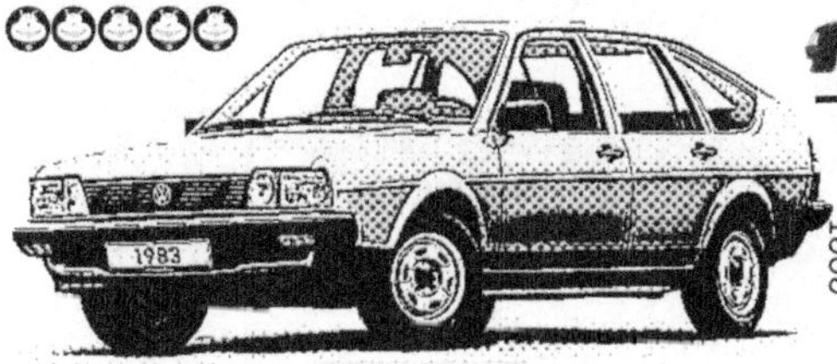

4435

1385

1685

Volkswagen Passat 1980 - 1988

Here's a big giant Golf to play with. Larger than ever, got Audi five cylinder carburettor engines in 1983 and then the diesels in 1985. Remarkably tough old things, the hatchback is always forgotten, but these were the best, we even go to the bother of listing the utterly overlooked Santana which only troubled the showrooms for a couple of years.

Engines: 1.6 • 1.8 • 1.9 • 2.0 • 1.6D **BHP**: 69-74- **MPH**:98- 102
MPG: 31-38 **Gearbox:** 5spd/Auto **Boot:** 470/1320 **Doors:** 5

Volkswagen Passat 1988 - 1996

The last truly dull and boring one, which for some reason ditched the hatch. Fitting the engine transversely meant an end to the 5 cylinder, see below. Incredible reliability and ability to rack up massive business mileages. Superb engines better to have a 2.0 petrol or the 19TDi, not exciting even with the VR6. High mile wear & tear to engine/suspension.

Engines: 1.8 • 2.0 • 2.8 • 1.6D • 1.9D **MPG**: 28-53.3
Gearbox: 5spd/Auto **Boot:** 465 **Seats**: 5 **Doors:** 4

Volkswagen Santana 1983 - 1985

Completely and utterly forgotten, yet it remains one of the smartest of the '80s saloons that UK customers stayed away from in droves. No diesel just the petrols on offer in this market. Depreciation was off a cliff which meant that second owners and beyond got a fantastic four door bargain. Just the usual look outs. Should last forever. See Cover.

Engines: 1.6 • 1.8 • 1.9 • 2.0 **BHP**: 69-138- **MPH**:98- 124
MPG: 31-33 **Gearbox:** 5spd/3spdAuto **Boot:** 440 **Doors:** 4

Volvo 440 1988 - 1997

This Dutch built Volvo with Renault engines is better than you think despite reliability hiccups in the early days. Essentially an unremarkable family hatch that is reasonably well equipped. Full on Volvo safety in 1993 when body reinforced, then airbag and pretensioners arrived. Rust plus coolant leaks, smoky engine and electrical mishaps.

Engines: 1.6 • 1.7 • 1.8 • 2.0 • 1.9D **MPG**: 32.7-36.8

Gearbox: 5spd/Auto **Boot:** 379/1027 **Seats**: 5 **Doors:** 4

Volvo 460 1989 - 1997

This is a 440 with a boot, so not sure why it merits a separate entry, but here we are. Some reckon it is more sorted than the hatch. Revised in 1993 for safety and style purposes, GLT and CD at the top of the spec tree, later ES Pack added alloys, sports suspension and metallic. Tired Renault engines can smoke, leak oil and coolant.

Engines: 1.6 • 1.7 • 1.8 • 2.0 • 1.9D **MPG**: 32.7-46.1

Gearbox: 5spd/Auto **Boot:** 453 **Seats**: 5 **Doors:** 4

BangerWagons - Great Estates

The 1980s turned out to be the a very good time to shift stuff provided buyers didn't mind using an estate because that was the format of choice. Like the '90s a serious chunk of models in the showroom were estates even if the rise of the hatchback was killing off the two door Shooting Brake estate.

First off the traditional working class estate would never go away, except oddly the late Cavalier did. Never mind, Sierras, Escorts, Astras and Maestros were around in significant numbers for the working rep. Most noticeable was the swathe of Japanese models introduced to entice the driver that preferred not to breakdown. These included the many Toyota Corollas and Nissan Bluebirds.

One interesting development was the creation of the so-called 'lifestyle' estate. Actual square footage out back was not as important as the estate being cool, quick and looking good possibly with a roof rack supporting a couple of surf boards. One of the best examples is the E30 3 Series Touring which certainly looked the part and was useful enough in the real world. Similarly the Alfa Romeo 33 Giardinetta was a very stylish thing. In many ways these were practical compact models without being downmarket hatches like those Euroboxes.

Then again, Audi were pioneering the Avant which was a big, giant hatch, with an inconveniently sloping rear roofline, except that that the 200 Turbo was quick and handsome. However, the mega, luxury, estate was a thing in the '80s. That would be the Nissan 280 and 300C, as well as the short lived Mazda based Lonsdale.

Oh and then there is the Talbot Rancho. Not four wheel drive, or even a crossover, essentially a large, two door estate with plastic accessories. This hinted at a raucous off road lifestyle and although it could never really deliver that in full, still looked very good, especially on the cover.

However, if buyers wanted a 4×4 may I refer you to another section of the Bangerpedia, although Subaru could certainly oblige. Oh and I've called all the Frenchie estates, breaks. Pretentious, moi?

Alfa Romeo 33 Giardinetta 1985 - 1990

Rebadged as the Sport Wagon in 1989. Effectively an early version of those lifestyle estates rather than a big lugger, but properly sporty. Now had a galvanised body, revised rear suspension, all had power steering and fuel injection. Fragile Alcantara trim after a few years. Engines need looking after as does the whole practical package.

Engines: 1.3•1.5•1.7. **MPG**: 35.8-36.7 **Gearbox:** 5spd **Weight:** 1200 **Boot:**: 290/1005 **Seats**: 5 **Doors:** 5

Alfa Romeo Alfasud Giardinetta 1978 - 1981

Here is a mini estate and this was arguably the coolest and rustiest of them all. Very rare in the UK and although it could out handle all comers, the reality was it's a Billy basic (4spd, rubber mats), rot prone package for the masses because not everyone had a TI. Three-door Giardinetta so hatchback from 1981 was the replacement.

Engines: 1.3•1.4 **MPG**:37-40 **BHP**: 63•70 **MPH**: 94-106 **Gearbox:** 4spd **Weight**: 915 **Boot:** 600 **Doors:** 3

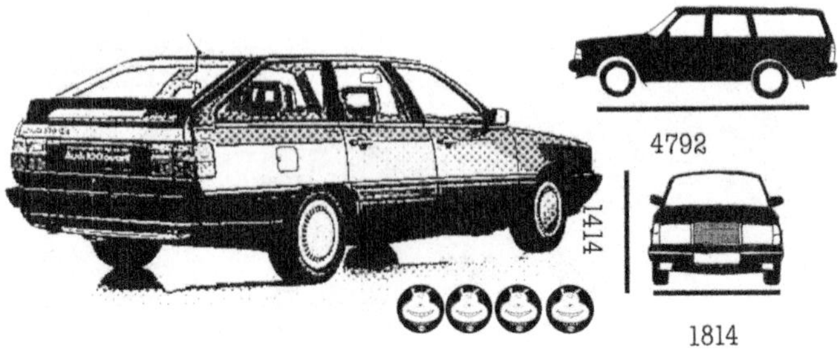

Audi 100 Avant 1983 - 1991

Technically the third generation 100 was not an estate but a sort of giant hatchback, hence the Avant name, but that sloping rear end was estate enough for most buyers who wanted to travel first class. Reliable in service can have starting issues and the old technology like ABS and other sensors are challenging.

Engines: 1.8 • 2.0 • 2.3 • 2.0D **BHP** 70-134 **MPH**: 109-125
0-60: 9.8-12.2 **MPG**: 31 **Weight**: 1140-1290 **Boot:** 390/643

Audi 200 Avant 1985 - 1991

200 spin on the Avant theme. Not identical to a 100, it had indicators in the front bumpers, there were proper door handles and the rear panel had wide integral lights. Inside, some unGermanic wood veneer, but extra gauges. Some added Quattro models with cruise control, air con. Significantly galvanised bodywork kept it for the long term. Big, Bargain, Baffling, estatehatchtype Banger.

Engines: 2.2 • 2.3 **BHP:** 138-182 **MPG**: 23 **0-60:** 7.6
MPH: 124-144: **Weight:** 1450 **Boot:** 390/643

Austin Mini Clubman 1969- 1982

Just possible to get what is a hatchback mini van with windows in the 80s, outlived the saloon as a 998cc, the van went onto '84. Pretty much van capacity too, but with carpets. Always good value used, bigger A series delivered a bit more urge. Inevitably rusty but easy to fix, blown head gaskets, collapsed suspension, rattly timing chain.

Engines: 998 • 1098 **MPG**: 34-37 **BHP**: 41-45 **MPH**: 75-82 **Turning**: 8.9 **Gearbox:** 4spd/Auto **Boot:** 523/999 **Seats**: 4

Austin Allegro Estate 1973 - 1983

Last Mark 3 gasp for the most unloved Leyland here in what's effectively its hatchback format. Upgrades mostly tinkering at the rusty edges, 1.3 HL tinted glass, bumper height rubbing strip, HLS protective rubbing strip in load area. The 1.5 had a modded gearbox. Vanlike with seats folded. Oddly cool, but still a bundle of mechanical trouble.

Engines: 1.3 • 1.5 • 1.7 **BHP:** 60-80 **MPG**:27-38 **MPH:** 80-96 **Gearbox:** 4-5spd/Auto **Boot:** 455/1500 **Doors:** 3

Morris Ital Estate 1980 - 1984

Company estate for losers. Gets the A Plus engine and 12K service intervals. Unofficially an in house cheapo rectangular headlight and matt black job rather than Ital themselves. Changes in '82 when 1.7 HLS discontinued model redesignations as the HL, became the SLX. Still very useful and cheap when new, proper lugging Banger.

Engines: 1.3 • 1.7 **BHP:** 61-77 **MPH**:91-97 **MPG**: 22-28 **Boot:** 88/104cu ft **Weight**: 985 **Turning:** 10.1

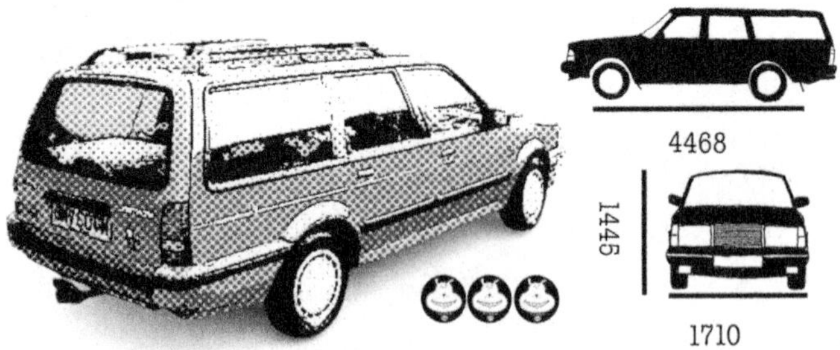

Austin Montego Estate 1984 - 1990

Surprisingly classy version, especially in Countryman spec. Rear facing child seats, so family friendly. Very easy to nick, used to be the fixable Banger of choice. Loads of specs Vanden Plas, MG and Countryman. Blown head gasket, noisy gearbox and most became terminally scruffy with the trim going missing or gaffer taped in place.

Engines: 1.6 • 2.0 • 2.0D **MPG**: 30.5-55.6 **Gearbox:** 5spd Auto **Boot:** 509/862 **Weight**:970 **Seats**: 5/7 **Doors:** 5

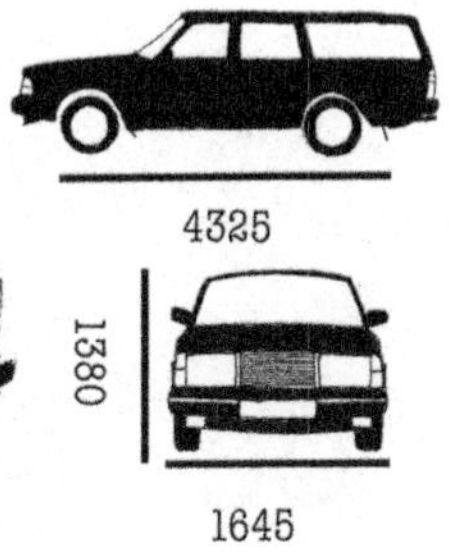

BMW 3 Series Touring 1988 - 1993

Ultimate lifestyle estate, so not designed for lugging bikes and bulky bollocks, but deserves its place here as one of the best pre modern Bangers. Great 6 cylinder engines, the fours will plod on though. Late model uprated specs SEs with cross spokes and spoilers. Killed by rot, blown head gaskets, worn out suspension and just general neglect in the old days.
Engines: 1.8•2.0•2.5 **BHP:** 115•129•171**MPG**: 30.1-35.3 **Gearbox:** 5spd/Auto **Boot:** 371/1125 **Seats**: 5 **Weight:** 1190

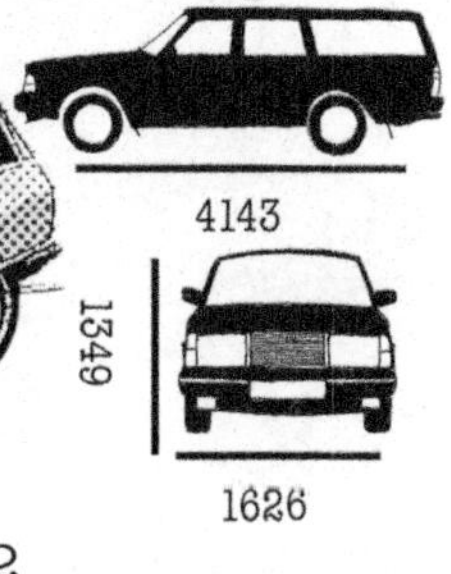

Citroen GSA Break 1972 - 1982

Absolutely colossal amount of easy access rear load space and the suspension makes it all the better suited to carrying especially with the rear seats folded. It has four disc brakes and CX like self leveling oleo-pneumatic suspension. Special model only at the end. Would deteriorate down the ownership chain with increasingly uninterested keepers.
Engine: 1299cc **BHP**: 65 **MPH**:99 **MPG**: 30 **Gearbox:** 4spd Man **Boot:** 707/1500 **Weight**: 920 **Seats**: 4/5 **Doors:** 5

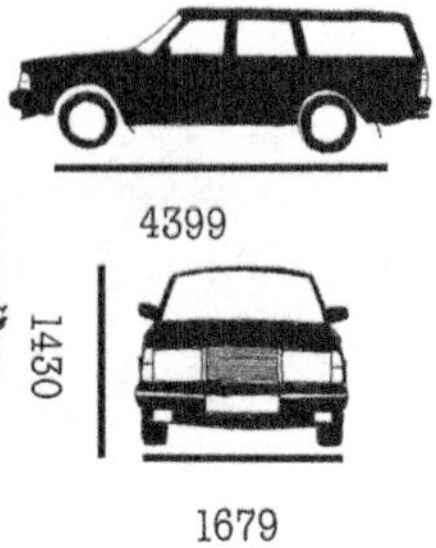

Citroen BX Break 1983 - 1994

These are very huge in so many ways. Super comfy, practical and used to be cheap because of the apparent complexities. The diesels are old school but great. Plenty to go wrong, suspension and steering, camshaft wear, snapped clutch cables, general electric upsets. Overall, '80s icon with a useful extension at the rear.

Engines: 1.6 • 1.9 • 1.7D • 1.9D **MPG**: 33.8-48.2
Gearbox: 5spd/Auto **Boot:** 512/1803 **Seats**: 5 **Doors:** 5

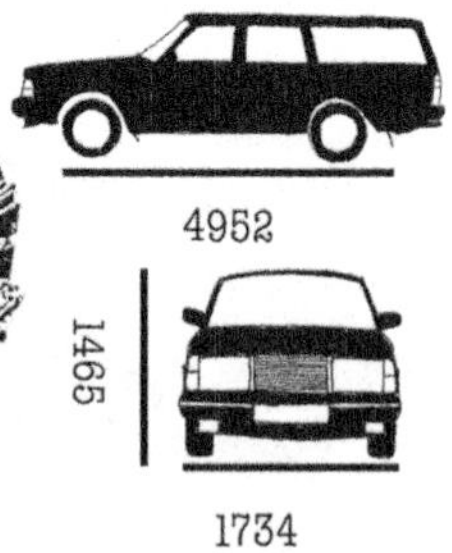

Citroen CX Safari/Familiale 1975 - 1989

Foot longer and 2m of load bay. Safari had 2 rows/5seats or as the 3 rows/7 seats Familiale version. New designation in '82 CX20, 22, 24 and 25D. In 1985, CX range adopted the same dash design, then in 2.5-litre models were fitted with ABS brakes. Gas spheres need changing, oil leaks from gearbox and metric TRX tyres rare.

Engines: 2.0 • 2.2 • 2.4 • 2.5D **BHP**: 101 **MPH:** 109 **0-60:** 12.4
MPG:26-30 **Weight:** 1330-1400 **Boot:** 507/2125

Fiat Miafiori Panorama 1978 - 1984

Replaced the 124 and effectively Fiat's Cortina, the cooking examples were pretty grim. Basic CL and electric window and central locking TC models. Added plastic over the years in '82 rectangular headlights, black sills to hide the rust. This useful model lived on after the saloon for six months. Bore wear and inevitable collapse of all the trim was rapid.

Engines: 1.6•2.0 **BHP**: 75-113 **MPH**:96-109 **MPG**:25-27
Gearbox: 5spd **Weight**:1060-1080 **Boot:** 640/1170

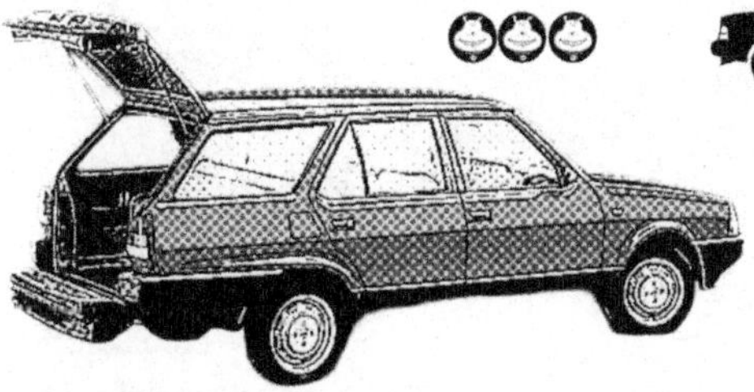

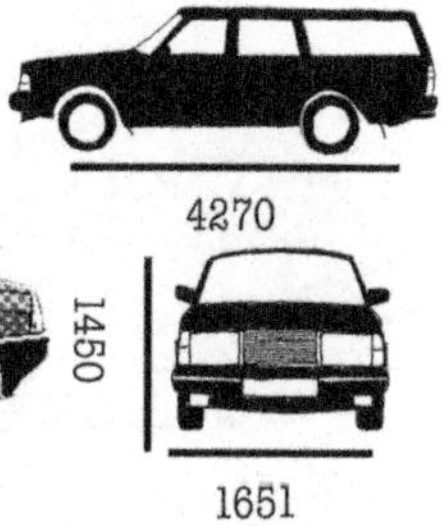

Fiat Regata Weekend 1985 - 1990

Rather cool horizontally split tailgate that you could sit on, otherwise a workaday estate. Came in Comfort specification, with rear wash wipe, two door mirrors, analogue clock and radio. Rectangular headlamps and an interior with reclining front seats and rear seatbelts. 1986, facelift with new doors and some modified body panels. Dullbutusefulbanger.

Engines: 1.6 **BHP**: 82 **MPH**:96 **MPG**: 33 **Boot:** 460/1400
Weight: 925 **Gearbox:** 5spd **Turning:** 10.3

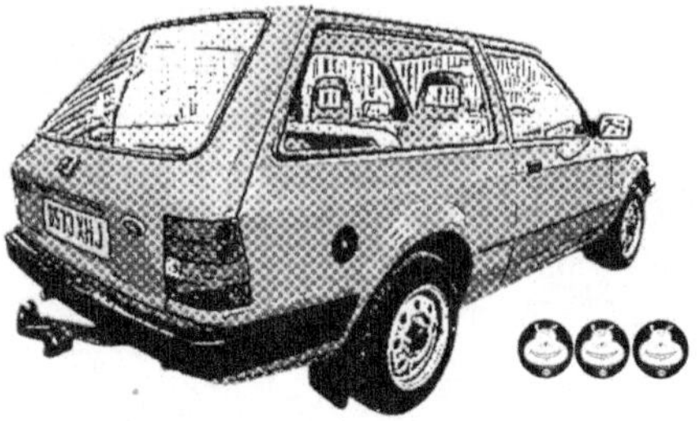

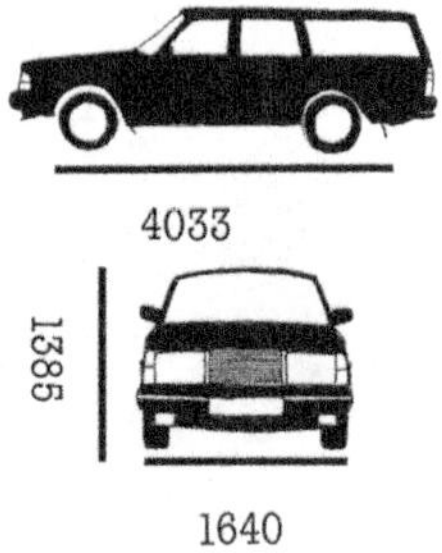

Ford Escort Estate 1980 - 1990

Escort Mark 3 switches to front wheel drive. Instant bestseller and huge range of model derivatives, basic models become Populars in 1986. got a sloping gum shield bonnet and polycarbonate bumpers. Inside a new dashboard and Granada stalks. After that just minor updates and more bits of plastic. Most run into the ground, but always a cheap fix.

Engines: 1.1 • 1.3 **BHP**: 53-59 **MPG**:29 **Gearbox:** 4spd-5spd **Weight**: 895 **Boot:** 360/1100

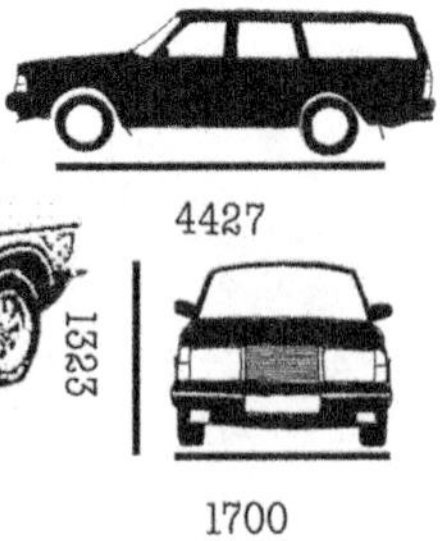

Ford Cortina V Estate 1979 - 1982

Last gasp Dustbin estate with slightly better rust protection which outlived the saloon by a couple of months. 2.3-litre V6 incorporated electronic ignition and boosted to 116bhp. Crusader run-out model in 1982 was a high spec best seller. Simple front engine, rear drive layout meant wear and tear is all fixable apart from terminal bodywork.

Engines: 1.6•2.0•2.3 **BHP:** 67-116 **MPG**: 28-31 **Gearbox:** 4spd Man/3spd Auto **Boot:** 934/1800 **Weight**: 1000-1130

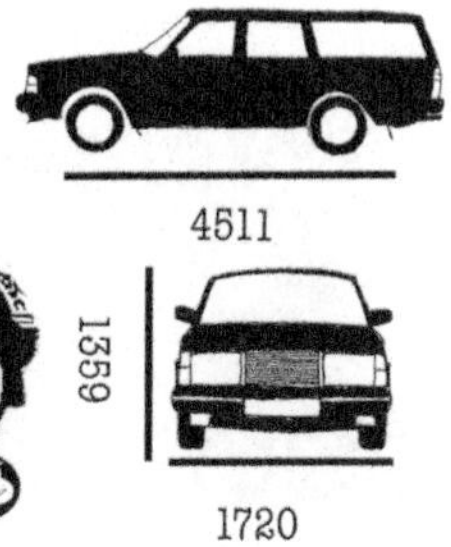

Ford Sierra Estate 1982 - 1993

Jellymould extension had lots of room and was certainly wildly popular as a hand me down from company fleets to families. It is like working on an old Cortina which makes it one of the better recent period Bangers. Loadsa specs and specials, but ok from the LX upwards. Wear and tear which is all fixable apart from terminal bodywork.

Engines: 1.6 • 1.8 • 2.0 • 2.9 • 1.8D **BHP:** 73-101 **MPG**: 26.1-38.7 **Gearbox:** Man/Auto **Boot:** 427/1958 **Weight:** 1110+

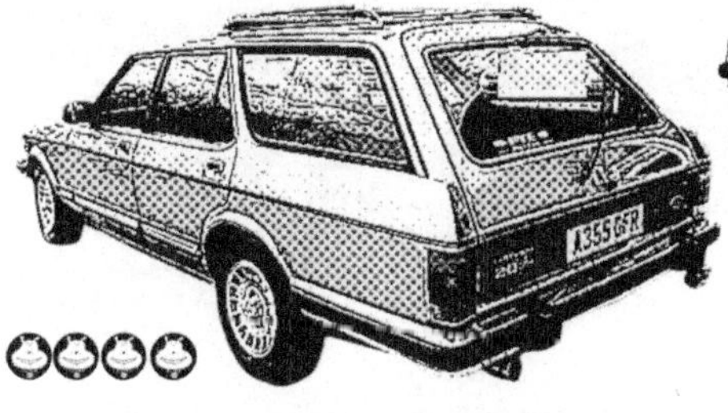

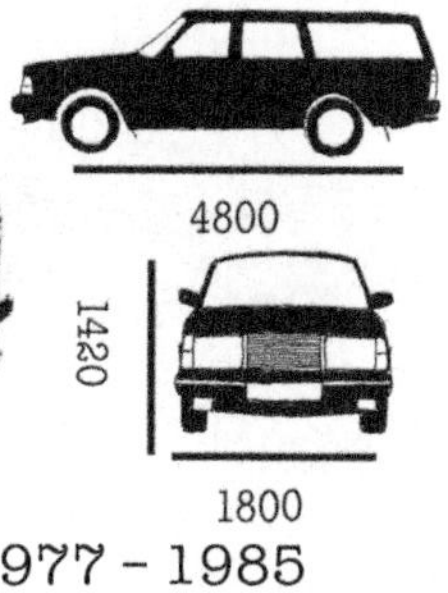

Ford Granada Mark II Estate 1977 - 1985

Rectangular estate Granny was always ready for work. Tough engines that now included 2.5 diesel in '82. Beyond the LX is the wonderful world of Ghia, electrical most things and air con from '82. 5 spd manual from '83. 3spd Automatic standard on 2.8 Ghia. Rot and neglect got most as for most it was just a posh Deutschland Dustbin.

Engines: 2.0 • 2.3 • 2.8 • 2.5D **BHP**: 104-135 **MPH**:104-118 **MPG**:24-28 **Weight:**1185-1365 **Boot:** 450/1800

FSO 125p Estate 1968 - 1991

A Lada built slightly closer to it's Italian homeland. Combi in Europe, but like the saloon, there isn't very much to say about what is a 1960s Fiat which was actually not half badly built, just very basic. Most problems like all used cars came with the subsequent owners who didn't give them very much love. Ancient owning + driving experience. Bangerpractical.
Engine: 1.5 **BHP**: 80 **MPH**: 93 **MPG**:29-31 **Gearbox:** 4spd
Weight: 1040 **Boot:** 500/1000 **Seats**: 5 **Doors:** 4

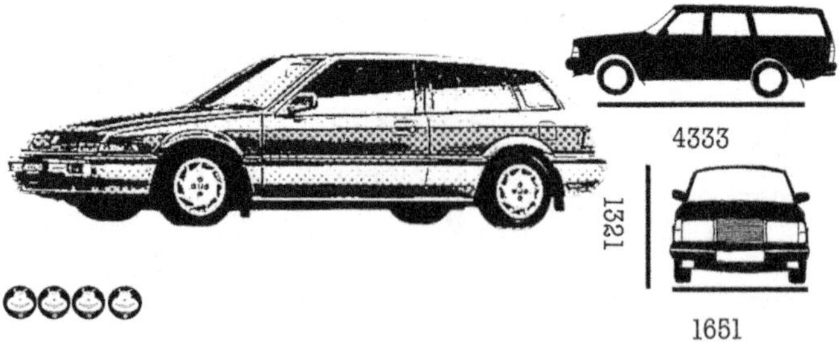

Honda Accord Aerodeck 1986 - 1989

It's just a three door hatchback, but that extension at the back and cool name means it is worth a mention as an '80s shooting brake. Bonus points for the pop up headlamps. Ultra reliable, practical estate for subtle cool cats. Around for a few years just EX and EXi. Outside chance of a blown head gasket, worn gearbox and leaky power steering.
Engines: 1955cc **BHP**: 106-122 **MPH**: 110 **0-60:** 10.2: **Gearbox:** 5spd/4spd Auto **Boot:** n/a **Weight:**: 1150

4064

1455

1613

Lada 1200-1600/Riva Estate 1970 - 1996

Cheap and cheerless old Fiat that was shockingly popular on account of its dirtcheapness. Actually quite useful as a compact load lugger that you can use on the tip run. Name change meant recessed door handles, coachlines and some front head restraints. 1.5 Riva from '85 with 5spd, classy chrome roof rails in '86. Noisy diff, knocking big ends.

Engines: 1.2 • 1.3 • 1.5 **MPG**: 29.7-31.5 **Gearbox:** 4/5spd
Boot: 500/1000 **Fuel tank**: 46.8 L **Seats**: 5 **Doors:** 5

4466

1370

1670

Lonsdale Estate 1983 - 1984

Mitsubishi Sigma originally, whilst saloon struggled, buyers liked the solidity and practicality of the estate, but this was a 1.6 and 2.0 from Japan whilst an import restriction dodge saw Aussie built 2.6s in the showroom. Basic but unburstable four cylinder engines with live axle and strut suspension. Badge rebrand lasted just over a year.

Engines: 1.6 • 2.0 • 2.6 **BHP**: 86-102 **MPG**: 24-28
Gearbox: 5spd/Auto **Weight:** 1153-1236 **Boot:** n/a

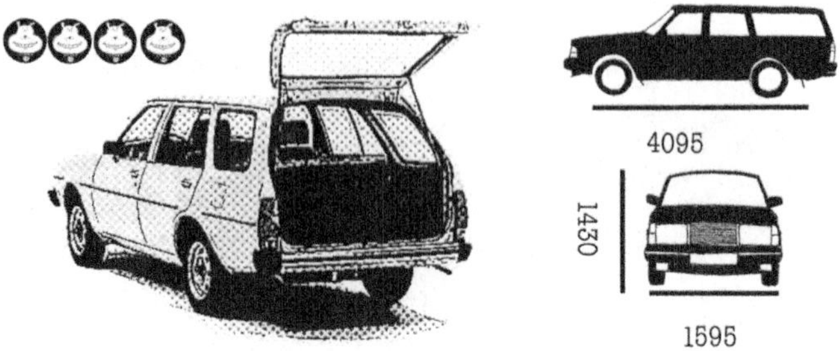

Mazda 323 Estate 1982 - 1986

Replacing the 1300 estate this is Mazza's first excursion down the front wheel drive route which combined with some brand new overhead camshaft engines to make a great hatch. 1.5 got a 5 speed from 1983 which was also the year for a bit of minor tidying up around the grille area, new steering wheel and better seats. Obviously reliable.

Engine: 1.5 **MPG**: 30 **Gearbox:** 5spd **Boot:** 240/1100 **Weight**: 920-**Seats**: 4 **Doors:** 3/5

Mazda 323 Estate 1987 - 1994

Forgotten, conventional small format estate which looked like a Ford Escort and was just as dull. This is a spot the difference scenario, the all new body does not look very new, after that, not very much happened apart from black bumpers. Overall incredibly reliable and hard to fault unless neglected or the servicing regarded as optional.

Engines: 1.5 **BHP:** 72 **MPG**: 33.8 **Gearbox:** 5spd
Boot: 378/1600 **Seats**: 5 **Doors:** 5

4590

1465

1690

Mazda 626 Estate 1987 - 1991

Very conventional small station wagon for the American market. Took the doors from the hatch and repositioned the rear lights to make a large tailgate that opened to the bumper. Large flat loading area. Super useful and practical especially as all the mechanicals are ultra reliable Mazzers. Not cool, just spacious, most run deep into the ground.

Engines: 2.0 **MPG**: 25 **Gearbox:** Man/Auto **Boot:** 430/1200 **Weight**: 1200 **Seats**: 5 **Doors:** 4/5

4575

1445

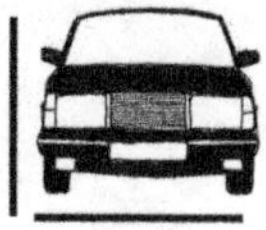

1689

Mazda 929 Estate 1981 - 1987

Well equipped and solidly put together middle order estate car which is incredibly reliable. GLX delivers most of the spec you need including electric door mirrors. '82 5 speed, '84 electric windows/central locking, '85 power steering. Not much goes wrong, if you can find one after it's done a seven figure mileage as a mundane superestateminicab.

Engines: 1970cc **BHP:** 90 **MPG**: 29.3 **Gearbox:** 5spd/Auto **Boot:** 484/1677 **Weight**: 1330 **Seats**: 5

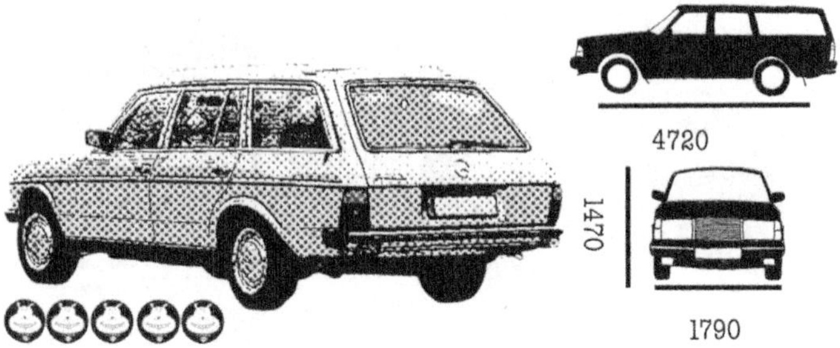

Mercedes 200T/TE 1975 - 1984

Best Banger estate ever. Self leveling suspension, load cover. '83 5spd, most seem to have sunroof, 60/30 split rear seat from '86. Chrome roof rails on the TE and rear wash/wipe. Always a top flight Taxi as a four, six cylinder and injected Es. Unarguably the ultimate Bangernomics mobile. Worn engines, suspension, rust are downsides.

Engines: 2.0 • 2.3 • (6)2.6D **BHP**:108-140 **MPH**: 90 -124
0-60:11.6 **MPG**:20-28 **Boot:** 523/879 **Weight:** 1490

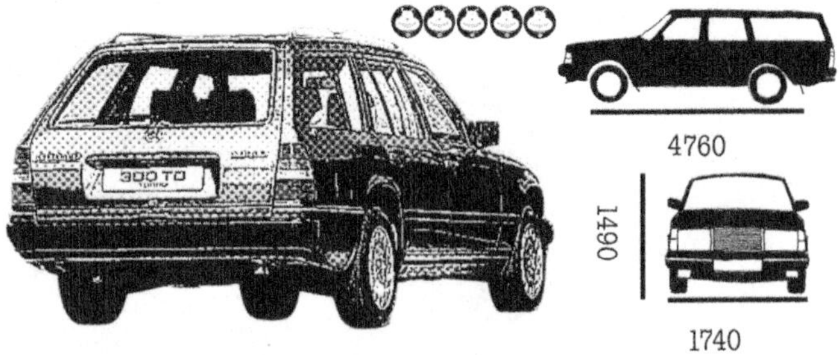

Mercedes E-Class Estate 1984 - 1995

Epically reliable, comfortable and nothing Merc has ever made since is as solid. Chrome roof rails, split rear seats, luggage cover, rear wash/wipe, ABS from '89. Rear facing kiddie seats option. Massive mileages and neglect take their toll, the expensive bits are automatic gearboxes and rear axle. Magnificent way to shift stuff.

Engines: 2.8 • 3.0 • 3.2 • 2.5D • 3.0D **BHP:** 90-190
MPG: 19.6-38.9 **Gearbox:** 5spd/Auto **Boot:** 530/1770

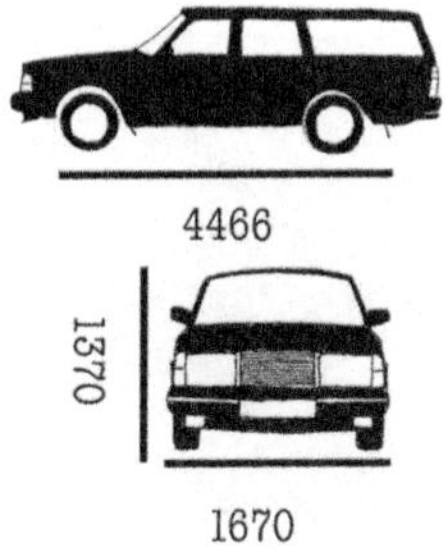

Colt/Mitsubishi Sigma 1983 - 1984

Designed as a top of the range lump and delivered to a confused UK marketplace that did appreciate the solidity of the estate. Much was made of the digital clock, front and rear reading lights, plus central armrest. Interestingly the 1.6 and 2.0 models came from Japan, an import restriction dodge saw Aussie built 2.6s estates in the showroom.

Engines: 1.6 • 2.0 • 2.6 **BHP**: 86-102 **MPG**: 24-28
Gearbox: 5spd/Auto **Weight:** 1219-1236 **Boot:** n/a

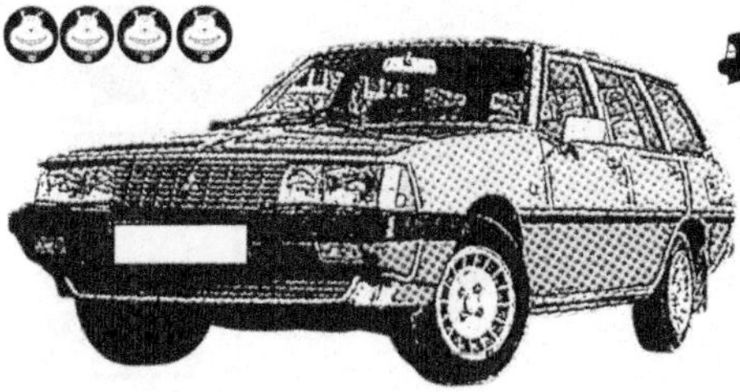

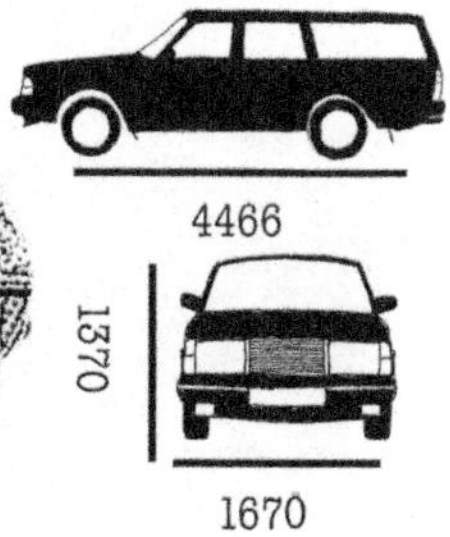

Colt/Mitsubishi Galant 1982 - 1984

Where have we seen this before? And in a different Banger category for some reason. Here is the Mitzi in it's original format. The estate is the practical one that makes the most sense, badged GLX with electric windows, remote door mirrors from '83, central locking six way adjustable driver's seat. Always reliable, practical and difficult to kill.

Engines: 2.0 **BHP**: 102 **MPH**: 98 **0-60**: 14.8 **MPG**: 31
Gearbox: 5spd/Auto **Boot:** n/a **Weight**: 1130

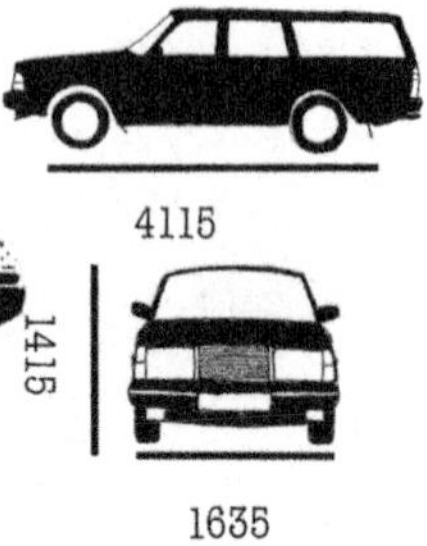

Mitsubishi Lancer Estate 1984 - 1989

The 1.5 came with a 5spd gearbox, but significantly there was also a 1.8 diesel across the range. Petrol 'economy' model deletes everything useful, electric windows, mirrors, central locking, power steering as does the diesel from '84. GLX from '85 power steering, electric windows, central locking and digital clock. Never broke down.

Engines: 1.5 • 1.8D **BHP**: 58-74 **MPG**: 28-47 **Gearbox:** 5spd **Boot:** n/a **Weight**:820

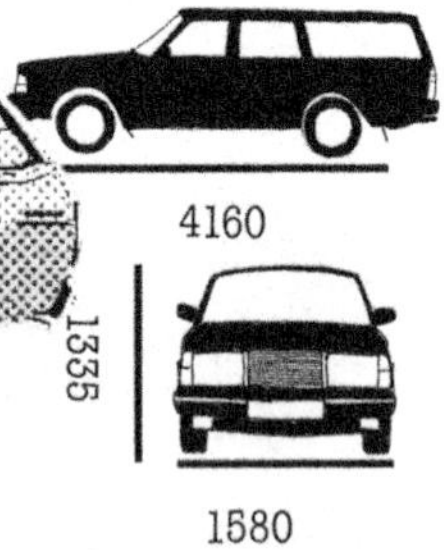

Datsun Sunny 120Y/140Y Estate 1977 - 1982

There was a van, plonked on top of the utterly ordinary front engined rear wheel drive, strut front suspension and live rear axle. The estate was just like the saloon, but rather more spacious. Same spec as the saloons. Fabulously extravagant wheel trims. Another practical family favourite which proved how terrible BL had become.

Engines: 1.2 • 1.4 **BHP**: 52-75 **MPG**: 28-35
Gearbox: 4spd/3spd Auto **Boot:** 400 **Weight:** 885-895

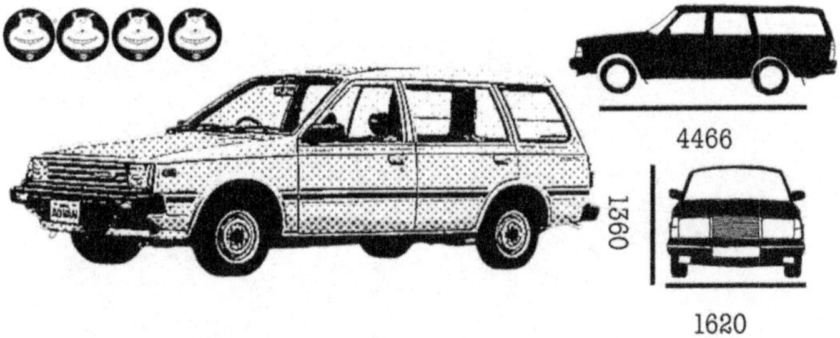

Datsun/Nissan Sunny Estate 1982 - 1986

Sunny goes rather square and also up to date with a transverse engine driving the front wheels. Not only that there was strut suspension up front and trailing arms at the rear. It also got the Cherry engines and this was a recipe for yet more utter reliability over the next four years which is all the buyers wanted.

Engines: 1.3 • 1.5 **MPG**:36-42 **Gearbox:** 5spd/Auto
Boot: n/a **Turning:** 10 **Seats**: 4 **Doors:** 2/4

Nissan Sunny Estate 1986 - 1991

As the hatch and saloon, except folding rear seats, single door pockets and no tinted glass. Engine uprate 1.6 went up to 94bhp uprated front suspension, revised grille and bumpers. Higher 5th gear and final drive ratio making it more economical. Old age means oil leaks, chirping camshaft and collapsing trim. Looks like an ordinary hatch though.

Engine: 1597cc **BHP:** 84-94 **MPH:** 99 **MPG**: 30
Gearbox: 5spd/3spd Auto **Boot:** n/a **Weight:** 1033

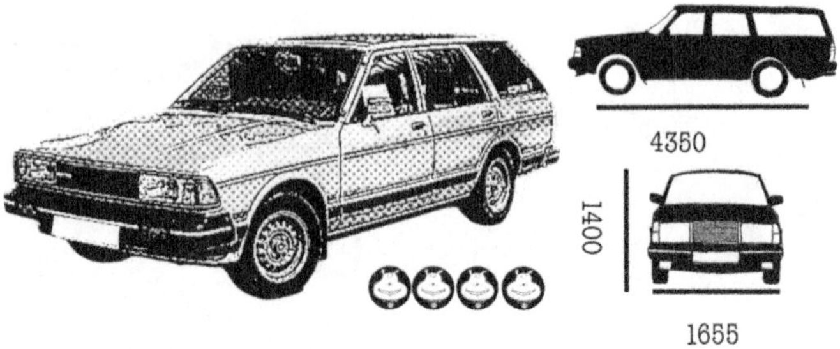

Datsun/Nissan Bluebird Estate 1980 - 1984

Same old Bluey underneath, on top it is all rather square, not hip. Rear wash/wipe, automatic not an option. This 910 series was resolutely rear wheel drive and same wheelbase. Proved very popular, got 5spd gearbox in '83, then black bumpers and bright metal inserts but what you have is the ultimate people's Banger estate.

Engines: 1770cc **BHP:** 88 **MPH:** 106 **MPG**:30 **Gearbox:** 4-5spd **Weight**: 1120 **Boot:** 420/n/a

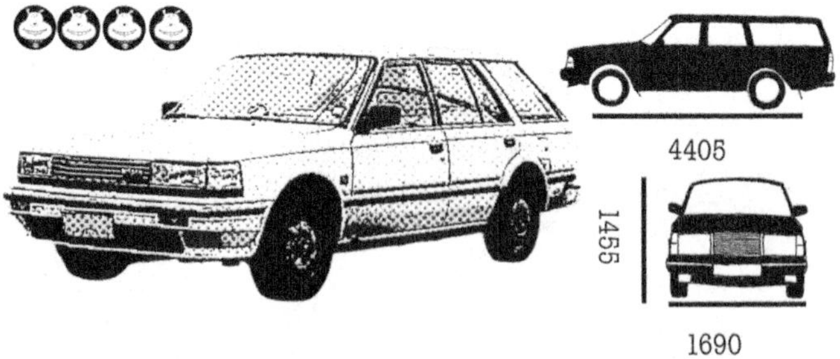

Nissan Bluebird Estate 1984 - 1986

Looks squarely similar to the Datsun, but underneath is a new age approach which means transverse engines driving the front wheels. Same 2.0 as before with a 5 speed gearbox. Badged as a GL it has body side mouldings, 2 speed intermittent wipers, two remote control mirrors, a digital clock, interior light dimmers and a centre console.

Engines: 1973cc **BHP:** 105 **MPH:** 105 **MPG**:34
Gearbox: 5spd/4spd Auto **Weight**: 1200 **Boot:** 410/n/a

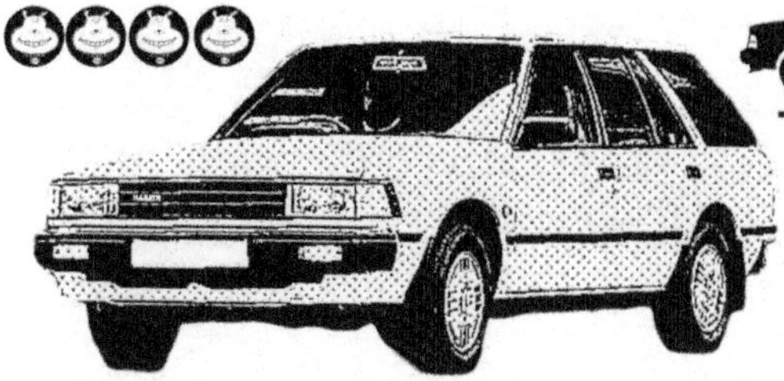

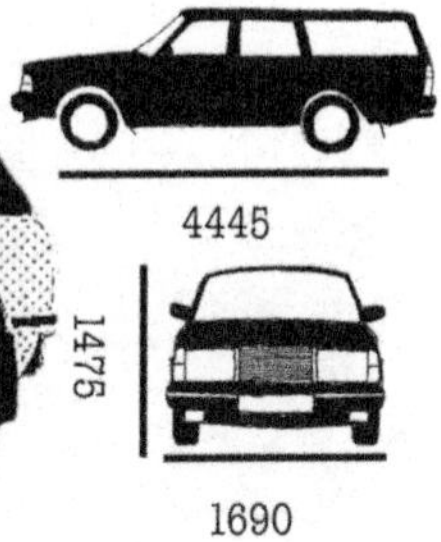

Nissan Bluebird Estate 1986 - 1990

Unarguably the most important brand new Banger Estate in Bangerpedia History. Introduced as DX with twin door mirrors, bright finish door handles, 2 speed intermittent wipers and tinted glass. Remote fuel flap, rev counter replaced by L in '88 with power steering. GL has the split fold rear seat, illuminated luggage area which is carpeted.

Engines: 1973cc **BHP:** 105 **MPH:** 105 **MPG**:33
Gearbox: 5spd/4spd Auto **Boot:** 504/n/a **Weight:**1123-1165

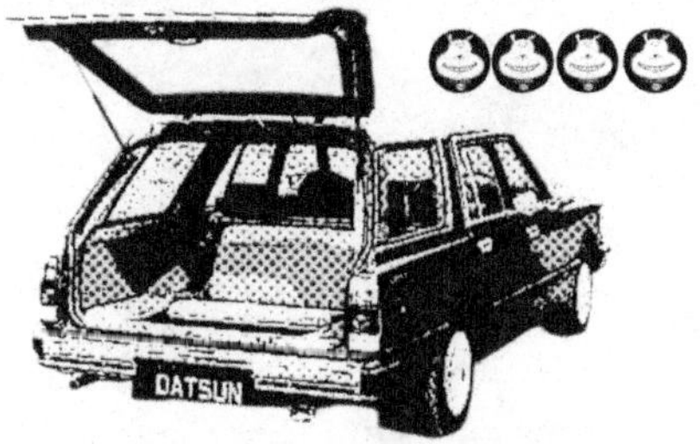

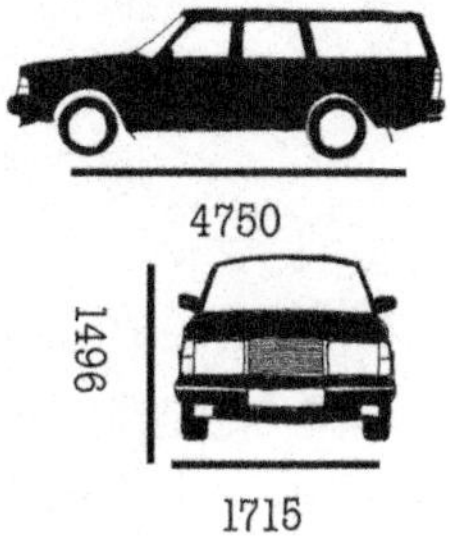

Nissan 280C/300C Estate 1980 - 1987

Here's the alternative Volvo/Granada luxury estate that everyone forgot about. The standout feature is twin rear wipers as well as standard air conditioning plus central locking and also the fact that the 3spd Automatic was an option and not standard like the saloon. Bigger engine from 1984, remote boot release and moquette trim. 7-seat option.

Engines: 2753-2960cc **BHP:** 125-155 **MPH:** 100-116
0-60: 13.8-11.6 **Boot:** 2162 **Weight:**1435-1450

Opel Rekord Estate 1977 - 1983

Pop along to your Vauxhall Open dealer and you could choose between the 'home grown' Carlton, or one of these estates. Both are Germans. Similar choice of petrol and a diesel engines, just better trim. Sold until 1986 but left the UK showrooms in 1983 to avoid any further confusion. Excellent underrated, premium Deutschland Banger Wagen. **Engines:** 2.0•2.3D **BHP**:69-99 **MPH**:99-112 **0-60:** 10.2 **MPG**: 25-35 **Boot:** 408/881 **Weight:** 1170-1295

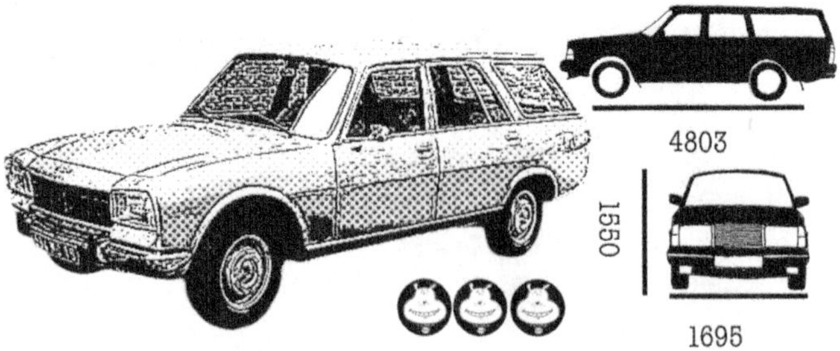

Peugeot 504 Break 1968 - 1983

Massive amounts of room and seven seats in the Famalie model. Seemed dated by the '80s, a sensible CX. Spacious, practical and proved to be impressively durable. Fuel injected 2.0 litre was impressive and the diesel provided solid, North African Taxi levels of utter dependability. Plenty of oil leaks and some random electrical issues. **Engines**: 2.0•2.2•2.3D **BHP**:69-78 **MPH:** 93-96 **MPG**: 26-37 **Gearbox**: 5spd/Auto **Weight:** 1238-1390 **Boot**: 1100

Peugeot 305 Break 1977 - 1988

Huge range of specifications and all the engines like the saloon. Facelift in '83, with a swept back-nose, lots more power options and the extra perky 105bhp 1580cc XU engine from the 205GTI. Stayed in production a year after the saloon. GT had tinted glass and sports steelies. Obviously they all, GL, GR, GT, GTX, GLD, rusted away.

Engines: 1.3 • 1.5 • 1.6 • 2.0 • 1.9D **BHP**: 67-102 **MPG**: 30-40
Gearbox: 5spd/Auto **Weight:** 975-1285 **Boot:** 412/n/a

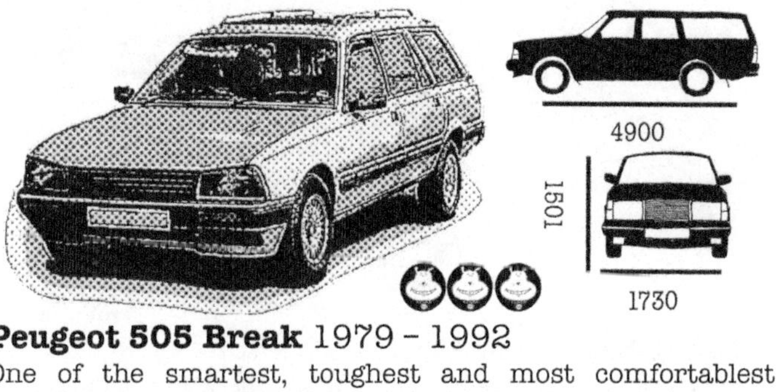

Peugeot 505 Break 1979 - 1992

One of the smartest, toughest and most comfortablest Bangers of the 1980s. Estate is great and three rows Family which also split seats gets 7 on board. All but the V6 and STi available. Petrols and diesels went on for six figure mileages. Transmissions either three-speed auto or four-speed manual, with five-speed from 1986 facelift. Value buys.

Engines: 2.0 • 2.2 • 2.3D • 2.5D**BHP**:96-168 **MPH**:97-107
0-60: 9.2-15.5 **MPG**:25- 31 **Boot:** 523/1104

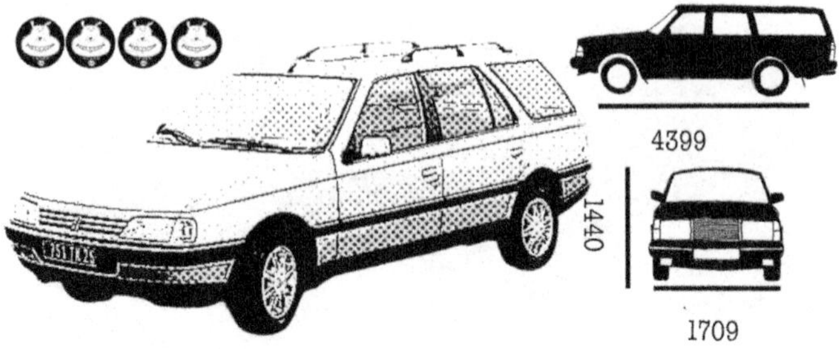

Peugeot 405 Break 1988 - 1996

Full of '80 French style in ultra useful Famailie format. Nice to drive, comfortable and spacious. Massive range, small petrols struggle but the turbo diesel fabulous for the time. GTX and Executive have all the spec. 1994 is when there were upgrades for safety including drivers airbag. Worn suspension, smoky engines are the high mile downsides.

Engines: 1.6• 1.8•2.0•1.9D **MPG**: 30.4-47 **Gearbox:** 5spd/ Auto **Weight**: 934 **Boot:** 425/1640 **Seats**: 5 **Doors:** 5

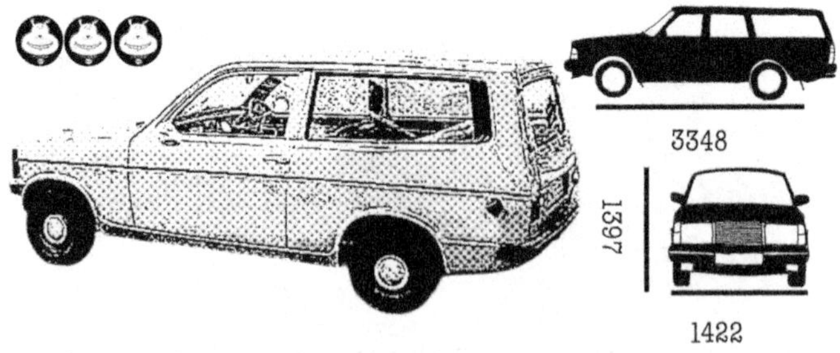

Reliant Kitten Estate 1975 - 1982

A Robin with a very useful extra wheel, in reality a side hinged doored hatchback. Same 848cc engine, otherwise identical from the rear with side opening door and wash/wipe. Longer gearstick as engine further forward. Amazing turning circle of rack and pinion steering was 25 feet in old money. More comfy/sharper DL model.

Engine: 848cc **BHP**: 40 **MPH:** 80 **0-60:** 17.6 **MPG**: 60 **Gearbox:** 4spd **Weight**: 538 **Boot:** 1200

Renault 18 1978 - 1986

In reality an old 12 in a curvy body and a whole bunch of other old engines, but 1980 Diesel 2068cc was very economical. Estate had folding rear seats and resulted in a flat floor too, so absolutely bags of room for bags. Mark 2 in '83 new front end and spoilers. Overall a very effective company estate that turned into a decent Banger.

Engines: 1.4 • 1.7 • 2.0 • 2.1D **BHP:** 64-110 **MPH**: 97- **MPG**: 33-38 **Gearbox:** 5spd **Weight:**940-1155 **Boot:** 481/1557

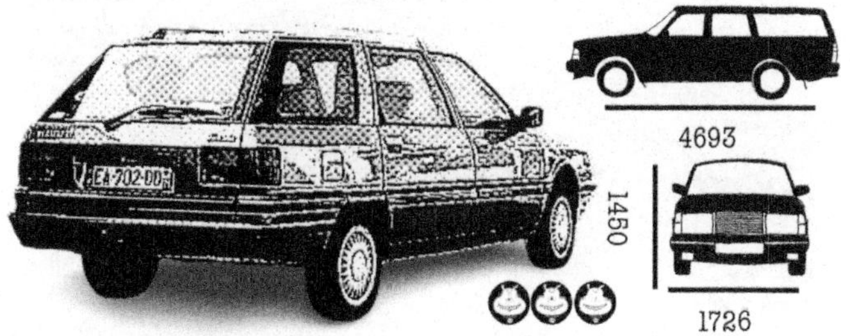

Renault 21 Savanna 1986 - 1993

Spacious and smooth riding, not very stylish and a bit flakey when it comes to reliability. Savanna from '87 has roof rails. '89 Phase II styling, smoked rear lamp lenses new grille bumpers. Top spec TXE, has alloys, electric sunroof, power steering, heated door mirrors, roof console, 60/40 split rear seat. What kills it is dodgy electrics and blown engines.

Engines: 1.7 • 2.0 • 2.1D BHP: 76-120 **MPG**: 30.9-46.3 **Gearbox:** 5spd/Auto **Weight:**1155 **Boot:** 674/1200

Subaru 1600/1800 Estate 1980 - 1989

Like most Subarus a bizarre offering at the time when most people didn't think they needed four wheel drive. 1.6 Became the L Series in '85 with rear wash/wipe and vinyl trim. 1.8 GLF becomes L dual range transfer box and automatic option. When ancient and worn out most were tossed away. Farmer's Super Duper Shopper.

Engines: 1595•1781cc **BHP:** 73-90 **MPH**: 93 **0-60**: 14.9 **MPG**: 25-30 **Gearbox:** 5spd/A **Weight**: 860 - 1126 **Boot:** n/a

Subaru Legacy Estate 1988 - 1994

Four wheel drive estate format made the most sense and this was the farmer's posh runabout. Incredible performance on road and slightly off. Basic spec Ecos are frill free, 4-Cam is the mad one. Not very exec really. Everything costs a fortune if broken. Wear and tear on the running gear and neglect if owned by someone outside the rural demographic.

Engines: 1.8•2.0•2.2 **MPG**: 27.8-29.3 **Gearbox:** 5spd/Auto **Weight:**1345 **Boot:** 420/700 **Seats**: 5 **Doors:** 5

Talbot Avenger Estate 1970 - 1981

Heated rear window on LS and nearside door mirror, GL has rear wash/wipe. Ruthlessly conventional with pushrod engines, strut suspension and four speed boxes, but that is what made them prime Bangers in the day. Certainly victims to wear and tear, rot and lack of any care at all. Alternative Cortina and always a bit cheaper.

Engines: 1.3•1.6 **BHP**: 59-69 **MPH**: 89-94 **MPG**: 30.9
Gearbox: 4-5spd/Auto **Weight:** 850-955 **Boot:** 538/n/a

Talbot Rancho 1977 - 1984

Underneath it's a Simca 1100 pick up, on top it is the SUV future (see cover). Lashings of matt black trim, roof rails, swiveling spot lamps and the front nudge bar helped the illusion. Pre LR Disco, rear passengers sat 4 inches higher. Not cheap new, almost £6K, but excelled as a Banger. Like a giant Tonka Toy the bits that weren't plastic rusted to dust.

Engines: 1442cc **BHP**: 80 **MPH**: 89 **0-60:** 14.9 **MPG**: 30.9
Gearbox: 4spd **Weight:** 1130 **Boot:** 340

Toyota Carina Estate 1977 - 1984

DX estate came with a rear wash/wipe. Revamped in 1980 adding 120mm to the car's length with bigger, more crash-resistant bumpers. In 1981 a five-speed gearbox was standardised. Third generation from '84, but same blend and Corollability, however the estate discontinued for a time, but it lived on in Bangerdom as one of the genuine legends. **Engines:** 1588cc **BHP**: 74 **MPH**: 93 **MPG**:32 **Gearbox:** 5spd **Weight:** 1005 **Boot:**450

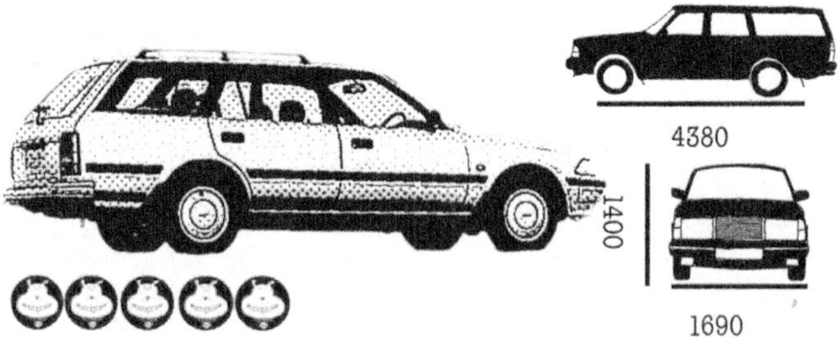

Toyota Carina Estate 1988 - 1992

5th Gen was all new, designed to be more spacious and economical and better to drive on crap UK roads with improved sixteen valve 1.6 engine. Intermittent wash/wipe but no front spoiler or automatic option. Central locking then unchanged until mild facelift in '90. Smoky high mile engines and worn suspension would bring them to a halt.
Engines: 1587cc **BHP**: 94 MPH: 109 **MPG**: 33
Gearbox: 5spd **Boot:** 535/n/a **Weight:** 1150

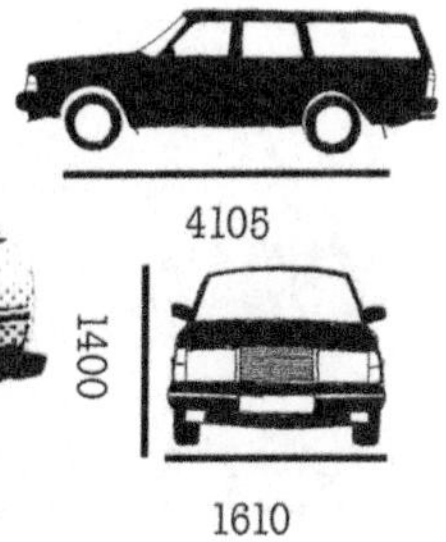

Toyota Corolla Estate 1979 - 1987

Estate kept the DX designation as the others were GL, only real difference was the load lugger had cloth rather than velour. After that nothing at all happened. The small engine soldiered on in the original RWD format until '87. The simplest of Corollas and mechanically indestructible, the body was another matter of course.

Engines: 1.3 **MPG**: 35 **BHP:** 60 **Gearbox:** 5spd/2spd Auto **Boot:** n/a **Turning:** 9.4 **Weight:** 885

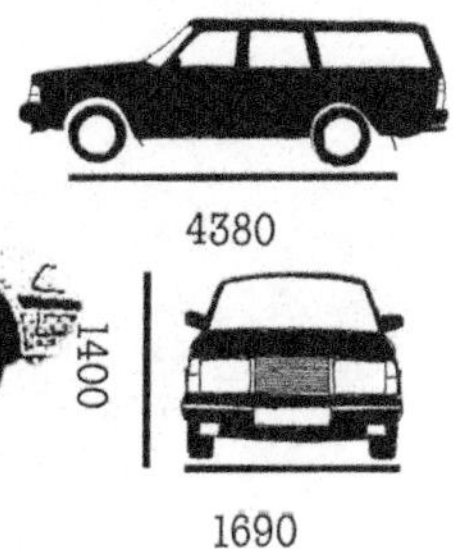

Toyota Corolla Estate 1987 - 1992

6th generation brought lots of bodywork options the station wagon was a decent holdall, if quite a rare sight. Actually a good vehicle to own and drive and not the deadly dull old thing history might have you believe. Power steering standard in 1990 and fairly classy, unlike later incarnations. Driven into the ground, yet they still survive.

Engines: 1.3 **BHP**:74 **MPH**:90 **MPG**:40 **Gearbox:** 5spd/3spd Auto **Boot:** 463/508 **Weight**:1020

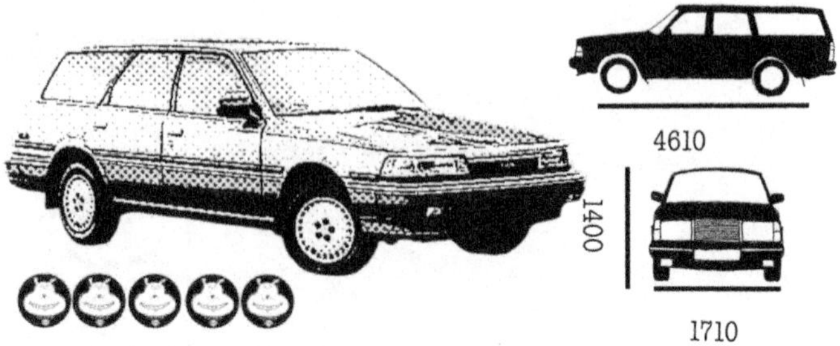

Toyota Camry Estate 1986 - 1991

Getting better at the Execugame, styling remains comatose but the engineering might win company car park arguments with twin cam Celica power. '87 Executive previously GLi. Auto. Outlived saloon, Built better than anything in Blightly or even Europe for that matter. Lots of specification to write home about such as air con and cruise. Banger Royalty.

Engines: 2.0 **BHP**:126 **MPH**:124 **0-60:** 9.4 **MPG**:32 **Gearbox:** 5spd/4spd Auto **Boot:**505/843 **Weight:** 1340

Vauxhall Chevette Estate 1975 - 1984

Luton's last design gasp on top of General Motors T world car platform, but sawing off 11 inches off the back end, fitting a hatch and the old Viva engine. Tidy on the road however rear drive seemed old hat by the '80s and arrival of the Astra meant loads of special editions to compensate, which at least delivered more standard kit. Vinyl trim only.

Engines: 1256cc **BHP**: 57 **MPG**:35-40 **Gearbox:** 4spd/3spd Auto **Weight:** 910 **Boot:** 400

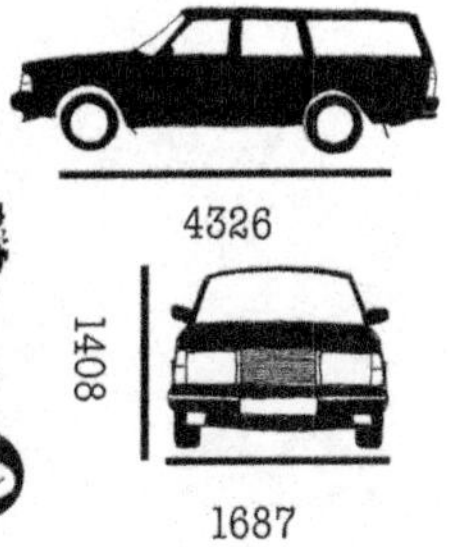

Vauxhall Cavalier Estate 1983 - 1988

Cavalier out Cortina'd the Sierra and won with it's front wheel drive, running tidily on MacPherson struts up front and torsion beam at the rear. Split fold rear seats, in base, L and LD specs. Overall very durable although noisy camshafts and hard valve stems, so smoke and drama as the miles built up. A cheap fix at the time.

Engines:1598cc/D **BHP**: 54-90 **MPH**:90- 93 **MPG**:30-38
Gearbox: 4spd/3spd Auto **Weight:** 990-115 **Boot:** 510+

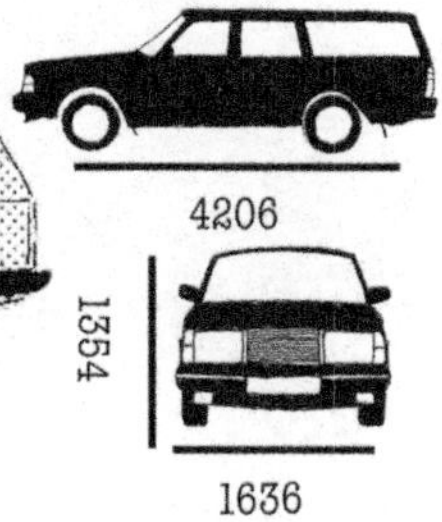

Vauxhall Astra Estate 1981 - 1984

Slogging diesel delivered amazing economy for the low level rep who needed an estate. '82 Rear wash/wipe and electronic ignition. A popular fleet and family vehicle which was cheap to fix and easy to look after. Worn brakes, suspension and smoking diesels are some issues. Most have been driven to destruction and none were cherished.

Engines: 1.3 • 1.6D **BHP**: 54-75 **MPG**: 34-48 **Gearbox:** 4spd
Boot: 470/720 **Weight:**905-1005

Vauxhall Astra Estate 1984 - 1991

Great range of petrol engines and the diesels (1.7D from '89) delivered amazing economy. A popular fleet and family vehicle which was cheap to fix and easy to look after. Worn, brakes, suspension and smoking diesels. Some special editions like 1.6 Swing with 50/50 seat and load cover.

Engines: 1.3 • 1.4 • 1.6 • 1.6D • 1.7D **BHP**: 54-90 **MPG**: 34-48
Gearbox: 5spd **Boot:** 470/720 **Weight:**905-1010

Vauxhall Carlton Estate 1980 - 1986

Opel Rekord with a Droop Snoot front. Facelift in 1982 brought in 1.8 L, 2.0 L carbs and 2.3 L diesel. A wider range of trim levels consisting of L, GL. An injected 2.0 L engine was introduced for the 1984 model year and replaced by a 2.2 L fuel injection engine for 1985. never mind all that just a big old comfy estate Banger that's easy to keep going.

Engines: 1.8 • 2.0 • 2.2 • 2.3 • 2.3D **BHP**: 71-115 **MPH:** 108
0-60: 11.2 **MPG**: 25-35 **Boot:** 481+ **Weight:** 1130-1285

Vauxhall Carlton Estate 1986 - 1993

The big family estate car, by 1990 ABS on the petrols, the Ls and GLs don't have much, so better get a CD or CDX. Diplomat and Diamond packs deliver upgraded trim of course. Non Turbo diesel a slug and 3000 'Lotus' Lugger. Not much appreciated at the time, so survivors will be worn out, suspension, brakes, engine and electrics.

Engines: 1.8 • 2.0 • 2.6 • 3.0 • 2.3D **MPG**: 24.4-41.6
Gearbox: Man/Auto **Boot:** 530/930 **Seats**: 5 **Doors:** 5

Volkswagen Passat Estate 1980 - 1988

Here's a big giant Golf to play with. Larger than ever, got Audi five cylinder carburettor engines in 1983 and then the diesels in 1985. Remarkably tough old things and massive choice of engines and specs, everything best suited to the estate format. Economy overdrive became standard on most models from '85. Even some limited editions like Country.

Engines: 1.6 • 1.8 • 1.9 • 2.0 • 1.6D **BHP**: 69-74- **MPH**:98- 102
MPG: 31-38 **Gearbox:** Man/Auto **Boot:** 470/1320+

Volkswagen Passat Estate 1988 - 1996

The last truly dull and boring one, so a great estate. Incredible reliability and ability to rack up massive business mileages. Superb engines better to have a 2.0 petrol or the 19TDi. High mile wear & tear to engine/suspension are the only things to look forward to. Find a GT which has a sunroof, there are also wide angle driver's door mirrors.

Engines: 1.8 • 2.0 • 2.8 • 1.6D • 1.9D **BHP**: 90-139
MPG: 28-53.3 **Gearbox:** 5spd/Auto **Boot:** 465/1500+

Volvo 240/260 Estate 1978 - 1993

Loads of models DL, GL injected GLE and GLT also V6 260, so plenty to choose and most eventually got 5spd and injection. Saloons gradually phased out, so this was the lead model. Ones that are not antique dealer time warps will have rotten bodies and engines that are smokey, cammy and all the ancillaries go pop.

Engines: 2.0 • 2.2 • 2.3 • 2.9 **BHP**:107-136 **MPG**: 27-29
Gearbox: 5spd/3spd Auto **Boot:** 1200/2151 **Weight:** -1470

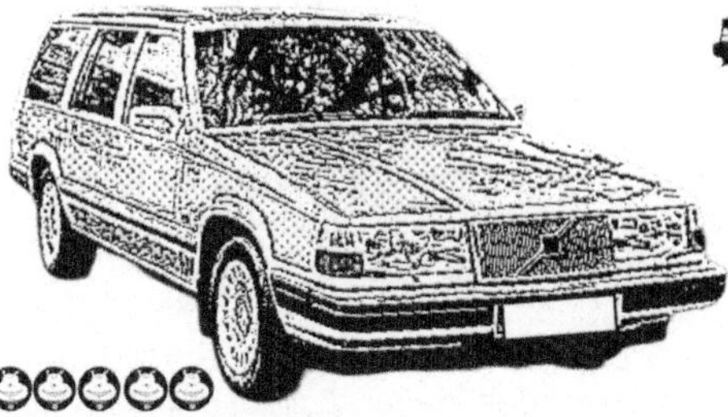

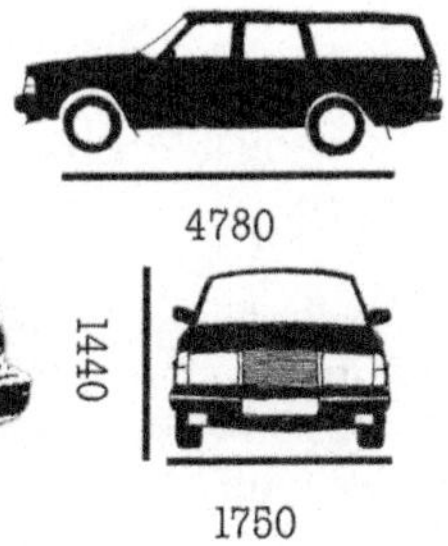

Volvo 700 Estate 1984 - 1991

Front wheel drive estate that was better than ever on the road and at lugging stuff.. A bunch of great 5 cylinder engines too, from adequate to outrageous and frugal. Loads of spec level combinations GL, SE,GLE,GLT, which were always being revised. Tired smokey diesels and worn suspension. Reliable and very useful old thing.

Engines: 2.0•2.3•2.9•2.4D **BHP**:114- 180 **MPG**: 25.2-46.7
Gearbox: 5spd/4spdAuto **Weight:** 1473 **Boot:** 792/1580

Space Ships - Banger Vans

The People Carrier is born, or was it? According to the historical timelines them Frenchie's came up with the Espace.

Previously if you wanted to shift a large family or tons of friends then it really was a case of borrowing a minibus or a van. For minibus, read Transit, Sherpa, Bedford CF, or Commer FC, or any number of medium sized panel vans that had added windows and seats. Indeed, if you are prepared to be patient then once all the Bangerpedias are finished, back to 1947 or thereabouts, you should have the opportunity to buy the Vanbangerpedia which will detail, most of the post war vannage up until 2000.

Otherwise there was no alternative but to wait until 1984. Except that if you just wanted seats then it was mostly the French to the rescue with their Break estates. In particular the Familales which had at least 7 seats in all.

In history, first there was the Plymouth Voyager which arrived months before the Renault. Manufactured first for the 1984 model year, this was known variously as the Voyager, the Town & Country, the Dodge Caravan and the Plymouth Voyager, only over here as an import.

As for the other boxes, some were vans the tiny ones from Daihatsu and Bedford, same thing really and Toyota Space Cruiser. The Japanese had it covered with the Nissan Prairie, the Honda Civic Shuttle that had the right name but only seated five. The Mitsubishi Space Wagon did better with seven.

Overall though, we didn't get anything American until the '90s, so yes the Renault Espace, was the first, but you really had to wait a few owners down the line until it was properly Banger affordable.

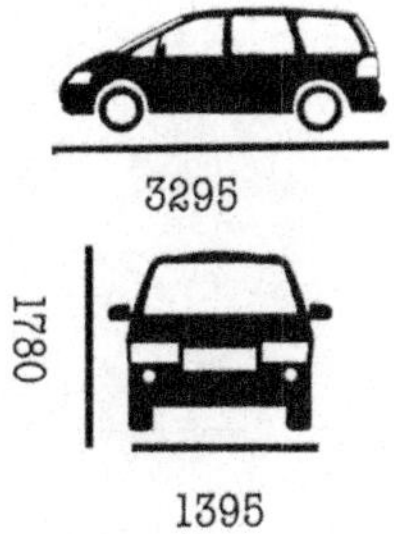

Bedford Rascal 1986 - 1993

Later badged as a Vauxhall (1990) joint venture between General Motors and Suzuki (Super Carry) and built in Dunstable. Most were vans, some became campers, a few had seats screwed into the payload area and became the cutest people carriers on the planet. Rust has killed most. Smoke and oil leaks and general neglect finished them off

Engines: 1.3 **MPG**: 38.0 **Gearbox:** 5spd **Payload:** 550kg
Weight: 755 **Seats**: 6 **Doors:** 5

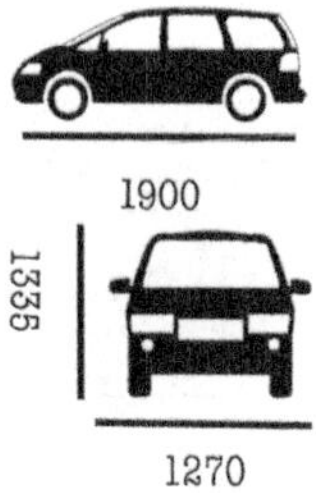

Daihatsu Hijet 1986 - 2004

A real micro van with more seats than are truly comfortable or safe. Considering its size the 1.3 engine is more than enough. Will seat six incredibly. Better enjoyed as a van, tipper or pick-up. Seem to buzz around well beyond their recorded time of death. Enjoy. Rust have killed most. Smoke and oil leaks and overused by a local handyman.

Engines: 1.3 **BHP:** 65 **MPG**: 38 **Gearbox:** 5spd Man
Boot: 560kg+ **Seats**: 6 **Doors:** 5

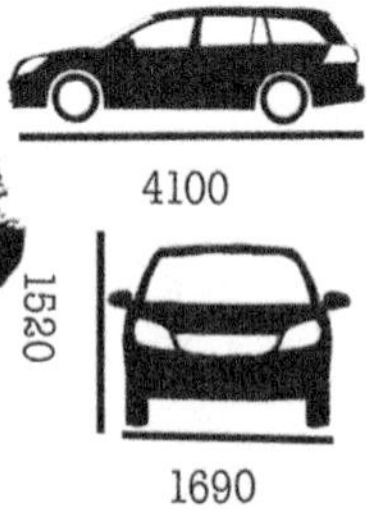

Honda Civic Shuttle 1984 - 1991

So called 'tall' vehicle which isn't quite an MPV more of a breeze block estate. There was a 4WD for a bit. Didn't catch on, not really space shuttley enough, Civic reliable though. Otherwise only around briefly in the 1990s before the name returned on a proper people shifter. This is just a weird Civic incarnation which now seems attractively oddball.

Engines: 1.4 • 1.5 • 1.6 **MPG**: 37.6-39.9 **Gearbox:** 5spd
Weight: 1050 **Boot:** 328/648 **Seats**: 5 **Doors:** 5

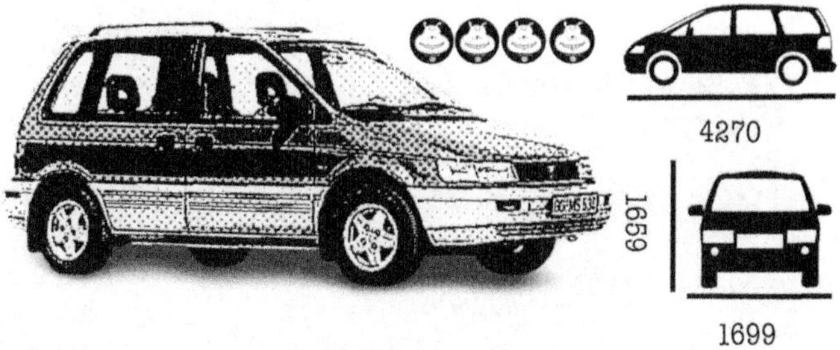

Mitsubishi Space Wagon 1984 - 1991

Runner seats 5 and the Wagon manages 7. The trouble is that it isn't that flexible and with 7 up, not any meaningful luggage space. That makes these simply a well built estate car with a high roof. Split/fold rear seat, Diamond Pack adds glass sunroof, roof rail and luggage cover. Suffers from rust, wear and tear, check exhaust and brakes.

Engines: 1.8 • 2.0 • 2.0D **MPG**: 30-6 -32.8 **Weight**:1228
Gearbox: 5spd/Auto **Boot:** 521 **Seats**: 5/7 **Doors:** 5

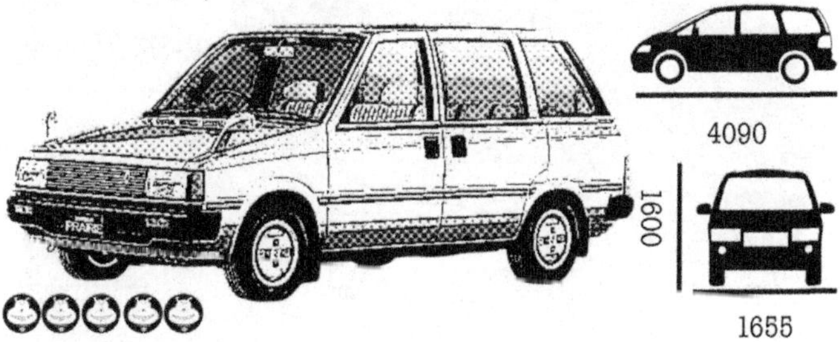

Nissan Prairie 1983 - 1989

Underneath it's a Sunny estate, not quite a van with windows, but certainly a typical box on wheels and historically pre-Espace and Dodge Caravan. Sliding commercial doors and missing B pillar means acres of access. Rear seats fold so that there's a double bed where they used to be. Rust victims. Brilliant year zero MPV.

Engines: 1.5 • 1809cc **BHP**: 74-89 **MPH**: 90-99 **MPG**: 29-30
Gearbox: 5 spd **Boot:** 1900 **Weight:** 1040 **Seats**: 7 **Doors:** 5

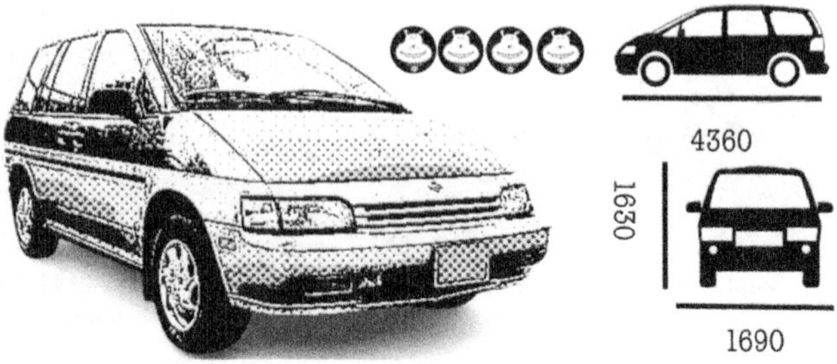

Nissan Prairie 1989 - 1991

Surprisingly short lived people van that looked the bees stylish knees, with sliding door convenience and tons of room inside. Usually front wheel drive, 4WD Japanese market models available for that go anywhere ability that UK buyers shunned. Super reliable and Bullet Train styling are the main plus points. Grey imports more common.

Engines: 2.0 • 2.4 **MPG**: 29-30 **Gearbox:** 5spd
Boot: 250/1800 **Seats**: 5-7 **Doors:** 5

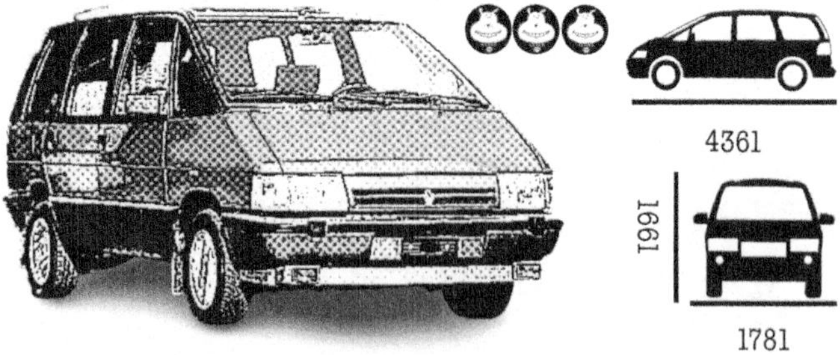

Renault Espace 1984 - 1991

The original model, a van for families, not completely original but certainly the most stylish. Apart from the driver's seat, all the others could be removed. The fronts even swiveled 180 degrees, Captain style. The second and last row of seats could have been reclined and form a king-size bed. Clutches can have a short life, smokey diesels.

Engines: 2.0 • 2.2 • 2.9 • 2.0D **MPG**: 26.4-35.8
Gearbox: 5spd/Auto **Boot:** 580/3060 **Seats**: 5/7 **Doors:** 5

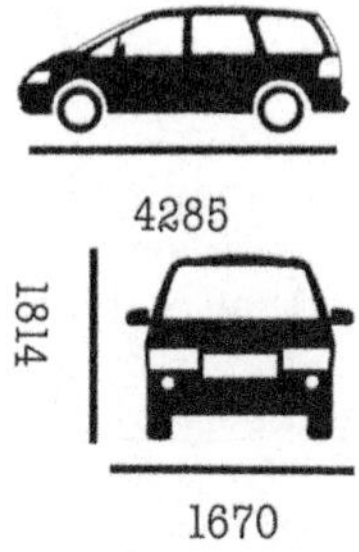

Toyota Space Cruiser 1983 - 1990

Actual van (LiteAce) with windows, but there was more to it than that, cleverly repackaged for up to 7. Drove like a van though which was never great. One sliding door, but did some tricks inside, the double bed one and could be specced with Captain's chairs for a swiveling meeting. Reliable mass family transportation. Excellent.

Engines: 1812cc•2.0 **BHP:** 75-87 **MPH**: 91 **0-60**: 16.2 **MPG**: 32 **Gearbox:** 5spd Man **Boot:** n/a **Seats**: 7-8 **Doors:** 4

BUVs - Banger Utility Vehicles

What we have here is mostly working vehicles. This is the era when people bought something with four wheel drive capability because they needed it for work. Maybe they were a farmer, a surveyor working on building sites or doing all that real lifestyle stuff with surfboards and fishing rods.

Obviously Land Rover were exploiting the fact they had sort of invented the premium off roader in Europe and buyers loved the Lord of Manor driving position. There were no other proper rivals as the Mercedes G was just an old army truck with MB-Tex covered seats. You could make a case for a well equipped Mitsubishi Shogun, but it just didn't have the kudos associated with a Landie.

Oddly enough at the other end of the utility vehicle game the Suzuki Vitara was starting to make an impact. Private buyers sticking a Rhino decorated cover on their spare wheel understood that there was a full on friendly cult around these alternative vehicles. Instead of a hot hatch for the youngsters, here was something that the whole family could enjoy and go on adventures together. Even if it was only to the new retail park.

Otherwise, everything 4 x 4 was largely utility, especially the cheaper stuff from ARO, Asia and the Daihatsu Traks. A lot of them looked like Med Holiday rentals but could really do the off road business. The Suzuki SJ413 led that little pack, despite an accusation they could fall over in corners, but that's all 4 x 4s really.

Further up the food chain, the Toyota Land Cruiser finally arrived en masse to keep well-off farmers on track. The Isuzu Trooper was also a contender which was bought by farmers who didn't need to show off, or break down in a Range Rover. Ditto the Nissan Patrol, which was a great big brick of a thing.

There was also the traditional Series Land Rovers which were updated for a new decade and were still simple enough to tow, lug and plug around difficult working environments. 90s and 110s had a new lease of life that pointed to a brighter utility focused future.

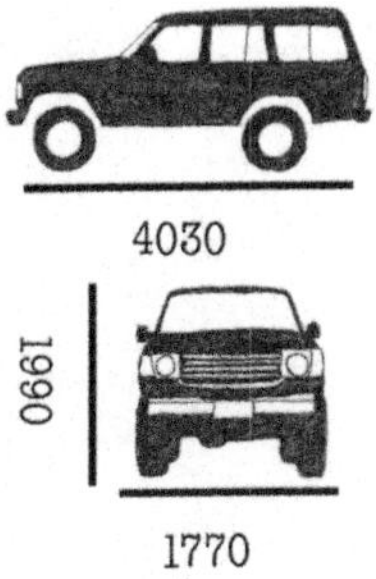

ARO 240 1978 - 1986

Utterly forgotten Lego style military spin off that dates from the '60s and briefly here to garner hard currency. Fitted with a big, low output diesel which worked well enough with the 4×4 system. The Mitsubishi power unit was rather marginal and later a slightly more lively Peugeot 2.2. Rebadged as a Ranger. Overall it's an uncivilised Duster..

Engines: 2.6D • 2.2D **BHP**: 30-59 **MPH**:68 **Gearbox:** 4spd **Weight**: 1650-2000 **Boot:** n/a **Towing:** 1450

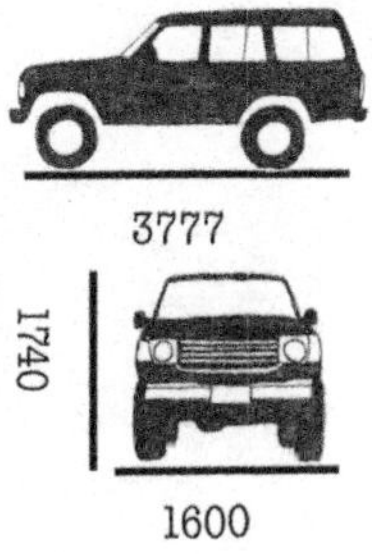

ARO Dacia Duster 1986 - 1996

ARO 10 as it was known in Romania came to the UK through the '80s and '90s and sold on price. Renault engines and the warning that it would be unwise to venture too far off road. Enough people bought them, either the convertible or the hardtop estate for imports to continue for some time. Tatty from the off, now retro cool if any survive.

Engines: 1.4 • 1.5D **MPG**: 25.7-34.8 **Gearbox:** 4spd **Boot:** Yes... **Weight**: 1280 **Towing:** 1000 **Seats**: 4 **Doors:** 3

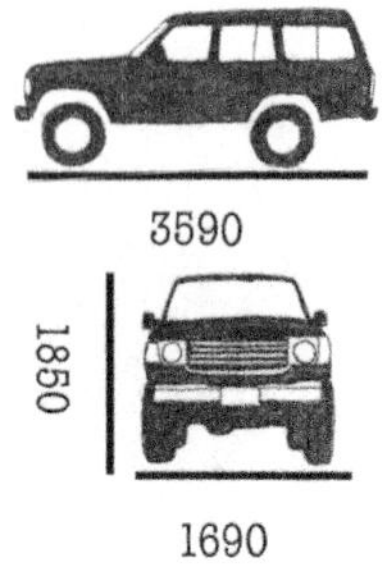

Asia Rocsta 1986 - 1997

A Jeep on the cheap, very basic, but owners swore by them. Powered by Kia engines, this is effectively the Korean army's 4×4. Available with hard and soft top and some say it was only available in the '90s, but actually dates from 1986. Not comfortable, just rather charming. An off roader as it is supposed to be. Finding rot and spares are the downsides.
Engines: 1.8 • 2.2D **MPG**: 23.5-35.3 **Gearbox:** 4spd
Weight: 1270 **Boot:** 110/470 **Towing:** 1000 **Seats**: 5

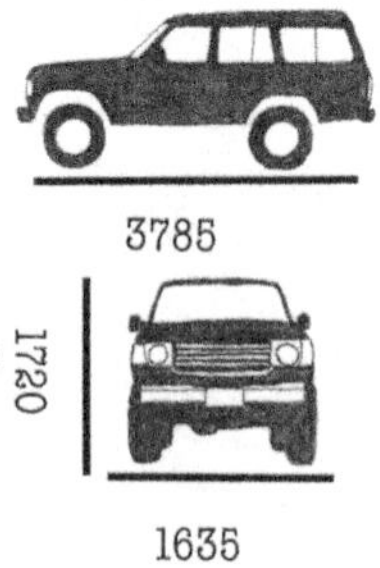

Daihatsu Sportrak 1989 - 2002

Lightweight version of the Fourtrak, sort of. Best suited to holiday hire duties somewhere sunny for the DX soft top one. A more grim location for the EL hardtop, which can certainly hack it off road. ELXi has freewheel front hubs. Restyled in '94 with revised suspension and specifications. Look for rust, wear and tear.
Engines: 1.6 **MPG**:27.8 **Gearbox:** 5spd **Boot:** 295/920
Towing: 1500 **Weight:**1206 **Seats**: 5 **Doors:** 3

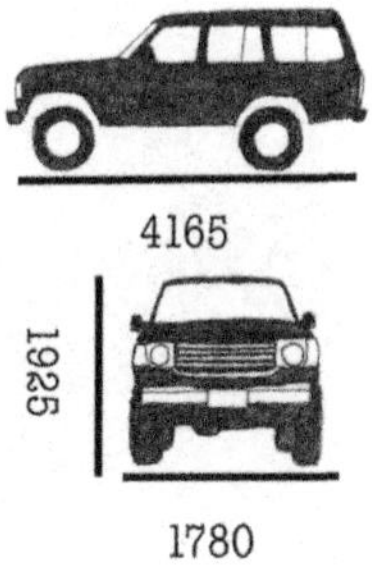

Daihatsu Fourtrak 1985 - 1997

First genuine altDefender 90. Farmers and builders bought these and quite right too. Really basic until the '90s with uprated brakes and running gear. Got independent suspension in 1993 and incredibly a seven seat version. Diesels replaced the petrol. Rust, wear and tear look out for old farm hacks which could be barely alive. Great workers.

Engines: 2.8 **BHP:** 72-87 **MPG**:30.1 **Gearbox:** 5spd
Boot: n/a **Towing:** 3500 **Seats**: 5 **Doors:** 5

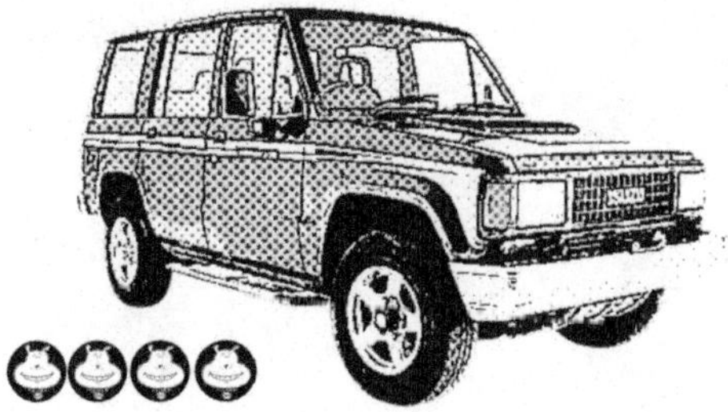

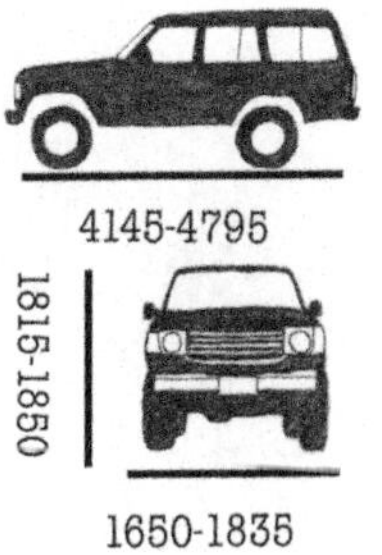

Isuzu Trooper 1987 - 1991

The Bighorn back in Japan and a Vauxhall Frontera in Blighty. Three door 2.3 petrol to start, then 2.6 petrol and 2.8 turbo diesel far better. Citation has gadgets like cruise and heated front seats. Farm hacks which could be barely alive, but underrated, utterly unkillable at the price. Zero image worked to it's under the radar advantage.

Engines: 2.3•2.6•2.8D **BHP:** 88-111: **Gearbox:** 5spd/Auto
Boot: 770-1190 **Towing:** 3500 **Seats**: 5 **Doors:** 3/5

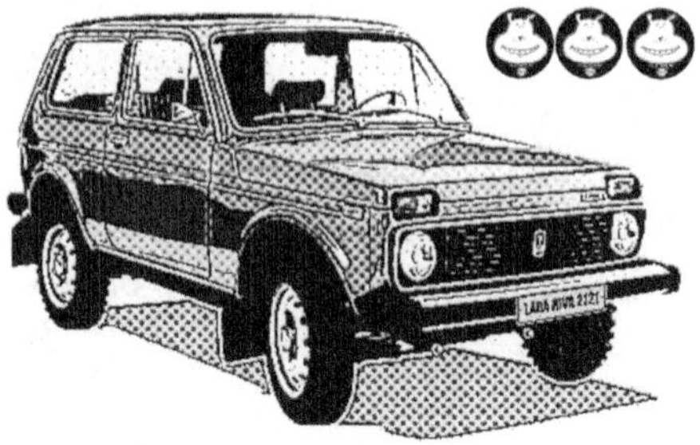

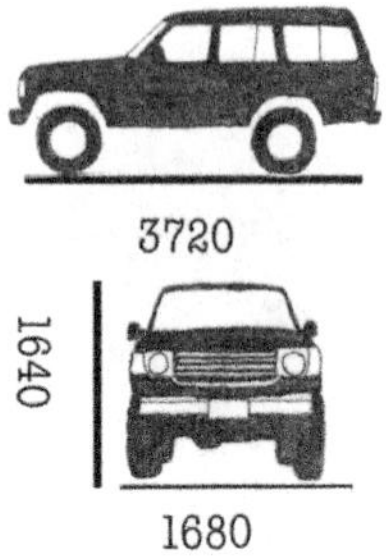

Lada Niva 1979 - 1998

A real word Defender that is rugged, excellent off road and properly basic. Cheap at the time and therefore expendable. LHD until 1983. Revamped in '86 with rear wash wipe, rear mudflaps and rubber insert bumpers. Cossack from '87 has bull bars, spare wheel carrier, glass sunroof, white alloys. Electrics and charging issues, rust of course,.

Engines: 1.6 **BHP:** 85 **MPG**: 21 **MPH**: 81 **Gearbox:** 4spd **Boot:** 420/780 **Towing:** 1000 **Seats**: 5 **Doors:** 3

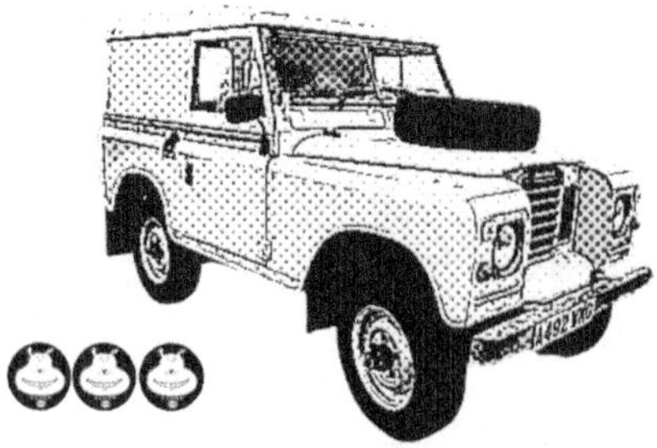

Land Rover Series III 1971 - 1985

Definitive working vehicle. It has the longest story ever told. The shape never changed much, just short "88 or long "109. 5 bearing 4 cylinder engines from 1980. Low compression V8 LWB meant to fend off Land Cruiser, but it remained an unsophisticated lorry, despite County spec good intentions. Rust, electrics. Once sorted very much a long termer.

Engines: 2.3•2.6•3.5•2.3D **BHP**: 62-91**0-60:**26-31 **Gearbox:** 4spd **Boot:** 1510+ **Towing:** 3500 **Seats**: 2/3/7/9+

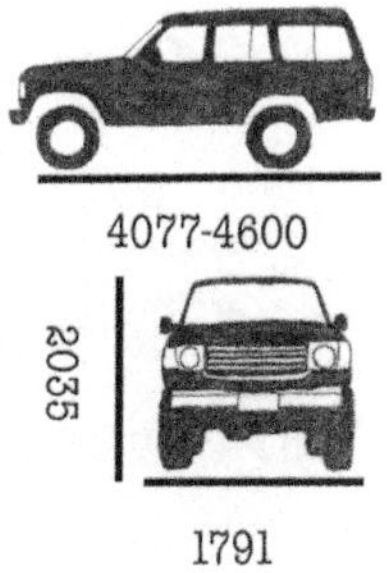

Land Rover 90/110 1983 - 1990

Into the 20th Century, 110 came first with coil springs, all synchro 5spd gearbox on 4 cylinders, full width plastic grille and flared arches on the outside. 90 in '84 (pretty much 93" wheelbase anoraks) also new 2.5 Diesel and V8 is back in '85. More changes with 2.5 petrol then a turbo diesel as it was turned into the Defender. Build still marginal.

Engines: 2.5•3.5•2.4D•2.5D **BHP:**83-134: **MPG**: 28.2 **Gearbox:** 5spd **Boot:** 2300 **Towing:** 3500 **Seats**: 2/7/9+

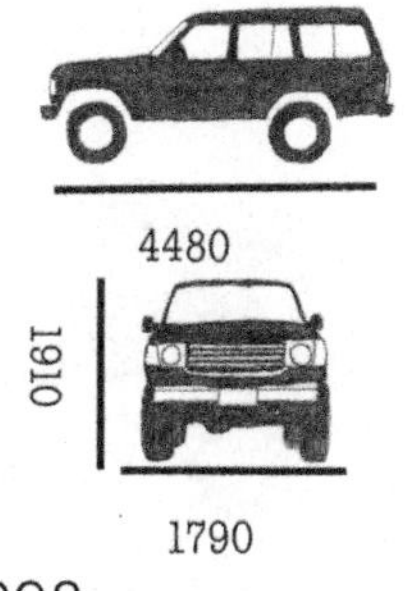

Land Rover Discovery 1989 - 1998

Range Rover with a different body on top, optional seven seats and some curious engine choices. The 300 TDi and V8s are the only ones worth considering as the tiny petrol dismally slow and troublesome. Spacious, refined and some decent XS and ES specs with twin sunroofs and alloys. Blown head gaskets, rot and electrical upsets. Better than II.

Engines: 2.0•3.5•3.9•4.0•2.5D **MPG**:17-34.2 **Gearbox:** M/Auto **Boot:** 881-1699 **Towing:** 3500 **Seats**: 5/7 **Doors:** 3/5

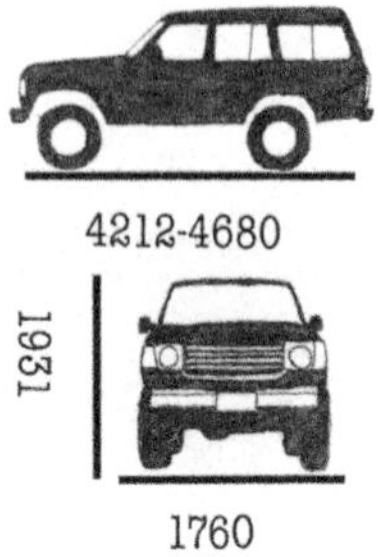

Mercedes G-Wagen 1979 - 1991

Old School Defender killer, but not remotely Range Rover comfy, just a boringly tough military go anywhere vehicle which was surprisingly decent on road. Best bought used had coil sprung live axles and the usual transfer low ratios when required. Last of the pre Blingers with zero creature comforts. As ever, watch out for worn out ones.

Engines: 2.3•2.8•3.0D **MPG**: 16.2-20.3 **Gearbox:** 5spd **Boot:** 530/900 **Towing:** 750-3500 **Doors:** 3/5

Mitsubishi Shogun 1983 - 1991

In case a buyer didn't want to break down all the time in a Range Rover/Disco here was the realistic on/off road answer in the boxy shape of the Shogun. Great on/off road and good for towing. Diamond Pack has more kit and V6 in '89 almost RR Vogue. Short or long models with row three and 7 seats. Soft Tops for a bit. Solid just fluid leaks and worn out parts.

Engines: 2.6•3.0 **BHP**: 102-139 **MPH**: 87-99 **MPG**: 17 **Boot:** 2100 **Towing:** 875-1800 **Weight:** 1740-1765

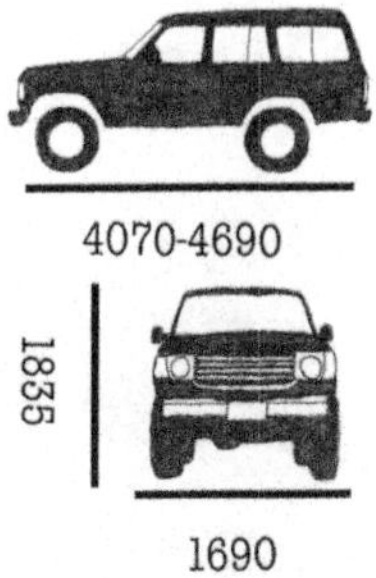

Nissan Patrol 1982 - 1991

A big tough old unit that is best off down on the building site. Not the most articulate chassis, so something of a rough road MPV. Two sizes and the five door will have 7 seats. Not great mpg even on the diesels, just a lump on the road. Zero finesse, but unlikely to stop going. Dull, but still more reliable than most LRs. Neglected ones should be left to rot.

Engines: 2.8•3.0•2.8D•3.3D **BHP**: 94-119 **MPH**:81-87 **MPG**:19-22 **Weight**:1835-1980 **Boot:** n/a **Towing:**750-3500

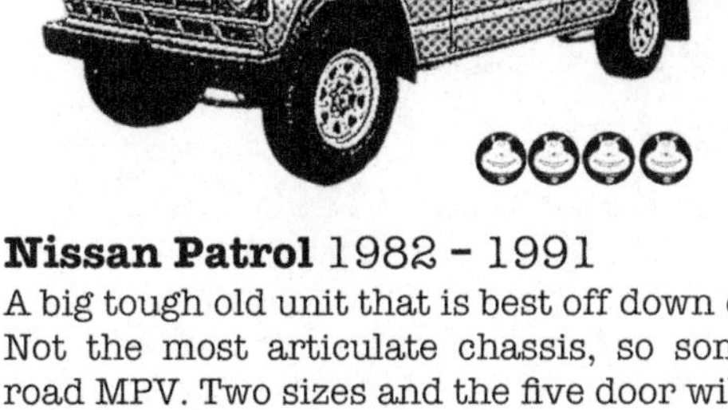

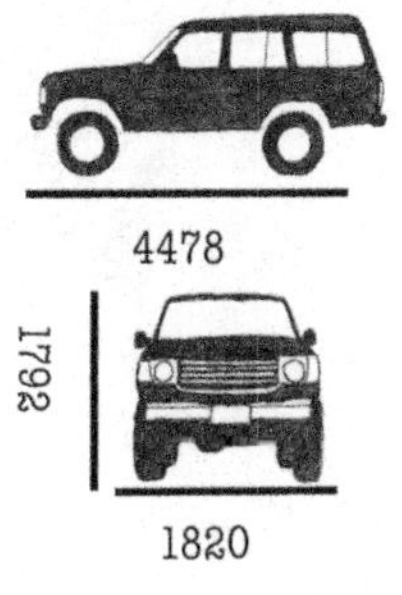

Range Rover 1970 - 1994

The poshification begins with the 'In Vogue' in '81, but welcome practicality is the four door. In Vogue 4 door has alloys and auto, then 'Vogue' standard from '84. 165bhp V8 in '85 and VM diesel in '86. Then Vogue SE which tells you everything, becoming a complicated liability for some and not the wisest Banger buy unless a basic V8.

Engines: 3.6•3.9•2.4D•2.6D **BHP**:106-168 **MPH**:93-108 **MPG**:12-23 **Boot:** 1020/2000 **Towing:** 750-3500

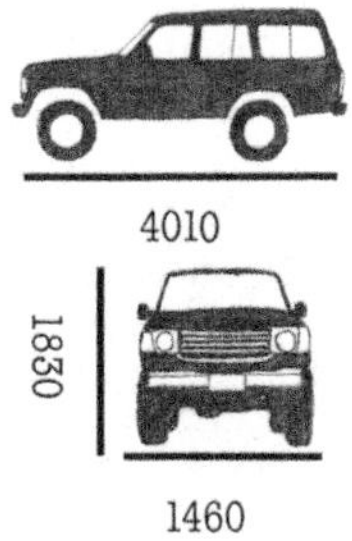

Suzuki SJ410/Santana 1982 - 1990

Buying one was like bringing your holiday rental home. Slow and allegedly deadly if operated too enthusiastically, but the marginal 45bhp kept drivers in check. Part of the import dodge, so made in Spain at which point (1987) it's a Santana. Surprisingly efficient off the beaten track. Holiday spoilt if engine smokey, suspension noisy and there's rot.
Engines: 970cc **BHP**: 45 **MPH**: 75 **MPG**: **Gearbox:** 4spd
Boot: 100ish **Towing:**1200 **Weight**: 890

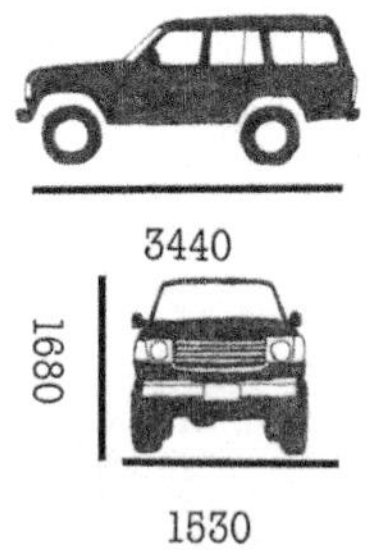

Suzuki SJ413 Samurai 1985 - 1996

Basic pint sized Jeep which excels as a holiday rental but will do so much more. A tough little nut with unbreakable engine, but Spanish built body as flimsy as you would expect in our climate. There's a hardtop, soft top and a longer one. Very underrated overall, poor on road but brilliant off for its size. Smokey engine, noisy suspension and rot.
Engines: 1.3 **BHP:** 63 **MPH:** 78 **MPG**: 28 **Gearbox:** 4spd
Boot: 100ish **Towing:** 1100 **Weight**: 924 **Seats**: 4 **Doors:** 3

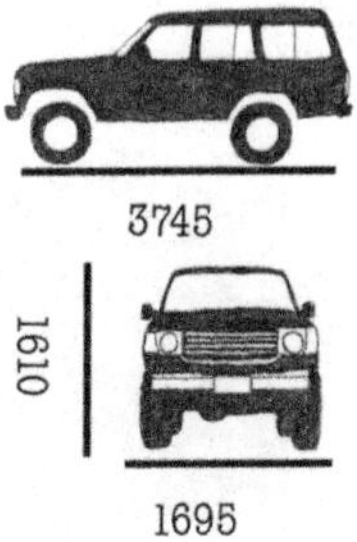

Suzuki Vitara 1988 - 1991

The vehicle responsible for the adoption of high rise family SUV of choice and what a great bit of kit. Tough, practical, stylish and usefully compact. Lots of models, this is the people's Landcruiser and potentially just as unbreakable, only the 3 doors until the '90s. Banger buyers check out minor electricals, coolant and oil leaks. **Engines:** 1.6 **BHP:** 75 **MPH**: 87 **0-60:** 16 **MPG**: 34.4 **Boot:** 202 **Towing:** 450 **Kerb:** 1005

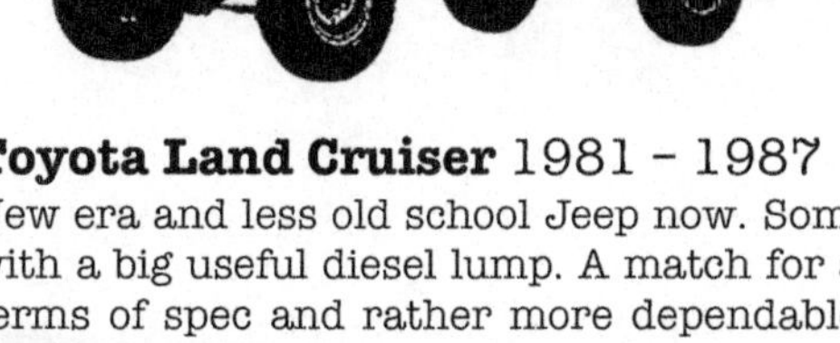

Toyota Land Cruiser 1981 - 1987

New era and less old school Jeep now. Somewhat gaudy but with a big useful diesel lump. A match for a Range Rover in terms of spec and rather more dependable. Not something readily adopted or understood. A bit more diesel output did not improve the mpg or its appeal at the end of the run. Niche Banger, rare and perfect for well-off caravanners

Engines: 3890cc **BHP:** 99-101 **MPH:** 95 **0-60**:19
MPG: 26 **Weight:** 2078 **Boot:** 11.7 cu ft **Towing:** 2500

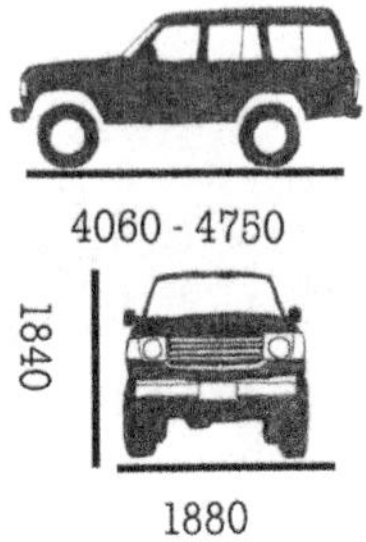

Toyota Land Cruiser 1987 - 1990
Becoming the Legendcruiser in the UK and clearly it was now being pitched as an Oriental Range Rover in five door format, and rather more suited to hard work. Superb at towing, lugging and just going where others struggle. Lasts forever with care and prices remained remarkably firm throughout an almost infinite life span. **Engine:** 3980cc **BHP**: 102 **MPH**: 87 **0-60**: 18 **MPG**: 22 **Boot:** 275/1100 **Towing:** 3500 **Seats**: 5/7

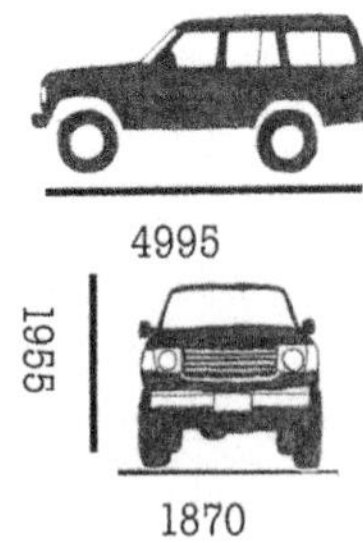

Land Cruiser II 1998 - 1992
Various size Cruisers worldwide so they finally tried the 'fun' sized one as sort of a mega Vitara. Sits on a Defendersque 90 inch wheelbase and the diesel turbo more than able on and off road. A good caravan and boat tug and became Banger material quicker than the five door. Lots to love like the altimeter and inclinometer gadgets.
Engines: 2446cc **BHP:** 89 **MPH:** 81 **0-60:** 23.8 **MPG**: 19 **Boot:** 331 **Weight**: 1700 **Towing:** 750-2500

Quattro Bangers - 4WD Style

Well this was interesting. Just when you least expected it, along came loads of cars that weren't just front or rear wheel drive, but all wheel drive. Just for clarification you will find Subarus in other sections, but that's what we expect of them, same with Suzukis too. Also all the usual 4×4s will be in the Utility section. What we are covering here are the manufacturers we mostly never expected to come up with a 4×4 system usually plumbed into a cooking saloon, hatch or estate.

Why did this happen? Well, rallying did, or more precisely Audi did. Usually a minimum of 200 models had to be made to qualify for the wonderfully bonkers Group B rally class. For Audi, dominant victories and two drivers' and manufacturers' titles with the 'Ur-quattro' in the World Rally Championship between 1982 and 1984 were important factors. It seemed a waste not to use that technology on the available models hence all those Quattros in the showroom at the time.

Not surprisingly the head of the VW Group got in on the act with their permanent 4×4 Syncro version. Just 26,000 four-wheel drive Golf Syncros were ever built and only 1000 were sold in the UK. This is separate from the excitingly supercharged G60, rather than the workaday four door hatch.

Then to everyone's surprise, there are the Alfa Romeos, Citroens and Peugeots that got in on the all wheel drive act. None were more successful than Ford. Then there is the wonderful Fiat Panda, all the 4×4 that anyone needs, plus the Sisley system appears to be fixable on a budget. There will never be such an exciting time to buy an old car. Probably.

Oh and why are these Bangers? Well, these are 'ordinary' models that once they have been through the used car process, end up being judged on their complication and running costs. Someone who just wants an old estate rejects a 4×4 because the mpg is going to be far worse. They slip down the ownership profile and became a risky Banger purchase, which might be good in the mud.

Alfa Romeo 33 QV 1985 - 1987

Only in the showrooms for eighteen months, the hard ride put some people off and the 1.5 output was marginal, so they bought Quattros. Estate format, rear wash/wipe tinted glass and central locking. Got alloy wheels in '86 otherwise not much happened. You simply used the lever in the centre console to switch from two for four wheel drive.

Engines: 1490cc **BHP**: 95 **Gearbox:** 5spd **Weight:** 990 **Boot**: 290/1005 **Seats**: 5 **Doors:** 5

Audi 80/90 Quattro 1983 - 1986

This is where it started and the first 80 had 136 bhp to play with. In 1985 though the 5 cylinder was replaced by the Golf GTI 1.8 with electronic ignition. The serious Quattro became the 90 in 1984 with 5 cylinders but just 136bhp. Exclusively available in saloon format, it became the more than capable Banger.

Engines: 1.8•2.0•2.2 **BHP**:112•115•136 **MPH**:120-124 **MPG**: 24 **Boot:** 505 /541 **Weight**: 1062-1300 **Doors:**4

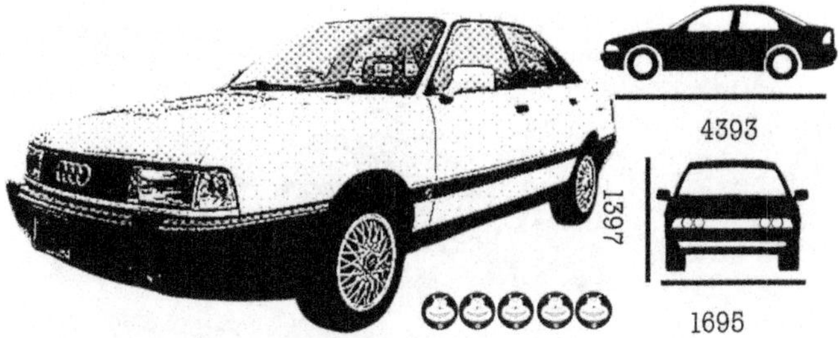

Audi 80/90 Quattro 1986 - 1991

Blunt styling for the mid '80s and still, saloon only. 80 got ABS as standard in '88 along with electric windows and mirrors. New catalytic equipped 1984cc engine in '89 along with power steering. '90 got a new 2.3 5 cylinder with a cat, velour trim and electric windows. Engines become smoky, with age, galvanised body largely keeps the rot away.

Engines: 1.8•2.0•2.3 **BHP**:112•113•136 **MPH**: 122-137 **MPG**: 23-28 **Boot:**373 **Weight**: 1149-1220 **Doors:**4

Audi 100/200 Quattro & Avant 1984 - 1991

Huge surefooted saloon and from 1985 there is an Avant as well along with 200 Turbo as the high performance incarnation that only lasted to '87. From '88 non turbo 200 version in saloon and estate. 100 takes over in '89 with cat engine and alloys. Default Wear and tear issues of brakes and suspension.

Engines: 2144•2226•2309cc **BHP**: 138-170 **MPG**: 23-24 **Boot:** Avant: 390/1430 Saloon:570 **Weight:** 1090-1260

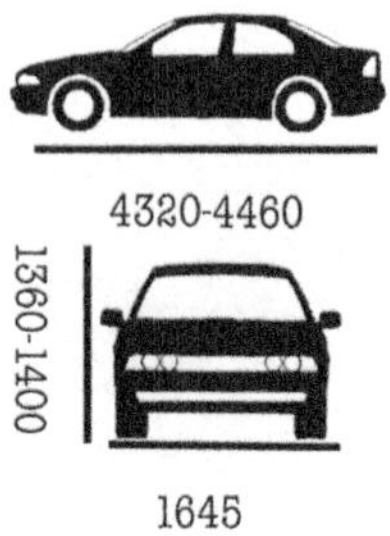

BMW 325iX 1985 - 1989

Here was a four wheel drive version of the 325i in two and four door models, available only as a special order which explains the short model run. Had flared wheel arches and added sill extensions. Oh and it was left and drive only. Front spoiler and foglamps plus a colour coded boot spoiler. Power steering from '88 along with catalytic kit.

Engines: 2494cc **BHP**: 171**MPH**: 135 **0-60:** 8.3
Gearbox: 5spd **Boot:** 404 **Weight**:1270 **Doors:** 2/4

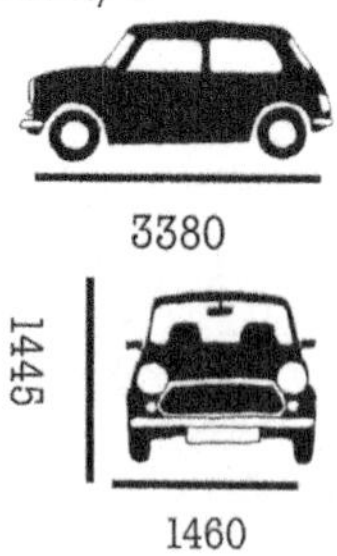

Fiat Panda 4×4 1984 - 1992

Steyr-Puch developed a 4WD system just for the Panda which could be driven with either the front or all wheels. It looked a bit different with a sump protection plate, more prominent side rubbing strips, extended wheelarches and a set of mud flaps. Apart from FIRE engine in '86 not much happened, although in Europe there was a van. Brilliant,

Engines: 965-999cc **BHP**: 48-50 **MPH**: 84 **0-60:** 17.5
Gearbox: 5spd **Boot:** 269 **Weight**: 805 **Doors:** 2

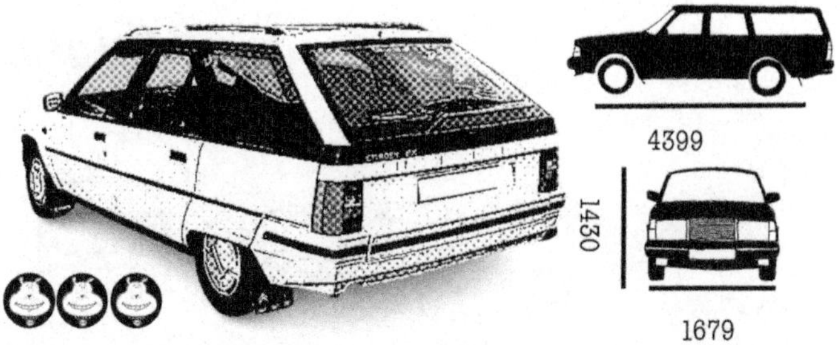

Citroen BX 4×4 Estate & GTi 1990 - 1994

Technically in and outside of the '80s Bangerpedia brief, but these were significant additions. Estate based on the TZS with permanent four wheel drive and rear differential with a limited slip. The GTi had a rear Torsen diff, ABS, power steering, central locking and electric windows plus a sunroof. A Banger because it's a complicated used Citroen.

Engines: 1905cc **BHP**: 107 • 125 **MPH**: 108-117 **MPG**: 24-31 **Gearbox:** 5spd Man **Boot:** Estate: 512/1803 GTi: 444

Ford Sierra XR4×4 1985 - 1990

The XR4i didn't hit the spot, but this did, first as a hatch and from '86 an estate. Alloys, electric windows. New V6 in '88, standard ABS in '89 and for '90 cosmetic changes with white front indicator lenses, smoked rear and black tail panel. Special editions, Ghia Plus, and 2.9. Handsome, useful and cheap, 'cos it's an old Jellymould Ford.

Engines: 2792 • 2933cc **BHP**: 150 **MPH**: 127 **0-60**: 8.8 **MPG**: 22 **Gearbox**:5spd **Boot**: Hatch: 385 Estate 427/1958

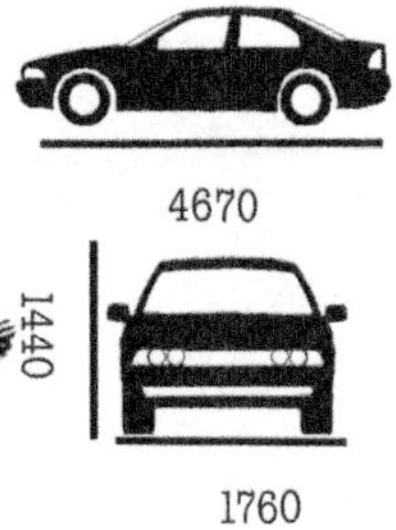

Ford Granada Scorpio 4×4 1985 - 1992

Executive all wheel drive with V6 power in Ghia and Scorpio hatchbacks. Uprated in 1987 with bigger engine, now as saloon (from 1990) and hatch. Leather trim, cruise control, but could de-specced to cloth, if the cops or a stingy fleet manager were involved. New MT75 gearbox in '88. Proper working blokes version of a 200 Quattro.

Engines: 2792•2933cc **BHP**: 148-150 **MPH**: 129 **0-60**: 9.0
MPG: 23 **Gearbox**:5spd/Auto **Boot**: 440

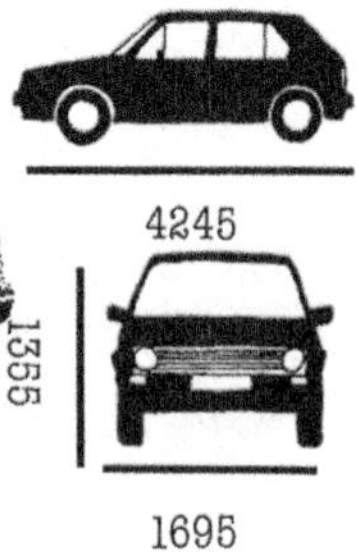

Mazda 323 1600 Turbo 1985 - 1989

An Integrale for the masses. A hot hatch with a homologation agenda, it was therefore not especially quick as the 4×4 piled the weight on. Electric windows, sunroof, headlight wash/wipe, tinted windows, central locking and 14" x 6" polished alloy wheel. New generation from 1988 painted all black with side skirts and electric sunroof.

Engines: 1597cc **BHP:** 148 **MPH**: 124 **0-60**: 7.8
Weight:1110 **Boot:** 325

Mazda 626 GLX Executive 1990 - 1991

Just on the '80s Bangerpedia cusp, a saloon and estate (from 1991) that no one knew they needed. There was no automatic option, but the spec same as the normal model with alloys, headlight washers, cruise control, electric mirrors, so it was well equipped. Good value and massively reliable of course. Good luck ever finding one.

Engine: 2184cc **BHP**: 116 **MPH**:114 **0-60**: 9.6
Gearbox: 5spd **Boot:** 467 **Weight**: 1305

Mercedes 300E/TE 4 Matic 1988 - 1992

Based on the standard 300E automatic, although a manual was a no cost option. Electronically controlled four wheel drive with Automatic Locking Differential. Also available in estate TE format. '89 headlamp wash/wipe, front centre armrest, leather gear knob and steering wheel. World of expensive pain if 4WD faulty, many just switch to RWD.

Engines: 2962cc **BHP**: 190 MPH: 135 **MPG**: 21-15 **Gearbox:** Automatic 4spd **Boot:** Saloon 520 estate 530

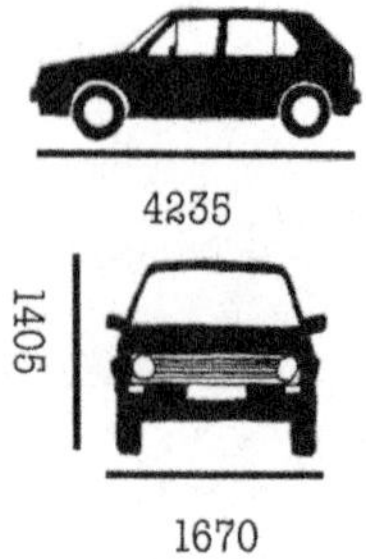

Mitsubishi Lancer 1800 GLXi 1989 - 1991

Applying the 4WD formula to smaller models mostly for the purposes of homologation. The Liftback, hatchback was first available in the UK now with multipoint fuel injection, full time four wheel drive and apparently a close ratio gearbox. Also alloy wheels, then 5 spokes in 1990 and a reflective tailgate, whatever that was. Ultra rare reliability.

Engines: 1755cc **BHP:** 95 **MPH**: 104 **0-60**: 12.6 **MPG**: 30
Gearbox: 5spd **Boot:** 337 **Weight**: 1135

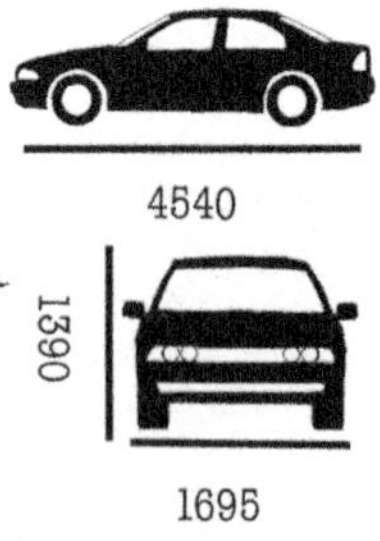

Mitsubishi Galant 2000 GTi 1989 - 1993

One to avoid if it goes wrong, but technically one of the most interesting from this period. Fuel injected 16 valve engine would be enough for most, but also have four wheel steering as saloon and coupe from 1990. Side mouldings and sill extensions set it apart. Good levels of kit, electric windows, mirrors and central locking.

Engines: 1977cc **BHP**:142 **MPH**:127 **0-60:** 8.8 **MPG**: 30
Boot: 415 **Weight:** 1335

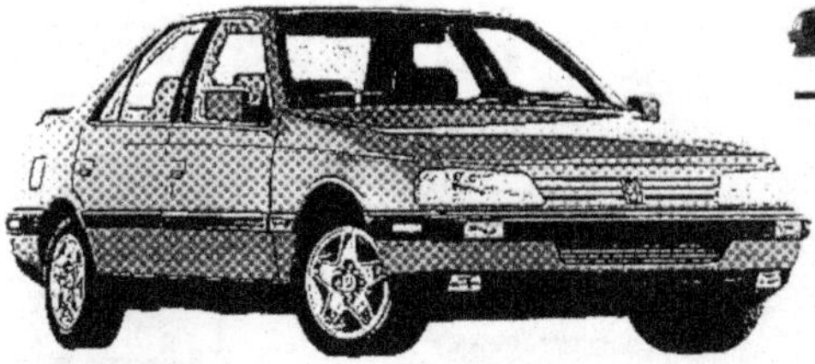

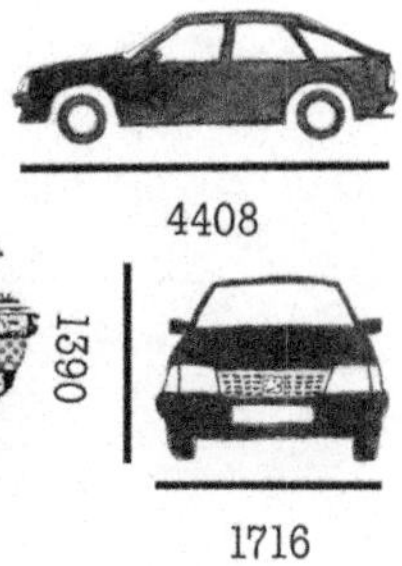

Peugeot 405 GL x4 1988 - 1996

Cooking 405 saloon with all wheel drive, great for building site surveyors on a budget. There was also an MI 16 x 4 for sports car drivers who needed to fit a baby seat. GL remains the oddity with power steering, self leveling rear suspension and central locking. In '90 it got body side mouldings, tinted glass, tweed trim and electric front windows.

Engines: 1905cc **BHP**: 110 **MPH**: 115 **0-60:** 10.6
MPG: 30.4 **Gearbox:** 5spd **Weight**: 1160 **Boot:** 470

Renault 21 Turbo Quadra 1990 - 1992

The 21 Turbo was all very well, but the problem was that get all the power through the front wheels was problematic, hence the Quadra. For the record it weighed 155kg more than the two-wheel-drive model, but the performance improvement was fairly marginal as the 0-60mph only dropped from 8.1sec to 7.8sec. Still fun though.

Engines: 1995cc **BHP:** 173 **MPH**: 138 **0-60**: 7.8 **MPG**: 25
Gearbox: 5spd **Weight:**1338 **Boot:** 490

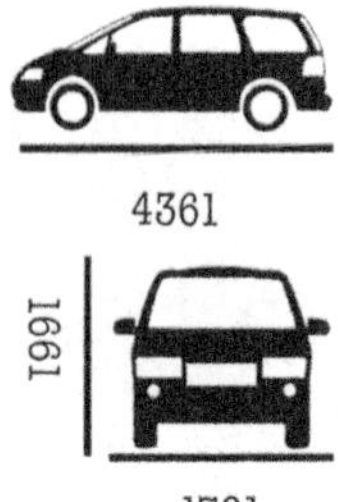

Renault Espace Quadra 1989 - 1991

No one would have thought they needed a four wheel drive MPV until they want to go to the Alps for a winter break. Before the SUV, this was the cool one. Available as a TXE with alloy wheels and side rubbing strips, also 2000-1 spec which meant double sunroofs and stripy trim. From '90 you could get leather trim, chrome roof rack & all that bollocks.

Engine: 1995cc **BHP**: 120 **MPH**: 96 **MPG**: 27
Gearbox: 5spd **Boot:** 580/3060 **Weight**: 1290

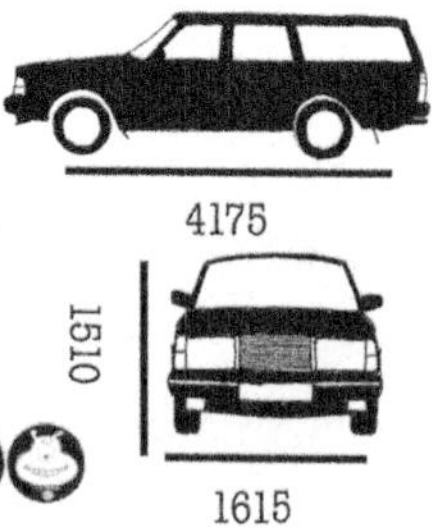

Toyota Tercel 4WD 1983 - 1988

The brochure said it was a 'new kind of car' and yes it was a crossover, not an SUV or Utility, but an estate with four wheel drive. Looks quite workhorse serious and unlike a Rancho actually delivered with an 'extra low gear' in 4WD. Split fold seats, split fold seats. Uprated in 1986: electric sunroof, remote boot + fuel flap release. Lasts forever in USA.

Engine: 1452cc **BHP**:71 **MPH**: 97 **0-60**: 15.2 **MPG**: 35
Gearbox: 7spd **Boot:** 991 **Weight**: 300/1200

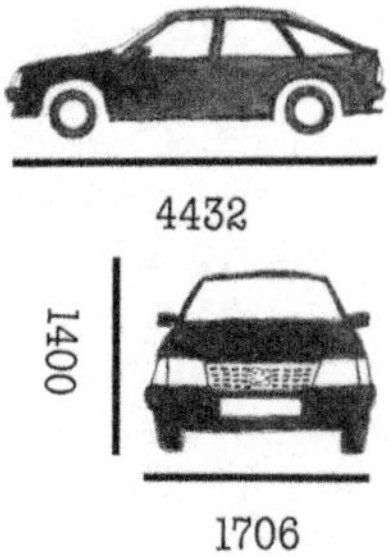

Vauxhall Cavalier 4×4 1989 - 1993

Not terribly successful but great for towing, it won awards for that. Billy basic with the L model (which had SRi engine), GSi delivered more especially with 150bhp. Got a cat in '90 and a security system, but not a lot else to report. Took a pasting because it was useful. Suffered oil leaks, ticking camshaft, smoky engine, worn gear linkage and suspension.

Engines: 1998cc **BHP**: 130 • 150 **MPH**: 129 **MPG**: 30
Gearbox: 5spd **Boot:** 384 **Weight**: 1265

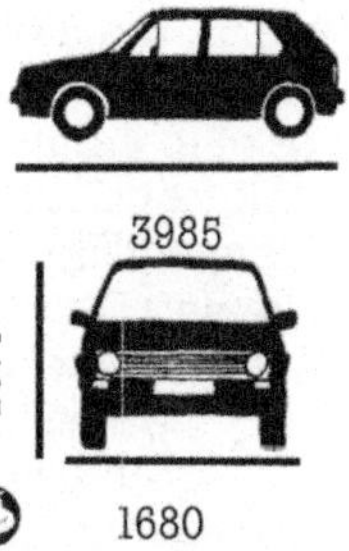

Volkswagen Golf /Jetta Syncro 1988 - 1991

A Golf and also a Jetta, but less likely to fall off the road. Permanent 4 wheel drive via viscous coupling. Power steering in '89 as the Jetta got stylish upgrades including colour coded bumpers deep, black arches, door sills and front spoiler. Can have oil leaks, blown head gaskets, snapped clutch cable. With winter rubber unstoppable.

Engines: 1781cc **BHP**: 98 **MPH**:109 **0-60**: 12 **MPG**: 30
Gearbox: 5spd **Weight:** 1070-1110 **Boot:** 380/ Jetta 527

BangerExecs - Management Motoring

If you were doing well in the corporate world, or your carpet cleaning franchise was booming, the executive cars you could choose now a stark choice. Very good, or truly terrible.

The '80s were all about the Germans and that meant the obvious pick was a 3 Series (new or an out of warranty Banger). A magnificent model on so many levels, great engines, especially the six cylinder, wonderful ergonomics and sharp handling. It helped if the buyers could afford to spec them decently as nothing was standard, but otherwise it was the perfect company car. BMW didn't get everything right as the E28 5 Series was well finished but quite dull. Those who wanted an accountant's saloon could always bag a W123 200, or an E Class. The new improved marque for consideration was the Audi range, from the compact 80 to continent shrinking aerodynamically advanced 100.

If those were the good Germans there were plenty of largely British '70s company car park hangovers that were worth avoiding, such as the Princess, Rover SD1 and Talbot Tagora. None of them made any sense at all as a premium buy whereas some middle order Japanese cars did. On the face of it, a Datsun Laurel had little to offer apart from a daft name, but the quality build, reliability and standard equipment appealed to the smartest business minds. Same thing with the equally dull Toyota Camry which was always a great long term investment, basically Bangers in waiting.

Other Europeans were sensible buying options. Volvo did offer the rather dated but comforting 240, whilst the more modern 740 which gradually had the hard edges rubbed off over the years was worth considering. Likewise the Saab 9000 a large hatch or saloon, both sensible and safe.

Back to the Germans, who built Granadas and Carltons, the more sensible and value choices, but at this level buyers wanted flair. That could be supplied by Lancias that no one also wanted, possibly an Alfa 75 or a Renault 25. Interesting enough, but truly terrible Bangers later in life.

Alfa Romeo Alfetta 1972 - 1984

Technically interesting saloon and the Gold Clover Leaf in 1982 had Electronic Fuel Injection and variable cam timing, not ideal for Banglongevity. Ditto the alloy wet linered twin-cam with rear mounted clutch and the couple of drive shafts to the wheels. Interestingly the underpinnings went on to support the SZ, too complex for its own good.

Engines: 1962cc **BHP**: 130 **MPH**:115 **0-60**: 9.7 **MPG**: 25 **Gearbox:** 5spd **Boot:** 479 **Weight**: 1140 **Seats**: 5 **Doors:** 4

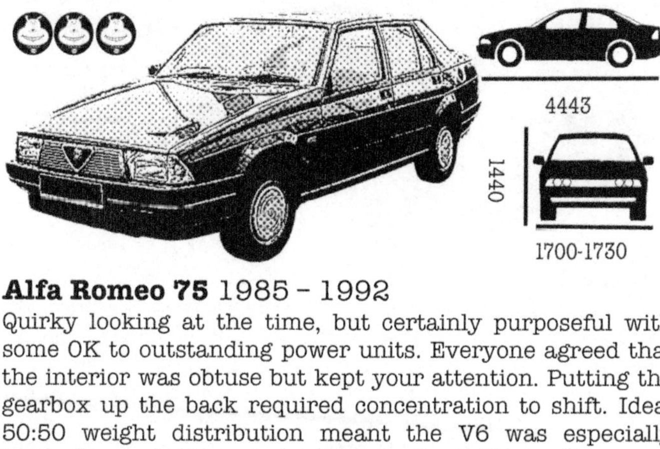

Alfa Romeo 75 1985 - 1992

Quirky looking at the time, but certainly purposeful with some OK to outstanding power units. Everyone agreed that the interior was obtuse but kept your attention. Putting the gearbox up the back required concentration to shift. Ideal 50:50 weight distribution meant the V6 was especially lovely. Rust, electrics, everything costly. Belissima?

Engines: 1.8•2.0•2.5•3.0 **BHP**: 106-188 **MPH:** 111-143 **MPG**: 27- **Boot:** 498 **Weight:** 1090-1250 **Doors:** 4

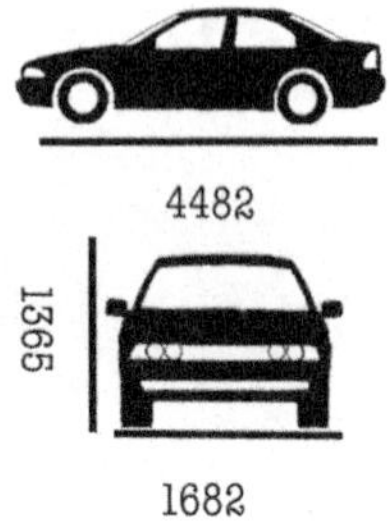

Audi 80 1978 - 1986

Coming into its own and no longer just a posher Passat. B2 era ushered in five cylinder engines for the CD model and arrival of the 80 Quattro. After the 2.1 a four cylinder 1.8 from the Sport was used before the 5-pot 90 series in '84. No diesels for the UK, this was a solid and sensible compact where you could still play the VW replacement part game.
Engines: 1.6 • 1.8 • 2.0 • 2.1 **BHP**:75-136 **MPH**: 99-120
MPG: 28-32 **Boot:** 505 **Weight**: 950-1190 **Doors:**4

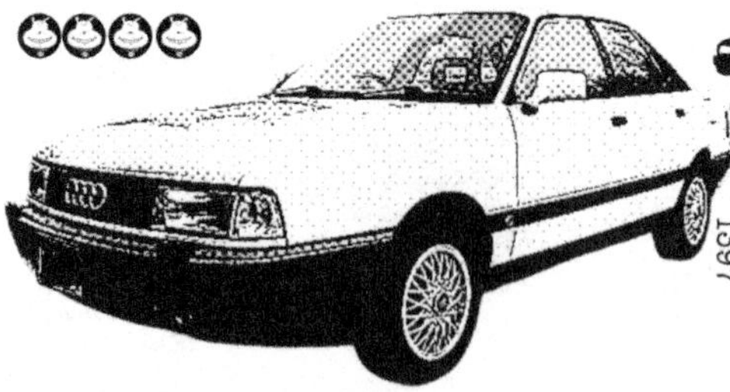

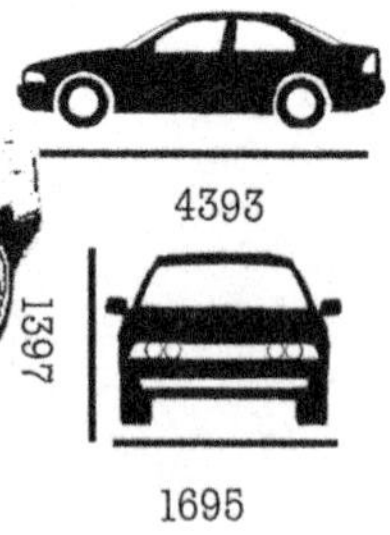

Audi 80 1986 - 1991

'70s wedge gone and now it's all very soap bar but beneath the surface there's galvanised metal which knocks the rot issue on the head. Front wheel and four wheel drive, plus a lot of petrol engine options. There was also the five cylinder 90s that ran until '91 as hardcore performance option, Turbo diesel more important model for Bangerists.
Engines: 1.6 • 1.8 • 2.0 • 1.6D **BHP**: 70-90 **MPH**: 104-110
MPG: 29.7 -36.8 **Weight**: 1204 - 1240 **Boot:** 453

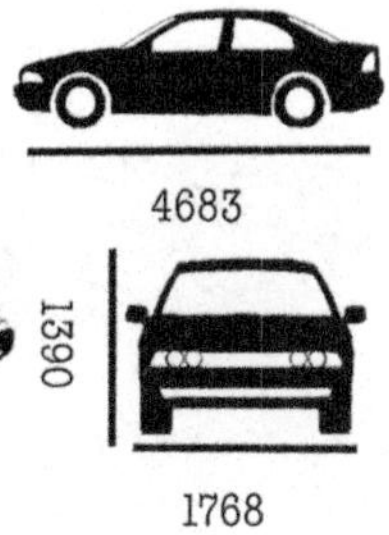

Audi 100 1976 - 1983

Front wheel drive, power steering and five cylinders wrapped up in a large square body wasn't everyone's idea of business class, but this is where it all started to come together. Flat floor meant tons of space, it was quick and comfy with decent levels of standard equipment. Always the bargain Banger buy compared to the Mercs.

Engine: 2.1 **BHP**: 116 **MPH**: 109 **0-60**: 11.5 **MPG**: 20.8
Gearbox: Man/Auto **Weight**: 1170 **Boot:** 643 **Seats**: 5

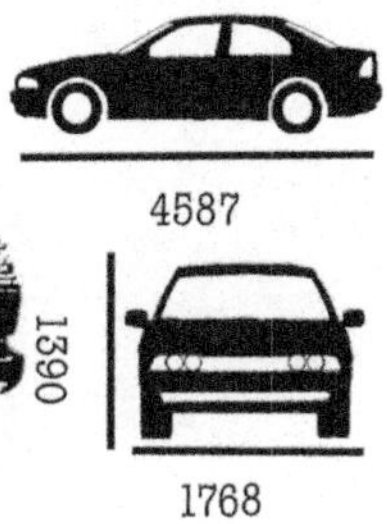

Audi 100 Avant 1977 - 1982

Back when a great big business premium hatchback made some sort of sense and technically for some it was a fastback. Plenty of engine options including the five cylinder diesel so potentially it was a proper working van. That meant it became a superior family Banger. Usual VW engine wear and tear and blue smoke. Important: not galvanised.

Engines: 1.6 • 2.0 • 2.2 • 2.0D **BHP**: 85-136 **MPG**: 20.8-36.1
Boot: 433/1113 **Weight**:1110 -1210 **Doors:** 5

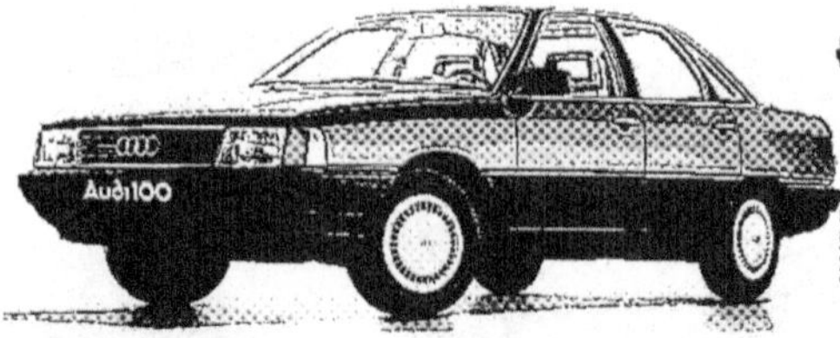

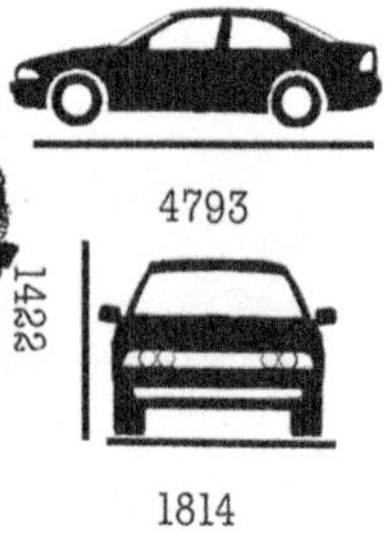

Audi 100 1983 - 1991

Here's the game changer cliché in all its galvanised glory. The point where the Cd figure of 0.30 became a thing. Four cylinder replaced by the 2.0 5 pot in '88 and there was turbo diesels, Quattro and petrol Turbos in the very large mix of models. Reliable in service can have starting issues and the old technology like ABS and other sensors are challenging.

Engines: 1.8 • 2.0 • 2.3 • 2.0D **BHP** 70-134 **MPH**: 109-125
0-60: 9.8-12.2 **MPG**: 31 **Weight**: 1083-1223 **Boot:** 570

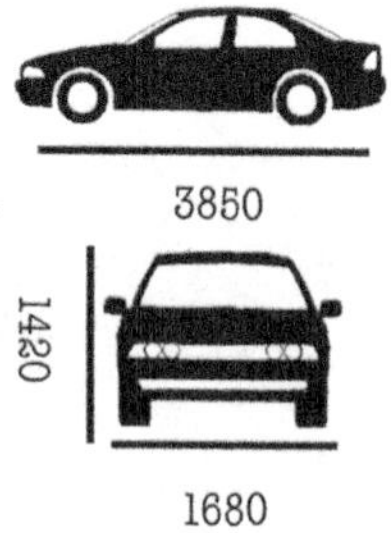

Austin Princess II 1978 - 1981

In comes the O Series in 1.7 and 2.0 size whilst the Es continued. Wedgetastic on the outside and the transverseness meant plenty of space on the inside. Hydragas comfy but never aged well once a Banger. 1980 late life fiddle about with specs and details to please the anoraks. Averagely awful as a retired Royal.

Engines: 1.7 • 2.0 • 2.3 **BHP**: 88-94-112 **MPH**:99-110
0-60: 12.6 **MPG**:24-29 **Weight:** 1145 -1215 **Boot:** 597

Austin Ambassador 1982 - 1984

Princess finally got the tailgate it had seemed destined for. Now just powered by O Series with two bhp outputs for the 2.0. Vanden Plas made do with the 92 and the HLS had 100, but no one cared, just 20K sales each year. A better banger than a Princess? Less about, marginally better build quality which isn't saying much. More practical less iconic.

Engines: 1695 • 1993cc **BHP**: 83 • 92 • 100 **MPH**: 100-104
0-60: 14.3 **MPG**: **Weight:** 1215 **Boot:** 597/1557 **Seats**: 5

BMW 3 Series 1975 - 1982

It's a premium two door saloon that just made it into the '80s with four or six cylinder power. Took a while to reach Bangerdom and by then the rot had set in. Overheating 6s and bore wear 4s, not everyone knew how to look after them, so it was worn out suspension and general neglect which finished them off before being proclaimed a classic.

Engines: 1.6 • 1.8 • 2.0 • 2.0 • 2.3 **BHP**: 89-141 **MPH**: 99-124
0-60: 13.8-8.7 **MPG**:23-30 **Boot:** 460 **Weight:** 1010-1110

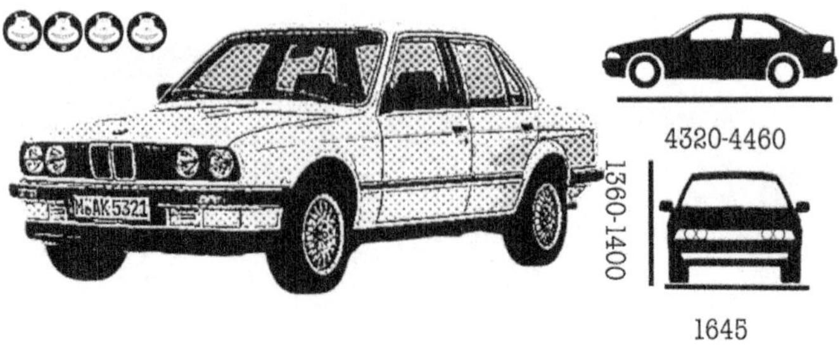

BMW 3 Series 1983 - 1991

Legendary saloon which defined the '80s deserves its place here as one of the best pre modern Bangers, even better with four doors. Great 6 cylinder engines, the fours will plod on though. Mid life matt black makeover for the '88 model year with dull bumpers. Killed by rot, blown head gaskets, worn out suspension and just general neglect.

Engines: 1.6 • 1.8 • 2.0 • 2.3 • 2.5 **BHP:** 89-168 **MPH:** 109-135 **0-60** 12.1-8.3 **MPG**:23-31 **Boot:** 425 **Weight:** 990-1180

BMW 5 Series 1972 - 1981

Seemed quite dated by the time it reached the '80s, but it was well finished with decent engines, the 518, 520, 525, 528 looked and felt like they were from the mid '70s, most had poverty spec trimmings as everything was an 'extra' new. Cheaper as a Banger than a W123 Merc, blown head gaskets and bore wear plus the inevitable rot.

Engines: 1.8 • 2.0 • 2.5 • 2.8 **BHP**: 89-175 **MPH**:99-129 **0-60**: 13.9-9.3 **MPG**: 22-29 **Boot:** 620 **Weight**: 1240-1410

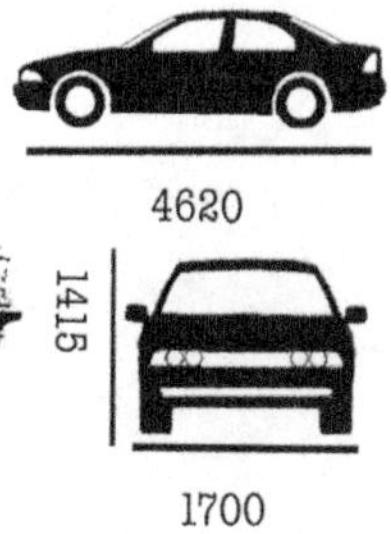

BMW 5 Series 1981 - 1987

Not the giant leap forward, a dull, conservative Bank manager spec 5 which meant that it became a Banger quicker. Grim 518, all the other 6s great, 525e misunderstood but perky and economical. Minor facelift in '84. Not much in the way of spec unless you bag an SE and it dropped down the ownership chain to Bangerdom sharpish.

Engines: 1.8•2.0•2.5•2.8•3.5 **BHP**:104-215 **MPH:**109-140 **0-60**:12.6-7.2 **MPG**:19-27**Boot:** 460 **Weight**:1160-1370

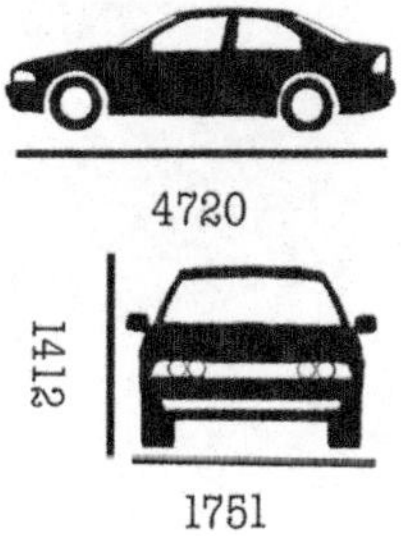

BMW 5 Series 1988 - 1996

Models goes up a few gears in comfort, quality and sheer presence, the premier Execubanger of the time. V8s are great, but a big 6 is the decent compromise. 518 can't cope, 530i can. Plenty to go wrong if not cared for, electronics, suspension bushes, injectors on diesels, whilst there is smoke and gearbox faults.

Engines: 1.8•2.0•2.5•3.0•3.5•2.5D **BHP**:111-215
MPH: 119-146 **0-60**: 7.7-12.4 **MPG**:33-40 **Boot:** 460

Chrysler 2 Litre 1973 - 1980

Here's a luxury company car with a 1981cc engine that peaked the year it was launched, fitted with Chrysler's American Torque-Flite automatic transmission and had a full length vinyl roof and spot lights as standard equipment. Even when everything else became Talbot this stayed a Yankee Chrysler. Just a big Avenger with poor mpg.

Engines: 2.0 **BHP**: 110 **MPH**: 107 **0-60**: 12 **MPG**: 22-29
Gearbox: 3spd Auto **Weight:** 1140 **Boot:** 400

Citroen CX 1974 - 1989

Wonderfully Dan Dare pilot of the future vibes even in the 1980s. New designation in '82 brought the CX20, 22, 24 and 25D. In 1984 the GTi Turbo shook things up a bit. In 1985, CX range adopted the same dash design, then in 2.5-litre models were fitted with ABS brakes. Gas spheres need changing, oil leaks from gearbox and metric tyres TRX rare.

Engines: 2.0•2.2•2.4•2.5D **BHP**: 101-166 **MPH:**109-135
0-60: 8-12.4 **MPG**:26-30 **Weight:** 1220-1385 **Boot:** 507

Citroen XM 1989 - 2000

Still delivering unconventionality by the bucket load it also meant supreme comfort. The manuals are a bit clunky, and 2.1 diesel agricultural but what a wonderful way to travel. Excellently space age interior and dash. Requires bravery to own with slipping auto gearboxes, broken clutches on the manuals and all sorts of fun with Hydractive suspension.

Engines: 2.0 • 3.0 • 2.1D • 2.5D **MPG**: 24.4-41.9
Gearbox: 5spd/Auto **Boot:** 435/1120 **Seats**: 5 **Doors:** 5

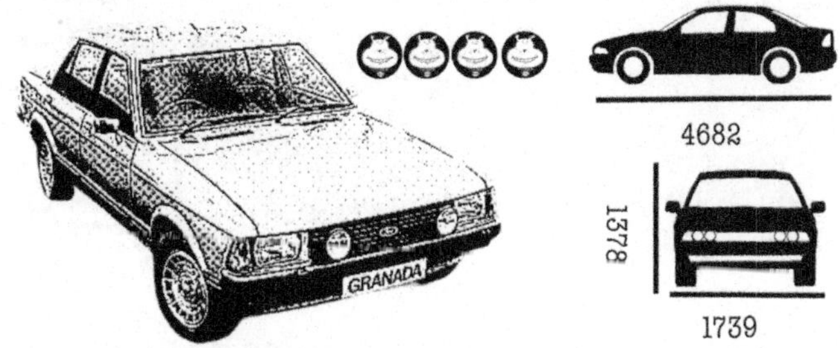

Ford Granada Mark II 1977 - 1985

The rectangular Granny was always ready for work, be it taxi, regional manager or chauffeur service. Tough engines now included diesel, that went from 2.1 to 2.5 in '82. Beyond the LX is the wonderful world of Ghia and Ghia X which were the top drawer Bangers. Rot and neglect got most as for most as a wunderbar Deutschland Dustbin.

Engines: 2.0 • 2.3 • 2.5 • 2.8 • 2.1D • 2.5D **BHP**: 104-148
MPH:104-118 **MPG**:24-28 **Weight:**1205-1412 **Boot:** 400

Ford Granada/Scorpio 1985 - 1994

Final shout for the Granny but an impressive line up. Hatches and the posher saloon which arrived in 1990 especially in Scorpio trim (above Ghia and Ghia X) with the full fat 2.9 24V. The turbo diesel is a bit of slug, 2.0 petrol best all round, lots of room, easy and cheap to fix. Smoke, worn cranks, wheel bearings and soggy suspension.

Engines: 1.8•2.0•2.4•2.8•3.0•2.5D **BHP**:89-192 **MPH**: 111-140 **MPG**: 24.8-35.6 **Boot:** 440 **Weight**:1225-1340

Fiat Croma 1986 - 1993

Centre section related to the Saab/Alfa/Lancia, variations on a 2.0 power plant, from normal to turbo. No one really wanted this Italian one, so cheap and neglected. The old thing was revised in 1991 with 'balancer' shafts so smoother and restyled slightly with marginally better interiors. Most dead, may have blowy turbos and worn out gearboxes.

Engines: 1995cc **BHP**:90-120-155 **MPH**: 103-131
0-60: 16.5 8.2 **MPG**: 34-39.3 **Weight**: 1142 **Boot:** 498

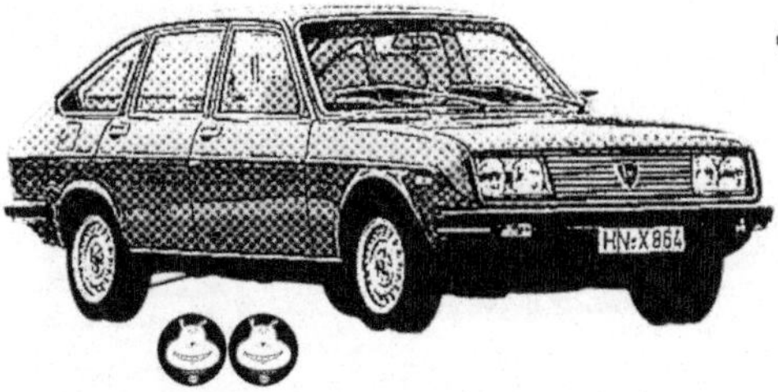

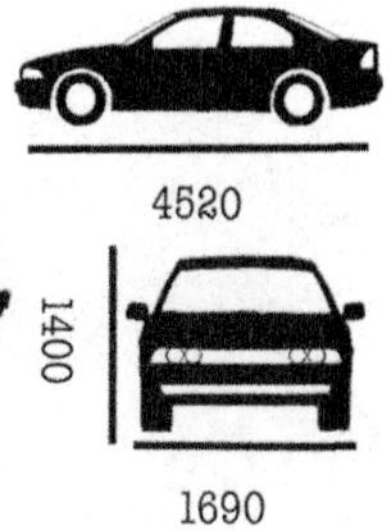

Lancia Beta 1972 - 1981

Here is the poster fastback saloon for the whole Italian rust tragedy of the '70s. The first of the Fiat Lancias it was a case of great twin cam engines let down by their surroundings. Same for most '70s saloons. Just a couple of engines available into the '80s, certainly better finished by then but the reputation was shot to pieces. Had a nice big boot.

Engines: 1.6 • 2.0 **BHP**:99-113: **MPH**: 106-112 **0-60**: 11.9 - 10.2 **MPG**:29-30 **Boot:** 500 **Weight**: 1145-1165

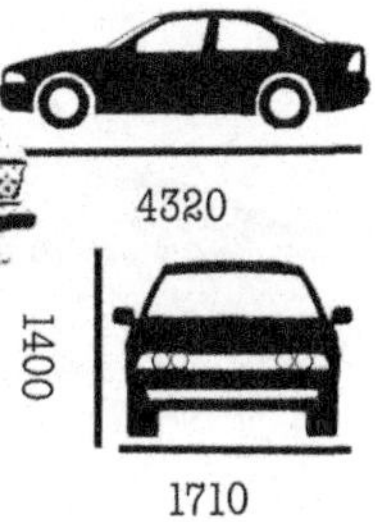

Lancia Trevi 1981 - 1984

A weirdly styled three box on top of a Beta floorpan with a name that now sounded like a footballer. Best known for its holy dashboard, or cheeseboard if you get the Gruyere gag. Ok to drive and an almost instant Banger at the time with only a handful sold at the time, laughing stock of the company car park, afterwards an OK Banger.

Engines: 1.6 • 2.0 **BHP**: 99-113 **MPH**: 103-112
0-60: 10.4-:9.4- **MPG**:25-29 **Boot:** 440 **Weight:** 1145 -1165

Lancia Thema 1985 - 1989

The sexiest of the Type Fours. i.e and LX versions of the 165bhp turbocharged 2.0-litre engine and also a 2.8-litre V6 injection automatic offered up to '88. On a practical level split/fold rear seats fold forwards, allowing access to the huge boot. Gears were always a weak spot with linkages breaking and fluid leaks, plus the usual electrical worries.
Engines: 2.0 • 2.8 **BHP**:114-173 **MPH:** 119 **0-60**: 8.1-10.4
MPG:27-34 **Boot:** 550/1000 **Weight**: 1120-1268

Lancia Thema 1989 - 1994

Second generation is a sort of Italian 5 Series. It had new headlamps and 16v engines, developing up to 200bhp. A further subtle facelift followed in 1992. Blown head gaskets, rust of course, always needed proper care, seldom got it from owner two onwards and turbo is especially fragile. Worn gearbox and driveshafts just some of the problems.
Engines: 2.0 • 2.8 **0-60**: 10-13.4- **MPH:**121-137
MPG: 30-34 **Gearbox:** 5spd **Boot:** 550/1000 **Doors:** 4

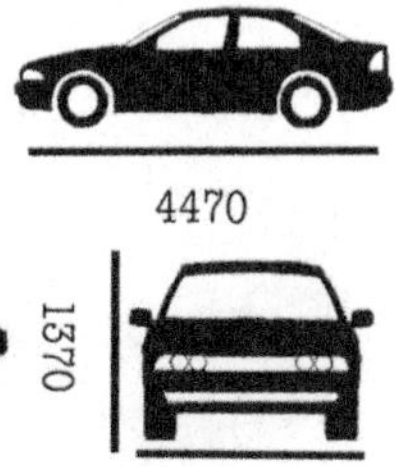

Lonsdale 1983 - 1984

UK already suitably confused by the Mitsubishi Sigma original. Most did appreciate the solidity of the estate, but these 1.6 and 2.0 saloons came from Japan whilst an import restriction dodge saw Aussie built 2.6s in the showroom. Basic but unburstable four cylinder engines with live axle and strut suspension. Badge rebrand lasted just over a year.

Engines: 1.6•2.0•2.6 **BHP**: 86-102 **MPG**: 24-28 **Gearbox:** 5spd/Auto **Weight:** 1208 **Boot:** n/a **Seats**: 5 **Doors:** 4

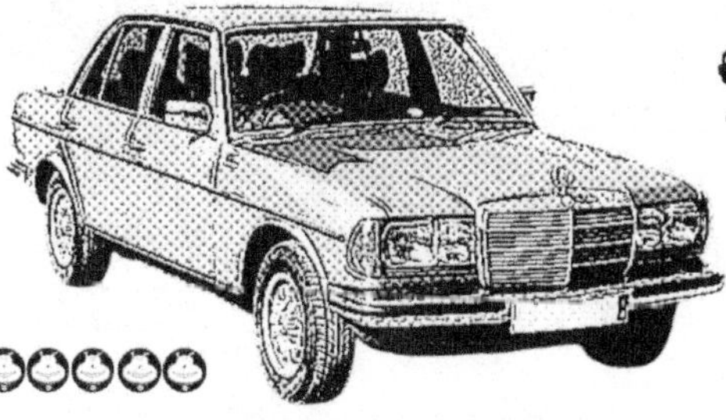

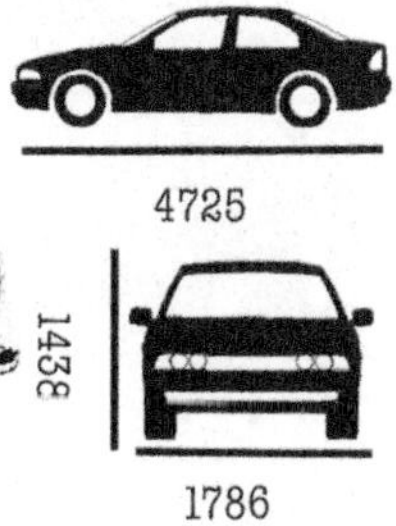

Mercedes 200 1975 - 1984

Best Beige Banger ever. Covered colossal mileages from a zero spec starting point. Always a top flight Taxi as a four cylinder the 6s and injected Es for posh duties. And most ordered with automatic gearboxes. Unarguably the ultimate Bangernomics mobile. Most were driven to 0,000,000 mileages, so it was always worn out engines, suspension.

Engines: 2.0•2.3•(6)2.6•2.8 **BHP**:108-182 **MPH**: 104-124 **0-60**:10.4-11.6 **MPG**:20-28 **Boot:** 500 **Weight:** 1340-1460

Mercedes 190 1982 - 1992

Best Beige Banger 2. Covered colossal mileages in some style and from a zero spec starting point. Despite being a top Taxi, tight inside but solid. Autos and 2.0 best, 2.6 subtle, small diesel sluggish. Overall though the perfect specimen for proper Bangernomics. Most were driven to star ship mileages, so it was clattery engines and suspension.

Engines: 1.8 • 2.0 • 2.5 • 2.6 • 2.0D • 2.5D **BHP**:71-164 **MPH**:99-135 **0-60:** 8.2-18.1 **MPG**: 30.2-43.5 **Boot:** 410

Mercedes E-Class W124 1984 - 1995

Premium E, yet another beige Taxi legend. Epically reliable, comfortable and nothing Merc has ever made since is as solid. Colossal number of engines. All injection engines from '88, ABS on the 300s from '89. Massive mileages and neglect take their toll, the expensive bits are automatic gearboxes and rear axle. Always worth fixing up.

Engines: 2.0 • 2.3 • 3.0 • 2.5D • 3.0D **BHP:** 102-188 **MPH:** 102-136 **0-60:** 13.7-8.4 **MPG**: 19.6-38.9 **Boot:** 465/665

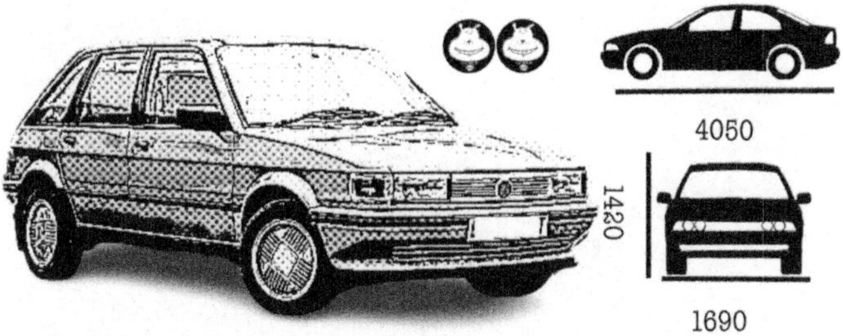

MG Maestro 1983 - 1994

First there was the 1600 for a year which was a pile of undeveloped old tat, a hot start, rough running disaster. In came the 2.0EFi, the irritating quirky talking dash dropped in '85. Averagely OK, but not properly hot hatch. Most left to fester before they ever became cool. Rotten sills blown head gasket and knackered suspension.

Engines: 1.6 • 2.0 **BHP**: 103 • 115 **MPH:** 111 • 113
0-60: 9.6 • 8.4 **MPG**: 30 **Gearbox:** 5spd **Boot:** 304/1091

MG Montego 1985 - 1991

Outclassed mildy warmish saloon, but at least the Turbo was fun. The second generation ones from late '88 were far better to drive and not as headstrong or untidy. Retuning the suspension was a revelation. Decent equipment levels by the end. However, by then no one was bothered by them as they rusted and blew head gaskets.

Engine: 2.0 **BHP**: 115-150 **MPH:** 115-124 **0-60:** 9.1-7.2 **MPG**: 25-30. **Gearbox:** 5spd **Boot:** 520 **Seats**: 4 **Doors:** 4

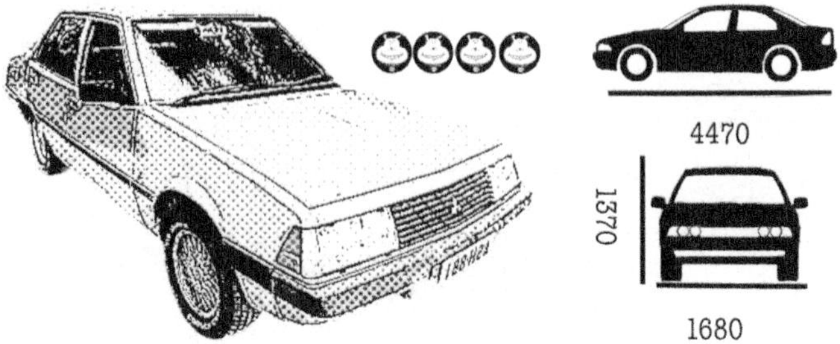

Mitsubishi Galant 1982 - 1984

Where have we seen this before? And in a different Banger category for some reason. Here is the Mitzi in it's original format. As before, the estate is the practical one that makes the most sense rather than this dated rear drive saloon. However, sticking a turbo on it to make 170bhp gives buyers a Mad Max four door Interceptor vibe. Reliable.

Engines: 1.6•2.0 **BHP**: 74-170 **MPH**: 98-124 **0-60**: 14.8-9.6 **MPG**: 31 **Boot:** n/a **Weight**: 1060-1210 **Doors:** 4

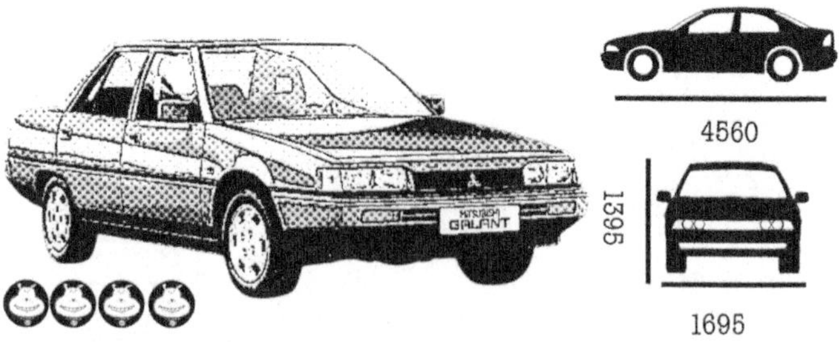

Mitsubishi Galant 1984 - 1988

After years of reliable rear wheel drive stagnation, here comes the front wheel drive revolution. It's a spacious comfy car where the strut front and independent rear suspension has the makings of a future rally contender. There's the turbo version for fun and a turbo diesel for the business users. Not a big seller but a solid one and a great Banger.

Engines: 1.6•1.8•2.0 **BHP**: 74-148 **MPH**: 99-124
0-60: 13.3-8.4 **MPG**: 30- 40 **Boot:** 430 **Weight**: 1020- 1130

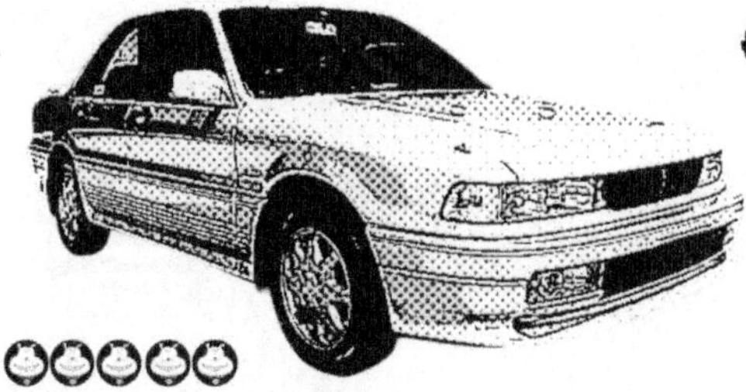

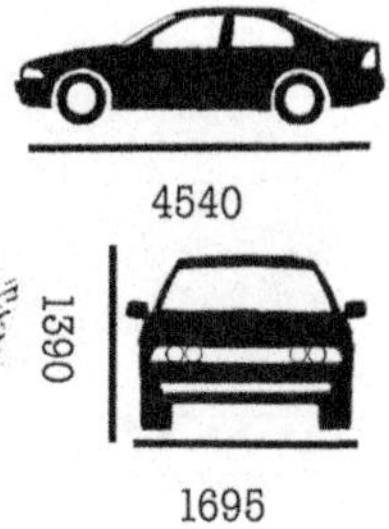

Mitsubishi Galant 1988 - 1997

It is the same Galant as before but with a new softer body plonked on top. Criticism of the old school interior by some, but the core values of granite tough mechanicals was always at the heart of its appeal. Diesel also a good ingredient, big depreciator and best to avoid the complicated 2000 GTi, but at least there was no turbo.

Engines: 1.8•2.0•1.8D **BHP**:85-144 **MPH**:104-127 **0-60:** 12.7-8.8 **MPG**: 30 **Boot:** 415 **Weight:** 1100-1200

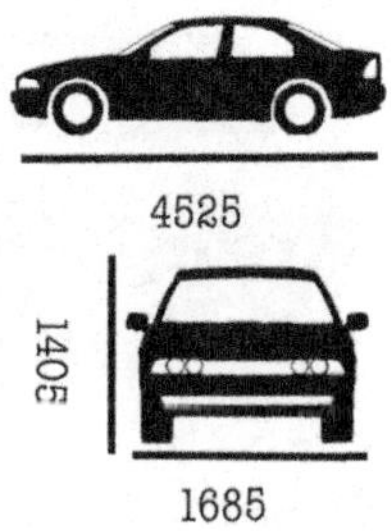

Datsun Laurel Six 1977 - 1981

Designed to sit somewhere between the Bluebird and Cedric using OAP names certainly worked it's magic for Datsun. Here was a spacious saloon that had an impressive level of standard equipment, like radios and heated rear windows which shamed the Euro equivalents. Not great to drive but reliable before rusting to dust. Lots of 4/6 pot engines.

Engines: 1.8•2.0•2.3•2.8•1.9D **BHP**:111-117 **MPH**:96-109 **0-60:** 13.5-20.7 **MPG**: 29-35 **Boot:** 410 **Weight:** 1150

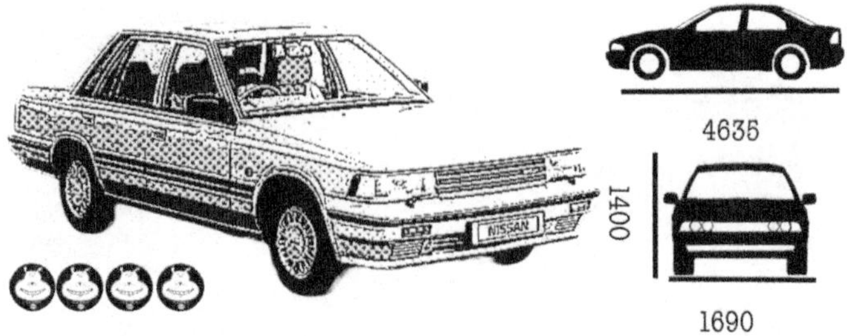

Datsun/Nissan Laurel Mark 2 1981 - 1989

Don't be fooled by the Mark II monicker, this is loads more of the same. Disappointing to new car nerds, for the Bangeristas it was the perfect barge. Live rear axle, uprated in '85 with injection and power upgrades and the usual shopping list of free stuff as standard including electric sunroof and alloys.

Engines: 2.0•2.4 **BHP**:96-128 **MPH**:112-115 **0-60:** 11.4 **MPG**:25-35 **Boot:** 410 **Weight:** 1150-1200

Nissan Maxima 1989 - 1994

Designed to take on the mid size Yank Tanks, in Amerika it had the 3.0-V6 single-cam engine under the 'hood' is similar to the one in the 300ZX. Had ABS too and moquette upholstery, SEL with leather. Driver's airbag from '92 after a short break. Good luck tracking one down, they will last as long as an owner needs them to.

Engines: 1.8•2.0•2.3•2.8•1.9D **BHP**:111-117 **MPH**:96-109 **0-60:** 13.5-20.7 **MPG**: 29-35 **Boot:** 410 **Weight:** 1150

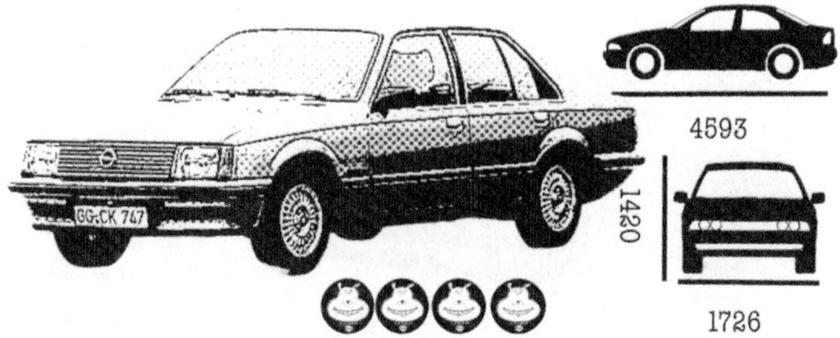

Opel Rekord 1977 - 1983

Pop along to your Vauxhall Open dealer and you could choose between the 'home grown' Carlton, or one of these. Both are Germans. Similar choice of petrol and a diesel engines, just better trim. This model sold until 1986 but left the UK showrooms in 1983 to avoid any further confusion. Excellent underrated, premium German Banger.

Engines: 2.0•2.3D **BHP**:69-99 **MPH**:99-112 **0-60:** 10.2 **MPG**: 25-35 **Boot:** 408 **Weight:** 1150-1250

Peugeot 505 1979 - 1992

One of the smartest, toughest and most comfortablest Bangers of the 1980s. A legend in Africa where it soaked up the unmade tracks was also built and soaked up the bumps. Petrols and diesels went on for six figure mileages. Transmissions either three-speed auto or four-speed manual, with five-speed from 1986 facelift. Value buys.

Engines:1.8•2.0•2.2•2.9•2.3D•2.5D**BHP**:103-168 **MPH**:97-127 **0-60:** 9.2-15.5 **MPG**:25- 31 **Boot:** 523

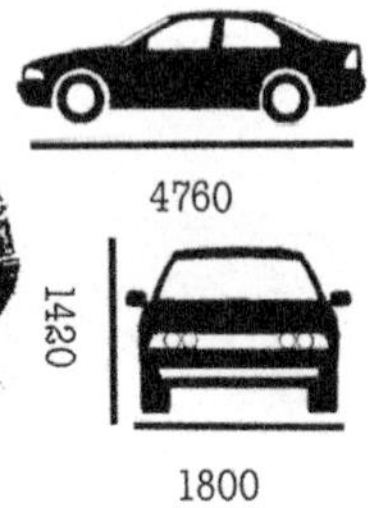

Peugeot 605 1989 - 1997

Here's a picture of depreciation which meant it became a taxi once retired from company car motorway duties. Otherwise best known for delivering comfort with a fabulously assured ride. The 2.0 turbo great and most went for the diesel anyway. SV had cruise and automatic ride control, SVE delivered leather. Clutch slip and suspension wear are just some of the possible issues.

Engines: 2.0•3.0•2.0D•2.1D **MPG**: 24.4-41.9 **Gearbox:** 5spd/Auto **Boot:** 497 **Weight**: 1475 **Seats**: 5 **Doors:** 4

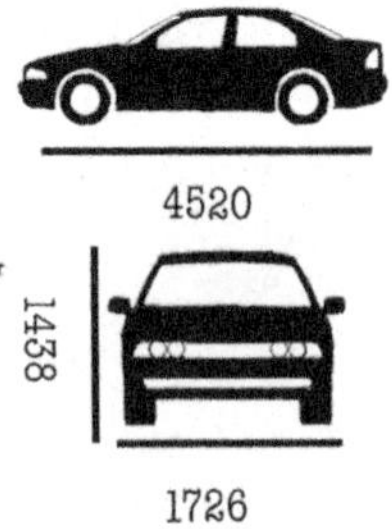

Renault 20 1975 - 1984

A 30 without the big engine got a revamp in 1980 when the Fuego dashboard was installed and later on the 1.6 was dropped in '81 replaced by a new 2.2 petrol. The largely similar big engined Peugeots were always more popular so these remained the cheapy FrancoBanger, Rot and shabby build and complication is what sent them to the scrappers.

Engines: 1.6•2.0•2.2 **BHP**:104-115 **MPH**:106-111 **0-60:**11.6 **MPG**:29-30 **Boot:**395 **Weight:** 1175-1220

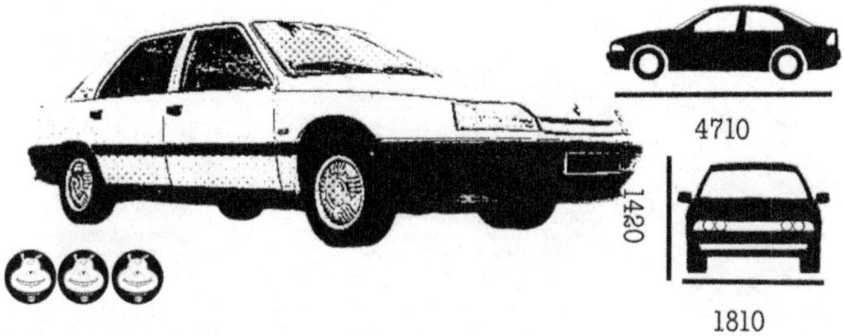

Renault 25 1984 - 1992

Francoluxury which means bags of space, comfort and a wonderfully smooth ride. No diesels, just a bunch of not especially frugal petrols plus late model Executives with lots of kit. 1988 revamp with a drop bonnet, bigger rear lights and some extra kit though the specs. Electrics, head gaskets, overheating, auto gearbox failure, everything really.

Engines: 2.0•2.1•2.5•2.7•3.0 **BHP**:103-152 **MPH**: 106-129 **0-60** 9.3-10.5 **MPG**: 19.2-32 **Boot:** 442 -1238

Rover SD1 1976 - 1986

BL put all the engines together in one big useless lump. V8 the most uneconomically interesting, VM diesel had a point, everything else blew a head gasket. Terrible as an exec express and just waiting to catch you out as a Banger. Not that spacious, or special. Looked good when parked, that's pretty much it. A crying shame all round.

Engines: 2.0•2.4•2.6•3.5•2.4D **BHP**:100-155 **MPH**:116-124 **0-60:**11.6 **MPG**:23-27 **Boot:** n/a **Weight:** 1270-1360

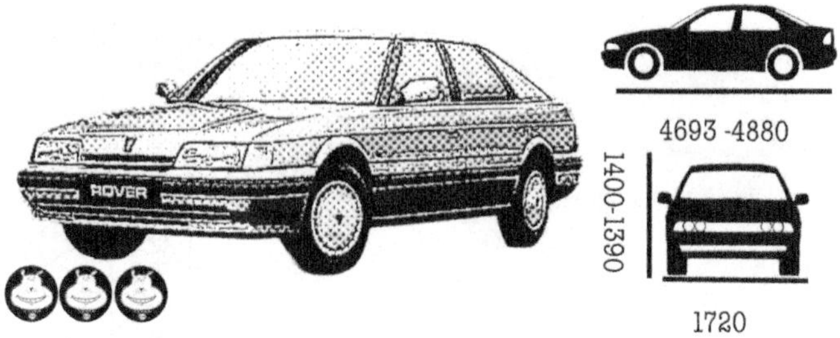

Rover 820 1986 - 1992

Smart enough and the Honda connection was the best thing about this new exec, O Series engine not initially great whereas the V6 always fitted the bill especially when it grew to 2.7. Fastback body backed up the saloon. Broken suspension, sticking electric windows are just some issues.

Engines 2.0 • 2.5 • 2.7 • 2.5D **MPG**: 27.3-42.6
Gearbox: 5spd/Auto **Boot:** 471-1405 **Seats**: 5 **Doors:** 4/5

Saab 99 1967 - 1985

Briefly into the '80s with the ice cream designation and what a wonderful collection of versatile models except that only 2.0 litre 2 and 4 door were left in GL spec. The two door became the 90 in '84 whilst according to the UK info it stayed a GL. Who cares, this was quite simply a solid sender of motor and the turbo was just a distraction.

Engines: 2.0 **BHP**:100 **MPH**:101 **0-60:**13.6 **MPG**:28
Boot:381/660 **Weight:** 1130

Saab 900 1978 - 1993

Ancient underpinnings, but a rock solid Banger legend that was outstanding. Five speed gearbox as standard from '85 made sense. Perky 16V from '88. Six figure mileages are a given with these. Non Turbo may be underwhelming, but less Banger bother. Strong as an Ox in a crash. Rattling timing chains, noisy camshaft, blowing turbos. Brilliant.

Engines: 2.0•2.0 Turbo **MPG**: 27.9-28.8 **Gearbox:** Man/Auto **Boot:** 650/1500 **Seats**: 5 **Doors:** 4/5

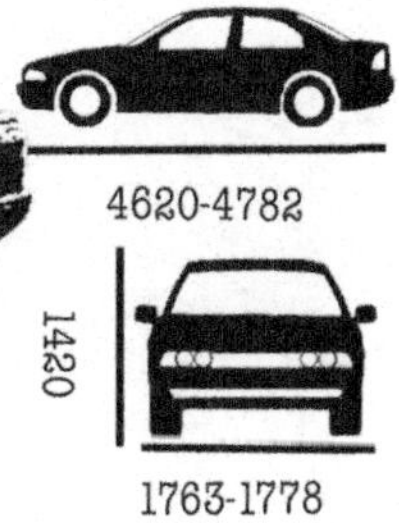

Saab 9000 1985 - 1991

The successful part of the ItalSwedo co-production. Excellent big saloon, or ginormous hatch. Got a larger body shell for this generation with uprated suspension. Lots of engine options and the Light Pressure ones are the best, V6 smoother and thirsty. Brilliant family Banger. Coil pack failure, air con issues, automatic 'box + suspension bushes.

Engines: 2.0•2.3•3.0 **MPG**: 29.2-32.3 **Gearbox:** 5spd/Auto **Boot:**486-556/883 **Doors**: 4/5**Seats**: 5

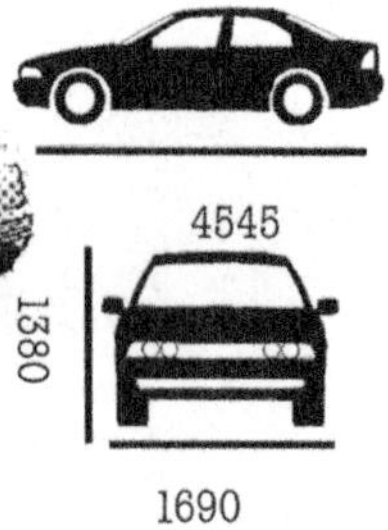

Subaru Legacy 1988 - 1994

Four wheel drive saloons at their rally winning best. Incredible performance on road and slightly off. Basic spec Ecos are spec free, 4-Cam is the mad one. Not very exec really and most rural buyers went for the estate anyway. Everything costs a fortune if broken. It will be wear and tear on the running gear if you can find one.

Engines: 1.8•2.0•2.2 **MPG**: 27.8-29.3 **Gearbox:** 5spd/Auto **Weight:** 1175 - 1335 **Boot:** 430/565 **Seats**: 5 **Doors:** 4

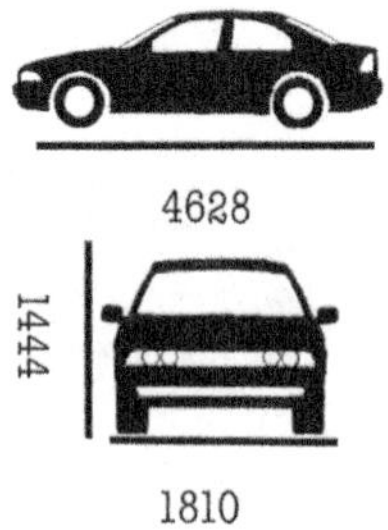

Talbot Tagora 1981 - 1984

A sign your business was in trouble, the old Tag was a big empty box of nonsense. Not nice to drive it dropped down the forecourt rankings to become the biggest depreciator and an instant used banger. Big engines not great for mpg, but a stop gap family car, an argument could be made for the Peugeot 2.2. Overall quality questionable.

Engines: 2.2•2.7 **BHP**:113-166 **MPH**:101 **0-60:**9-11.6 **MPG**:24 **Boot:** 572 **Weight:** 1227-1255

Toyota Camry 1983 - 1986

Solid saloon in a comatose body, the standard layout is transverse engine and front wheel drive. Just a bigger Corolla really now with some small petrol and turbo diesel units that were pretty nippy. Totally unaspirational, even if it was well put together and didn't break down. One of the best Bangers of the 1980s because of its sheer forgettability.

Engines: 1.9 • 2.0 • 1.9D **BHP**:89-83 **MPH**:109-106
0-60:13.7**12-** **MPG**:31-39 **Boot:**524 **Weight:** 1014-1108

Toyota Camry 1986 - 1991

Getting better at the Execugame, styling remains comatose but the engineering might win company car park arguments with its twin cam Celica power and in 1989 there was the 24 valve V6. Built better than anything in Blightly or even Europe for that matter. Lots of specification to write home about, such as air con and cruise. Banger Royalty.

Engines: 1.9 • 2.0 • 2.5 • 1.9D **BHP**:126-160 **MPH**:124-131
0-60:9.0-9.4 **MPG**:32-39 **Boot:**505 **Weight:** 1159-1334

Vauxhall Carlton 1976 - 1986

Opel Rekord with a Droop Snoot front and only available in L trim. Facelift in 1983 brought in 1.8 L, 2.0 L carbs and 2.3 L diesel. A wider range of trim levels consisting of "L", "GL" and "CD". An injected 2.0 L engine was introduced for the 1984 model year and replaced by a 2.2 L fuel injection engine for 1985. Big old comfy Banger and easy to keep.
Engines: 1.8 • 2.0 • 2.2 • 2.3 • 2.3D **BHP**: 71-115 **MPH:** 108
0-60: 11.2 **MPG**: 25-35 **Boot:** 481 **Weight:** 1130

Vauxhall Viceroy 1980 - 1982

No one remembers this one which was the halfway house between the Royale Saloon and Carlton. Effectively another spin on the Opel Commodore and only available with the carburettor 2.5 litre engine. It had ribbed velour though, heated rear window, radio cassette player and twin remote door mirrors in '81. A Carlton with knobs on.
Engines: 2490cc **BHP**: 114 **MPH:** 118 **0-60**: 12.2
MPG: 25. **Gearbox:** 5spd Man/Auto **Boot**: 478 **Weight**: 1246

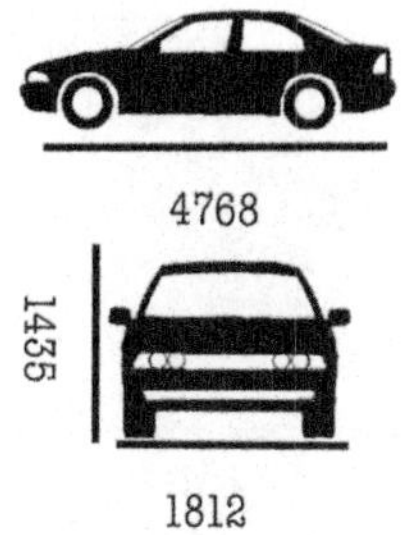

Vauxhall Carlton 1986 - 1994

Omega in Europe, here it is with a couple of six cylinder 12 valvers although the bread and butter ones are the range of petrol four potters. The basic 100bhp 2.3 diesel plodded on. Probably the best of the large family Bangers at the time which had German build quality, decent kit beyond the GL. Wear and tear suspension, brakes, engine and electrics.
Engines: 1.8 • 2.0 • 2.6 • 3.0 • 2.3D **BHP**: 90-150 **MPH**: 129
0-60: 10.5 **MPG**: 24.4-41.6 **Boot:** 530/930

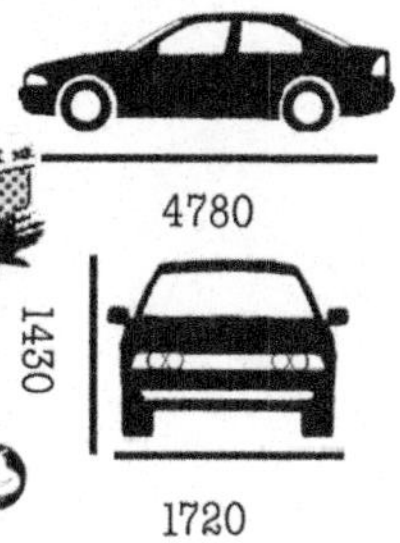

Volvo 240 1978 - 1991

It came from 1977 and by 1990 had the fuel injected engine and whilst the estate soldiered on for a few more years, the saloon was available in GL and GLT. From 1988 galvanised bodies but all the cross members and panels still need to be checked. Look for rotten bodies, engines that smoke are, cammy, also the suspension goes bang after a million miles.
Engines: 2.0 • 2.3 **BHP:** 107-155 **MPH:** 111 **0-60:** 9.7
MPG: 27-29 **Boot:**395 **Weight:**1274 **Seats**: 5 **Doors:** 4

4785

1410

1750

Volvo 740 1984 - 1991

New era brick that eventually had it's sharp edges rubbed off in 1987. Far more successful Swedoluxosaloon than previous attempts with a wide range of power units both petrols, turbo petrols, turbo diesels. Wide spec, GL, GLE, GLT and SEs includes electric most things. This made it a prime Banger because of inbred durability and practicality.

Engines: 2.0 • 2.3 • 2.4D **BHP**: 103-160 **MPH**: 115-121
0-60:9.4-11.5 **MPG**:29 **Weight:** 1309 **Boot:**470

BangerCoupes - Cool 2dr Runnings

Yet again what a time to be alive and be in the market for coupe. There were absolutely dozens to choose from. A rich tapestry of two and three door options that are going to suit just about everyone however wild or bizarre their tastes. Not only that, just about all of them became Bangers once out of warranty, a few owners and dents down the line.

The good news was that if you wanted a Capri, the Germans were still making it for you, just like the Opel Manta. Simple, sensible and largely reliable. Not as clockwork faultless as a Mazda 626, but then no one really wanted one of those.

What everyone did want was a Porsche. Never mind all the Volkswagen/Audi parts bin jibes, it had the right badge, pop up lights and looked great. Yes we are talking about the 924 which got cheap very quickly and the upscaled 944 wasn't too far behind a decade after they were brand new. Otherwise there was the genuine VW thing in the shape of the Scirocco which was a stress free ownership experience until the rot set in.

Genuinely weird offerings stayed quite rare because coupe buyers are not stupid. Who in their right mind is going to want a chopped up 2-door Volvo that isn't an estate? Never mind, a turbo Isuzu with a daft name and bankrupt importer soon meant that they were almost given away whilst the XT was from another planet. Instant risky Bangers.

Coupes were once a British strength and now looked like '70s leftovers and had gone very cold. MGB was in runout mode whilst the Lotus Elite seemed to have zero appeal and as fragile as anyone would expect. Calling it an Eclat doesn't make much difference. Other fantastic plastic creations from Reliant were really estates, but luckily none of them were Lancias. They made bad Beta Bangers, one rebranded as a High Performance Estate, except that Honda Prelude was also available.

Buying a Banger Coupe was never complicated.

Alfa Romeo Alfasud Sprint 1976 - 1990

What a beauty from Ital Design, even though the styling became more cluttered and black plastic over the years, but it remained a dream drive. Light, simple and flat four engined fun. They fell into disrepute as fast as any other Alfa and succumbed to rust and neglect as the pasta based wiring disintegrated. Deep neglect was not good.

Engines: 1.3 • 1.4 • 1.5 • 1.7 **MPG**: 34 **Top Speed:** 115
0-60: 9.1 **Boot:** 325 **Weight**: 915

Alfa Romeo GTV & 6 1976 - 1987

Underneath an Alfetta with a shorter wheelbase, on top Italdesign pretty, cramped but practical. In the '80s just decent 2.0 litre power. However, the GTV6 from '81 is the real L jetronic deal with a bump in the bonnet to fit it all in. A grown up Sprint with attitude and all the same issues when things go a bit rusty when it gets old and creaky.

Engines: 1962 • 2492cc **BHP:** 130 • 150 **MPH**: 118-127
0-60: 9.8-8.6 **MPG**: 34 **Weight:** 1080 **Boot:** 325

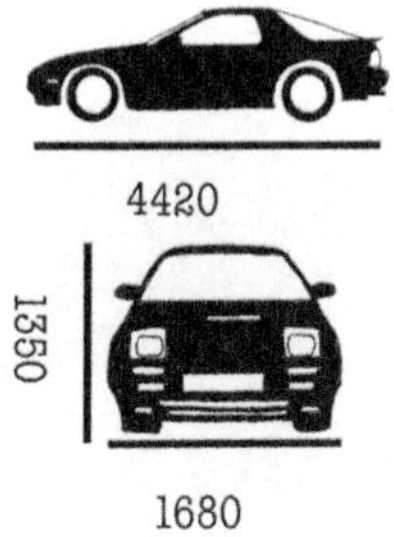

Audi Coupe 1980 - 1988

Right angle '80s styling which came without all the complicated Quattro plumbing and flared arches. Strong five cylinder and GTI engines make life easier as does the XXL hot hatch bodywork. Proper old fashioned GT in effect. Just the usual wear and tear and rust took care of most owners who did not realise how special it was.

Engines: 1.8•2.0•2.2 **BHP:** 90-136 **MPH**: 121 **0-60**: 8.7 **Gearbox:** 5spd/Auto 3spd **Weight:** 950-1050 **Boot:** 494

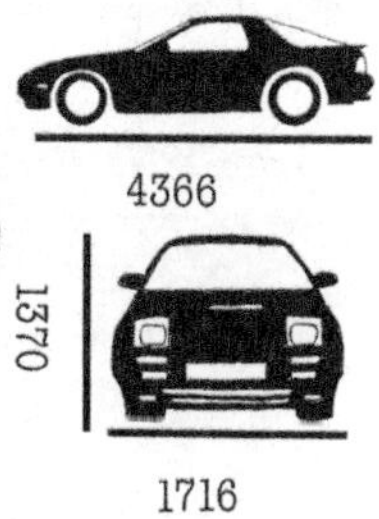

Audi 80 Coupe 1989 - 1996

Podgy but spacious, this is a full four seater, and the late '80s originals did not handle very assuredly until a '91 revamp which tickled the suspension. Top end was the 20V Quattro and S2, but the simpler ones were solid buys. Camshaft wear and knackered steering racks, mostly any seriously shabby ones will always cost a fortune to sort out.

Engines: 2.0•2.3•2.6•2.8 **MPG**: 27.4-32.9 **Top Speed:** 121-154 **0-60:** 5.9-12.9 **Gearbox:** 5spd/4spd Auto **Boot:** 494

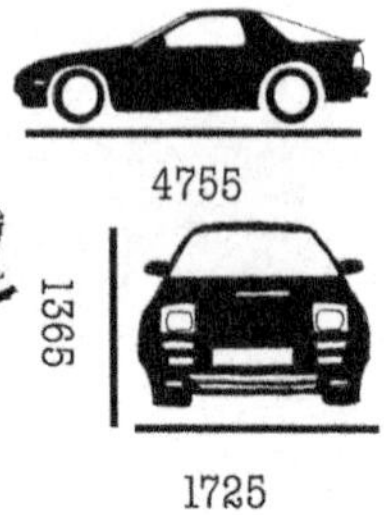

BMW 6 Series 1976 - 1989

Pretty, but rather ancient old thing by the '80s and the 633/628 revamped substantially in 1982 putting it on top of the 5 Series chassis. Range simplified to just the 628 that no one bought so a banger quicker and the 635 remained the prime buy. Neglect and rust took them to the back of the lot fairly quickly. Comfy flashy thing that's expensive to fix.
Engines: 2.8 • 3.0 • 3.2 • 3.5 **BHP**: 181-220 **MPH**: 129-140 **0-60:** 12.7-7.3 **Weight**: 1475-1490 **Boot:** 413

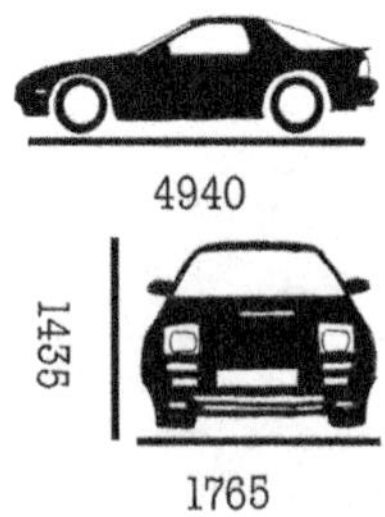

Bristol 412 1975 - 1982

Worth a mention as one of the bespoke classics that fell into disrepute which had a prehistoric 1940s chassis FFS. Became a Banger due to spectacularly thirsty Chrysler V8, terrible '70s Zagato slab styling and the first Brigadier General owner had died. Same thing with the Beaufighter that took over from it in '82, just didn't look the posh part.
Engine: 5900cc **BHP**: Dunno **MPH**: 135 **0-60**:7.8 **MPG**: marginal **Gearbox:** Always Auto **Boot:** Yes +flap for battery

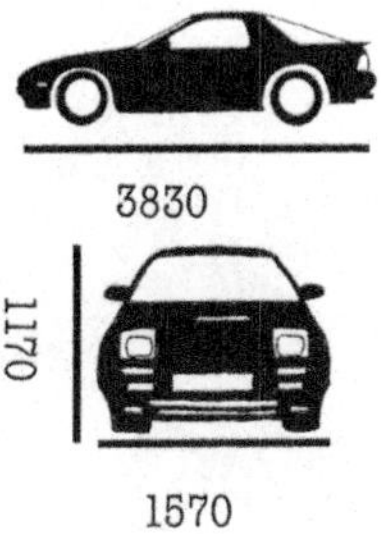

Fiat X1/9 1978 - 1989

This is a cracker of course, a beauty from Bertone that depreciated because it was an old Fiat. Baby Ferrari cliché always welcome even if the tepid power plants were not. The only real change was the 1.5 engine otherwise VS and Gran Finale Editions that had a bit of lippy (leather, decals, two tone paint). Best fun Banger ever, but rot and neglect...

Engines: 1498cc **BHP**: 85 **MPH**: 115 **0-60**: 10.4 **Weight**:920 **Boot:** 198 **Gearbox:** 5spd

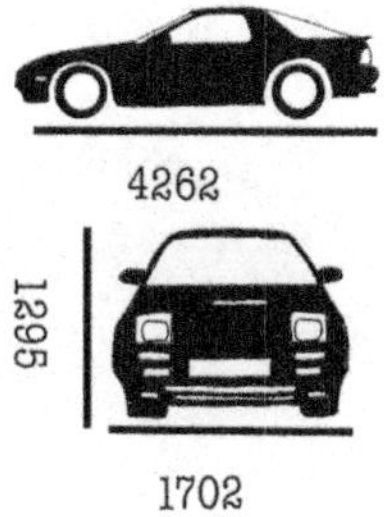

Ford Capri Mark III 1977 - 1986

Last gasp of the old girl that survived on public demand and made in Germany. 1600L survived to '82 as did vinyl roofed Ghia. Meanwhile Laser 1600/2000 '84-88 were the proper Bangers. 2.8 Special had a bit more survival street cred. Faded away quickly once the rot and bore wear set it. Along with the blue smoke came apathy. Not very Professional.

Engines: 1.6•2.0•2.8 **BHP**: 73•101•160 **MPH**:99-123 **MPG**: 25 **Boot:** 260 **Weight**: 1040-1170

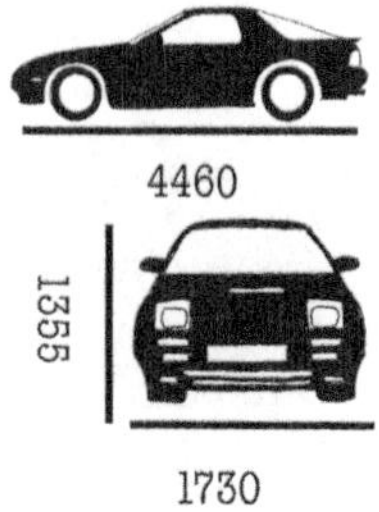

Ford Sierra XR4i 1983 - 1985

Effectively a Capri Mark 4, but jellymould and the problem was the Capri still existed. Only around for a couple of years and the story sort of continued with the XR 4×4. For the moment though it remained a three door Sierra with a weird extra side window and some bonus rear spoilers. Having the 2.8i engine helped but in the car market it flopped. Banger+

Engines: 2792cc **BHP**: 150 **MPH:**131 **0-60**:8.4
Gearbox: 5spd **Boot:** 410 **Weight**: 1175

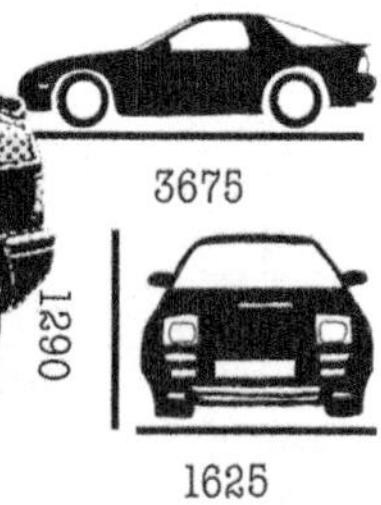

Honda Civic CRX 1984 - 1986

Well, this was fun, rather like a really well engineered X1/9, certainly had a lot more oomph, even though the styling was not as pretty. The basis as always was a great little engine, a 12 valver that delivered a useful 100bhp to hardly any weight at all, always a great ratio. The five speed gearbox certainly helped, with more close ratios. Perfect package.

Engines: 1488cc **BHP:** 100 **MPH**: 112 **0-60**: 8.5 **MPG**: 42
Gearbox: 5spd **Weight**: 820 **Boot:** n/a **Seats**: 2

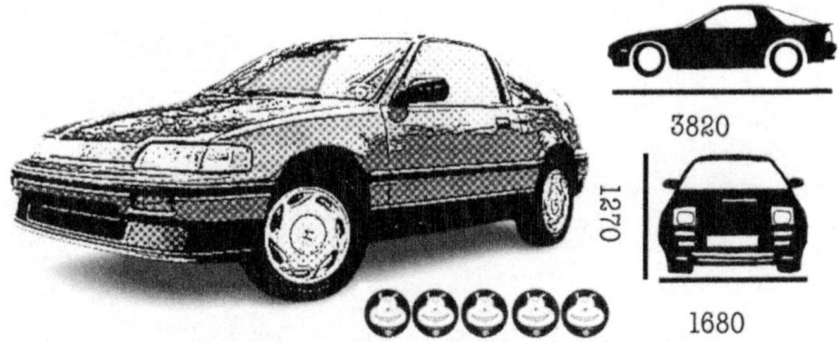

Honda Civic CRX 1986 - 1991

Stubby and rather brilliant road rocket. Arguably a hot hatch rather than coupe, but it is sporty enough justify a stand alone entry. VTEC engine is all very exciting at 7000rpm and the chassis is up to the job. Many were Max Powered to oblivion. Caution needed then, plastic interior survives even if rotting body doesn't. Wonderful.

Engines: 1.6 **MPG**: 42.2- **Top Speed:** 137 **0-60:** 7.3
Gearbox: Man/Auto **Boot:** 197 **Weight:** 905 **Seats**: 2 + 2

Honda Prelude 1978 - 1983

In the beginning Honda simply made the cooking Accord a bit more sexy. Creating the Prelude was a good thing and here it starts life as a runaround for the double income no kids twentysomethings and retirees delivered the no hassle experience that made it so sucessful. Electric glass sunroof, alloys and a digital clock. Rustification terminal.

Engines: 1602cc **BHP**: 80 **MPH**: 106 **0-60**: 11.5 **MPG**: 34
Gearbox: 5sp/3spd Auto **Boot:** 258 **Seats**: 2+2

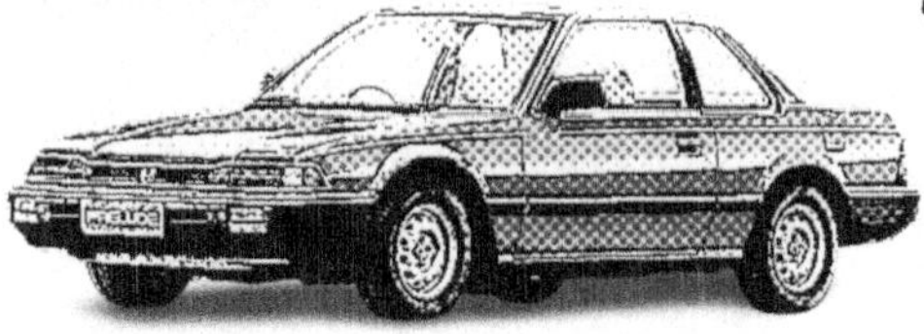

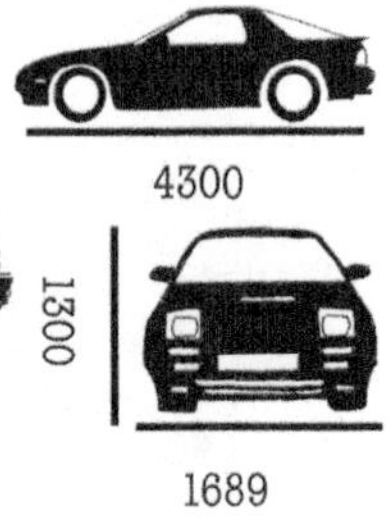

Honda Prelude 1983 - 1986

More of the reconstituted Accord magic, with wishbone suspension and pop up lamps. Under the bonnet was a bigger engine, but the idea wasn't to be outrageously fast. Rear wash/wipe, tinted glass, remote mirrors, folding rear seat, remote mirrors with radio and digital clock, Executive model too. Otherwise, it just started first time, every time.

Engines: 1829cc **BHP**: 106 **MPH**:115 **0-60**: 9.5
Gearbox: 5spd/Auto **Boot:** 314 **Seats**: 2+2

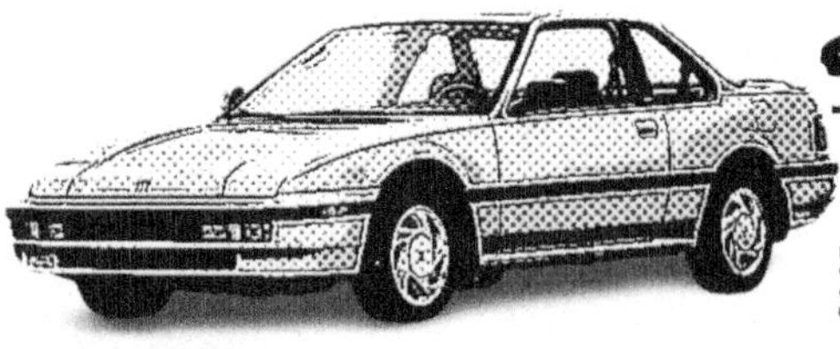

Honda Prelude 1987 - 1992

Third generation wedge, sort of- micro NSX which was a few years away, but had mechanical four wheel steering tech as an option. Pop up lights always delightful. Relatively light and consequently handles sweetly with those wonderful VTEC engines. Few took it that seriously or acted fast enough to stop the rot. Perfect, coupe Banger.

Engines: 1.8•2.0 **BHP**: 150 **MPH**: 118 **0-60:** 9.2 **MPG**: 29.4
Gearbox: 5spd/Auto **Weight**: 1065 **Boot:** 379 **Seats**: 2+2

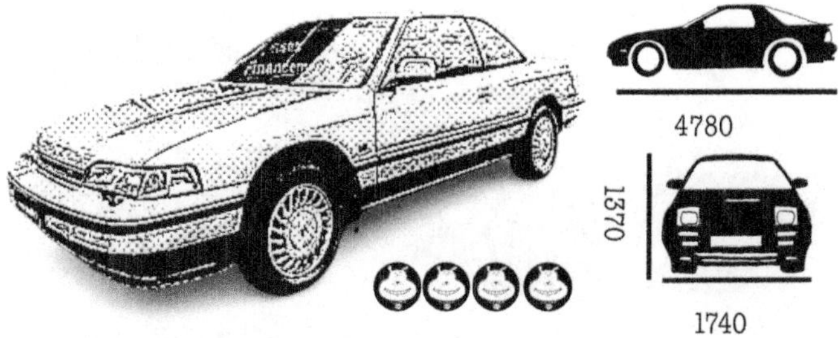

Honda Legend Coupe 1988 - 1991

It's an Accord+ also Rover developed in Coventry with Rover 800 inner body panels, but a 2.7 Honda V6 under the bonnet. Comfortable and well equipped, most had leather and electric everything, but just did not connect with the buying public as a big luxury Honda with two doors. Honda elements fine, everything else rusts to bits.

Engine: 2675cc **BHP:** 177 **MPH:** 132 **0-62:** 8.1 **MPG**: 28 **Gearbox:** 5spd/4spd Auto **Boot:** 440 **Seats**: 4

Hyundai S-Coupe 1989 - 1996

An unremarkable thing, the LSi had alloys and bucket front seats whereas the GSi glued on a spoiler and some bits of trim. Second generation from '92 had revised suspension, electric mirrors and now forced induction. Turbo SE in '95 had lower suspension. Bought on the basis of a low price they had blowing engines/scrappy bodies and cost buttons.

Engines: 1.5•1.5 Turbo **MPH:** 107-121 **0-60:** 9.1-12.5 **MPG**: 32.1-35.4 **Gearbox:** 5spd/Auto **Boot:** 261 **Seats**: 4

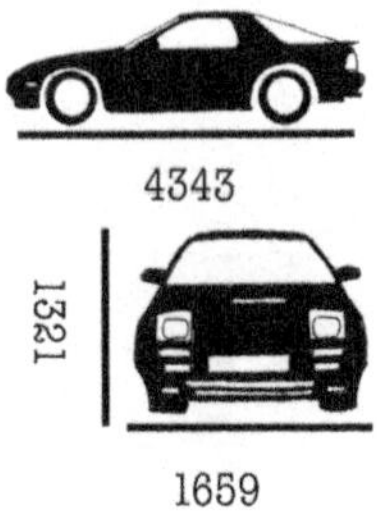

Isuzu Piazza 1986 - 1990

Sort of DeLorean done right, with a Handling by Lotus connection too. Grim early life left them stranded unsold on an airfield. Better than it appeared to be and decent performance, rapidly became the biggest bargain Banger coupe on the block. Nervous buyers worried about parts, but here's a brilliant Giuigiaro original for buttons in 1999.
Engine: 1994cc **BHP:** 150 **MPH:** 130 **0-62:** 8.4
Gearbox: 5spd **Weight:** 1247 **Boot:** n/a **Seats**: 4

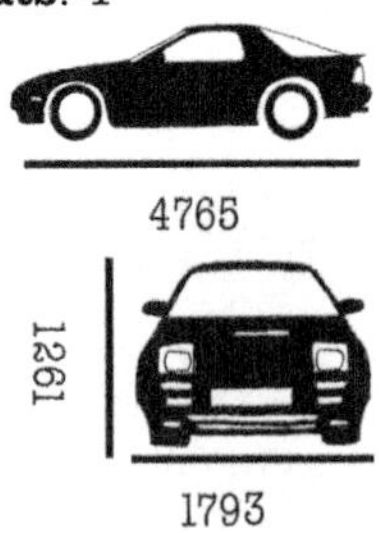

Jaguar XJS 1975 - 1991

Last gasp for the '70s survivor and these were old rotters. Despite simplified construction they still oxidise. Revised AJ6 engine is better, complicated V12 is a world of pain if not firing on all cylinders. Low miles can be fatal, they need exercise. Smoke, leaking coolant + oil, worn suspension and radius arms. Were cheap for a while, now mostly trouble.
Engines: 3.6 • 4.0 • 5.3 • 6.0 **BHP**:285-295 **MPH**: 141-161
0-60: 6.6-7.8 **MPG**: 18.8-24.3 **Gearbox:** 3spdAuto **Boot:** 480

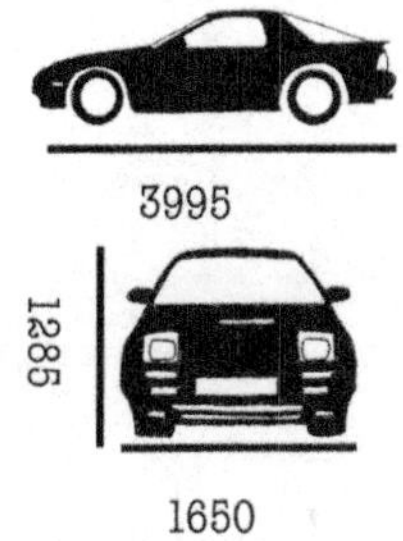

Lancia Beta Coupe 1973 - 1984

Amazing to think that these pretty coupes and even the semi convertible Spiders would ever be classed as Bangers. S2 model introduced in 1976. Colossal amount of engine options over the years, by the early '80s though it was just the 1.5. Nightmare then to buy and run and now to restore. Worth it in the end though.

Engines: 1585cc **BHP**:108: **MPH**: 100 **0-60**: 11.9
MPG:29-30 **Boot:** n/a **Weight**: 1000

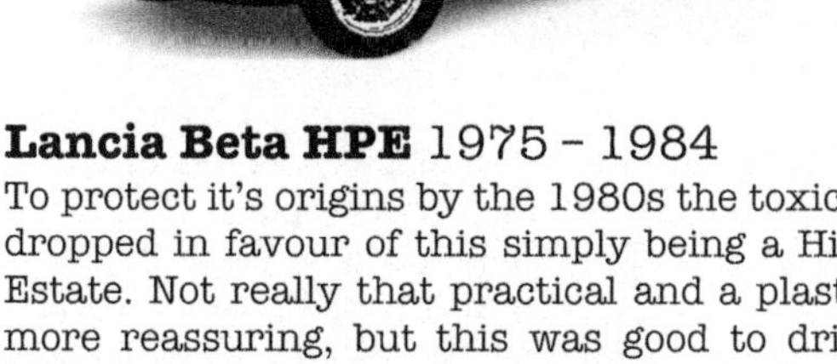

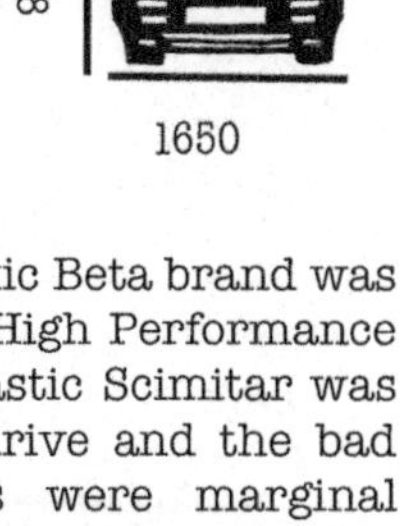

Lancia Beta HPE 1975 - 1984

To protect it's origins by the 1980s the toxic Beta brand was dropped in favour of this simply being a High Performance Estate. Not really that practical and a plastic Scimitar was more reassuring, but this was good to drive and the bad associations meant that future values were marginal enough. Became a Banger pretty quickly then disappeared.

Engines: 1585cc **BHP**:108: **MPH**: 107 **0-60**: 11.9
MPG:29-30 **Boot:** 1200 **Weight**: 1060

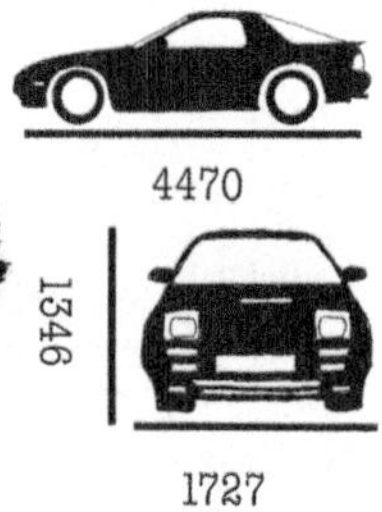

Lancia Gamma Coupe 1976 - 1984

Hard to think that such a big beautiful Pininfarina bad boy was the wrong sort of coupe at the time. Just a shorter Gamma saloon and not as quick as you'd think. Past the first caring owner they struggled when half parked on the pavement without a friendly metric spanner for years. Like all the others rust and general flakey build killed the brand.

Engines: 2484cc **BHP**: 140 **MPH**: 121 **0-60**: 10.1 **MPG**:24
Gearbox: 5spd **Boot:** 470 **Weight:** 1270

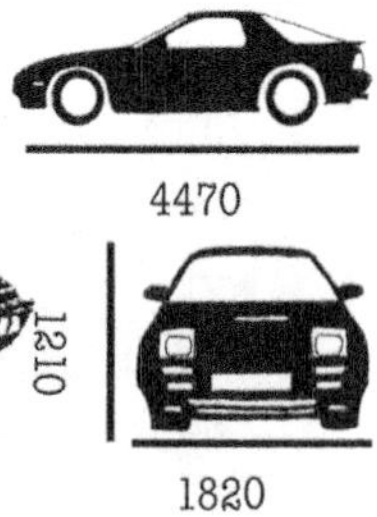

Lotus Elite 1974 - 1983

The trouble with Lotuses wasn't that there was lots of it, but usually the first problem stuck it under a tarpaulin in a front garden. The most neglected of the moderns demo'd the Lotus 2.0 engine that went up to 2.2 from 1980 along with a proper Getrag gearbox instead of the Austin Maxi related one. The mechanicals & neglected electrics caused trouble.

Engines: 1973•2174cc **BHP**: 142•160 **MPH**: 124 **0-60**: 7.5
Gearbox: 5spd/Auto **Boot:** n/a **Weight:** 1060

Lotus Eclat 1975 - 1985

This is a fastback Elite with less plastic which must have pleased Colin. Otherwise it was the same old story of hardcore unreliability. The fact that it was easier on the eye and a bit more nifty didn't matter. Also an Eclat wasn't 007's Esprit, which had the same issues but clung onto far more residual value. Subsequent Excel less neglected.

Engines: 1973 • 2174cc **BHP**: 142 • 160 **MPH**: 129 **0-60**: 7.5
Gearbox: 5spd/Auto **Boot:** n/a **Weight:** 1055

Mazda Montrose/626 1978 - 1982

Sexy Montrose monicker for the UK just some numbers everywhere else. Not wasted on this big, cool, metal box of a coupe sitting on coil springs at the back and struts up front which was pushed along by single cam engines connected to either a five speed manual or three speed automatic on the 2.0. 1.8 not offered in UK.

Engines: 1.6 • 2.0 **BHP**: 74-89 **MPH**: 99 **MPG:** 30
Gearbox: 5spd/Auto **Boot:** n/a **Weight:** 1060-5

Mazda 626 1983 - 1987

Now just a number, but an impressive one which added up to the sort of quality and the generous equipment level that the '80s buyer was now demanding in coupe flavours. There was a new 2.0 engine in '84 available in carburettor (102bhp) or injection (120bhp) form. Hard to kill and set the Mazda standard, a Banger of the best quality.

Engines: 1.6•2.0 **BHP**: 74-120 **MPH**: 99-112 **MPG:** 29-33
Gearbox: 5spd/Auto **Boot:** 467 **Weight:** 995

Mazda 626 1987 - 1992

Coupes are meant to be somewhat exciting and this was hyper competent. High tech thoroughbred with a decent amount of kit. Based on GT model with GLX Executive equipment, front/rear spoilers. All wheel steering could get you places/into spaces. '90 a boot lid spoiler and automatic no longer an option. Mazda build quality exceptional.

Engines: 2.0 **BHP**: 146 **MPH**: 130 0-60:8.3 **MPG:** 33
Gearbox: 5spd/ 4spdAuto **Boot:** 467 **Weight:** 1065

Mazda RX-7 1978 - 1986

The last Wankel in the UK brochures was this pretty 2 + 2 coupe which was as utterly reliable as you would imagine. Wasn't as quick as you might imagine sadly, although there was a slight bhp boost to 115. Otherwise it was just a stylish, reliable, slightly thirsty coupe which depreciated because of the scary rotors. Less bother than a neglected Capri.

Engine: 2292cc **BHP**: 105-115 **MPH**: 119 **0-60**: 8.5 **MPG**: 17.3 **Gearbox:** 5spd **Boot:** n/a **Weight**: 995

Mazda RX-7 1985 - 1992

Buyers are inevitably attracted to the oddest of coupes, but should of course run the other way. Despite being well built, the Rotary engine is a harbinger of oil leaks and expensive doom sometimes with an added turbo. Despite the cleverness of it all and the initial depreciation, it tempted some to sign up for Rotund Bangerdom.

Engines: 2354cc **BHP**:148-200 **MPH**: 131-143 **0-60**: 8.4 **MPG**: 17.3 **0-60:** 8.4 **Gearbox:** 5spd **Boot:** 200

Mercedes SLC 1972 - 1981

This classy icon just made it into the '80s. Underneath it is as SL convertible but it has been stretched from 14' 4" to 15' 7" in old money. Just the 450 by this point. They had headlamp wash/wipes, tinted glass, twin door mirrors, velour trim, central locking and not much else apart from veneers from those stingy Germans. Banger for a while.

Engines: 4520cc **BHP**: 220 **MPH**: 140 **0-60:** 8.5-
Gearbox: 4spd Auto **Boot:** n/a

Mercedes CE 1980 - 1988

Lopping 3 old inches off (W123) floor created a coupe of wonderful proportions and quality. For the 1980s the elegant old girl kept her looks but got the great fuel injected straight six. Not a huge seller, just for those who wanted something subtle and four seat practical. The few owner ones still depreciated most attractively.

Engines: 2.2 • 2.3 • 3.0 • **BHP**: 136-188 **MPH**: 125 **0-60:** 9.4
Gearbox: 5spd/4spd Auto **Boot:** 500

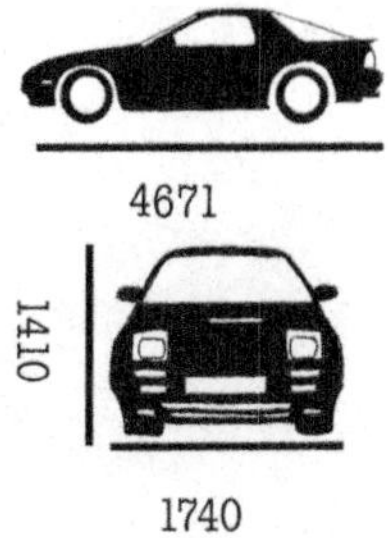

Mercedes CE/E 1988 - 1996

Accountant's idea of a Grand Tourer in W124 wrapping. From August '93 badged as Es with mild facelift and spec upgrade for 1995 which meant walnut trim, hole alloys and headlamp wash/wipe. Model run outs in '96 got cruise and anti-skid. Other worldly build quality, but not immune from early ECU failure and shonky auto boxes

Engines: 2.2 • 2.3 • 3.0 • 3.2 **BHP**: 136-188 **MPH**: 126-147
0-60: 7.5-10.6 **MPG**: 25.3-33.3 **Boot:** 480

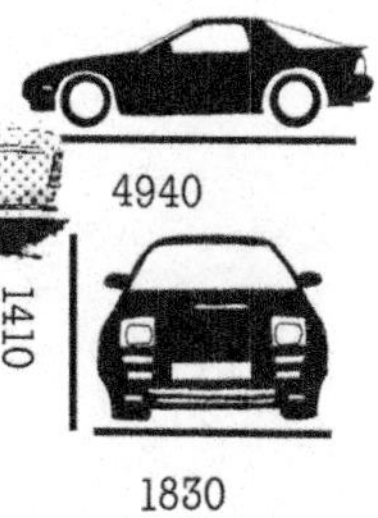

Mercedes SEC 1979 - 1992

Colossally accomplished over the top and identified by nerds as C126. Indeed they would claim its a mildly reworked W116, so despite the high techness added over a couple of decades (ABS, cruise) it is relatively uncomplicated. Putting one right will make a large fortune quite small. Probably worth it though.

Engines: 3.9 • 4.2 • 5.0 • 5.6 **BHP:** 218-300 **MPH:** 149
0-60: 7.2 **MPG**: 20 **Gearbox:** Auto **Boot:** 510

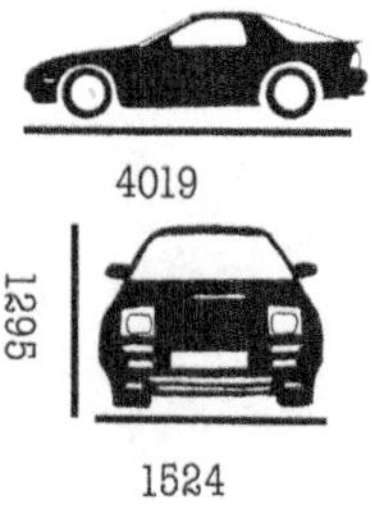

MGB GT 1974 - 1980

At the end of its life the MGB is bulked up with Federal bumpers and what are now very ancient underpinnings. That contributed to the rapid decent into modern Bangerdom. Arrival of the Limited Edition in '80 only meant buyers parked them in lock ups. Otherwise this was an outdated old fossil rather than a hot hatch.

Engines: 1798cc **BHP:** 95 **MPH**: 105 **0-60**: 12.1 **Gearbox:** 4spd overdrive on 3rd/4th **Boot:** 401 **Weight:** 1048

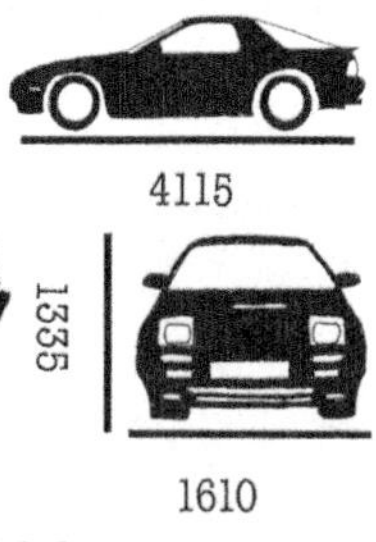

Mitsubishi/Colt Celeste 1976 - 1982

Groovy looking Celeste was an alternative to the Ford Capri, and Vauxhall Cavalier GLS as underneath there was a basic model in this case a Lancer so dull as a brick. By the '80s 1600ST and 2000ST although not especially quick, but tidy through the bends. Became cool retro coupe, had fold flat rear seats and tinted glass. Shabby and neglected in service.

Engines: 1597 • 1995cc **BHP:** 75 • 86 **MPH:** 106 **0-60:** 12.7 **Weight**: 990 **Boot:** n/a **Gearbox:** 4 speed

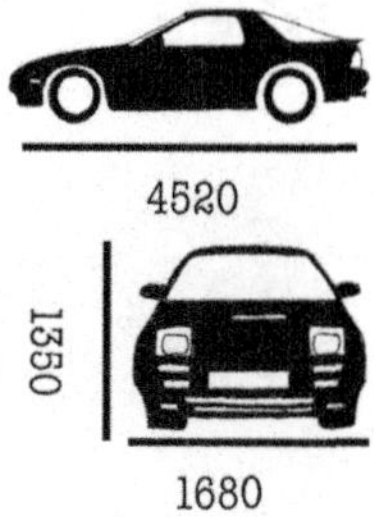

Mitsubishi /Colt Sapporo/Cordia 1982 - 1989

AKA the Cordia, GSR/GSL and Turbo in UK. An oddity with a game console digital dash and if ordered, turbo power, so this could not have been more 1980s. Underneath there's a Tredia, which didn't make it especially reliable. 1800 Turbo from 1985 with power steering, twin electric door mirrors, bucket seats and one of those digital clocks.

Engines: 1597 • 1795cc **BHP:** 75 • 113 • 134 **MPH:** 124
0-60: 9.8 **Boot:**n/a **Gearbox:** 4 speed/2speed final drive

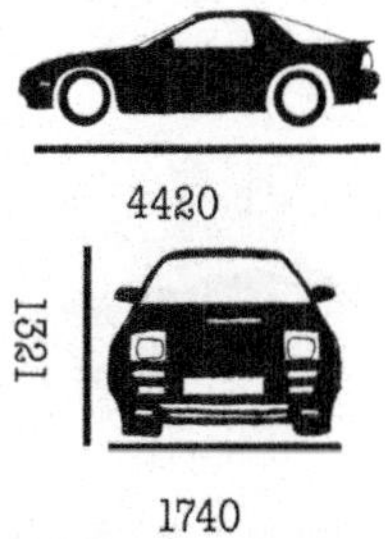

Mitsubishi/Colt Starion 1982 - 1989

Better than a Cordia, which isn't saying too much, but Turbo power and MacPherson struts make a potent enough package. Not the Japanlish model name mash up according to legend, simply an astral one. 2000 replaced by the 2.6EX in 1989 which was around for about a year when customer indifference killed it off. Good old fashioned turbo lag fun.

Engines: 1997cc **BHP:** 170 • 177 **MPH:** 133-134
0-60: 6.9-7.0 **Weight:** 1220 **Gearbox:** 4 speed

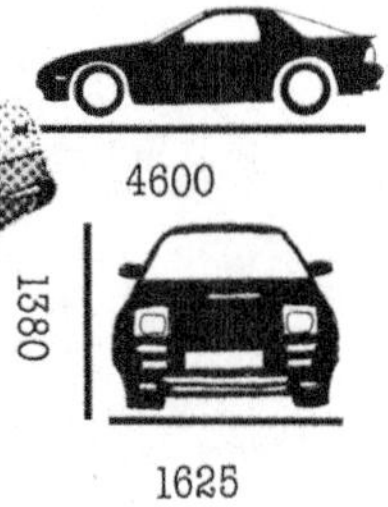

Datsun Skyline 1977 - 1981

Legend of course, except that at the time the 240K, as it was first known, struggled because it was expensive, thirsty and road testers said it could have been tidier through the bends. Coupe and six cylinder only in the UK Skyline went away before anyone realised it was cool. Incredibly a pretty instant Banger so expensive to run, but reliable.

Engines: 2393cc **BHP**: 127 **MPH**:116 **0-60**: 10.2 **MPG**:23
Gearbox: 5spd/3spd Auto **Boot:** n/a

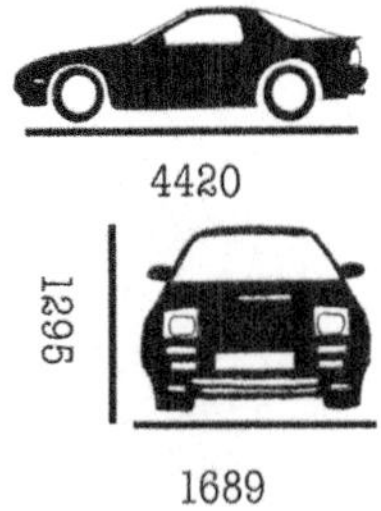

Datsun 280ZX 1978 - 1983

Lumpy follow up to the 260Z because it was aimed at the Americas. Despite getting the fuel injected one, and revised suspension still something of a slow old lump. 2 + 2 option and pop out targa roof panels. Apart from fiddling with upholstery and trim colours not much really happened during its import run. Had split/fold rear seats though.

Engines: 2753cc **BHP**: 140 **MPH**:114 **0-60**: 10.3 **MPG**:
Gearbox: 5spd/3spd Auto **Weight**: 1415-1450 **Boot:** 235

Nissan Sunny GSX/ZX 1987 - 1991

This is important, the ZX had a twin cam engine that was fairly lively, whereas the GSX had a single cam unit that was a bit slower and took 3 seconds more to 60. 1.8 from 1989 with bigger brakes, uprated springs and clutch plus alloys and bronze tinted glass. Sunroof deleted in 1990. An unremarkable and forgotten weird coupe Banger.

Engines: 1597 • 1809cc **BHP**: 84 • 122 • 125 **MPH**: 128
0-60: 8.3 **Gearbox:** 5spd **Weight**: 1080 **Boot:** 409

Datsun Sunny 140Y 1977 - 1982

Officially it is a coupe, looks like fastback hatch with utterly ordinary front engined rear wheel drive, strut front suspension and live rear axle layout underneath. For 1980 the Coupe got a rev counter and single piece black grille, then a push button radio and GLS badge. New model briefly in '81 is 1.5GL, coupe gets a 5 speed gearbox. Bangerlicious.

Engines: 1397 • 1488 **BHP:** 63-70 **MPH**: 99 **MPG**: 28-35
Gearbox: 4-5spd/3spd Auto **Boot:** 310 **Weight:** 790-885

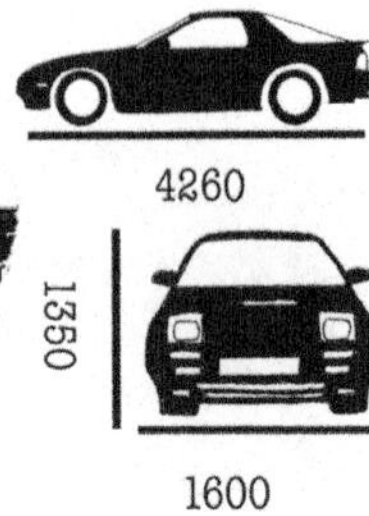

Datsun 160J Violet 1977 - 1981

Saloon based coupe which looked more like a Mustang than the Sunny version. Had split rear and fold velour rear seats. Heated rear window, tinted glass and a very useful door mirror. Also came with a 5spd gearbox. Old age means oil leaks, chirping camshaft and collapsing trim like all the other dustbin Datsuns from that era. Bangerlicious x 2.

Engines: 1595cc **BHP**: 81 **MPH**: 100 **0-60:** 12 **MPG**: 29-
Gearbox: 5spd **Boot:** n/a **Weight:** 891

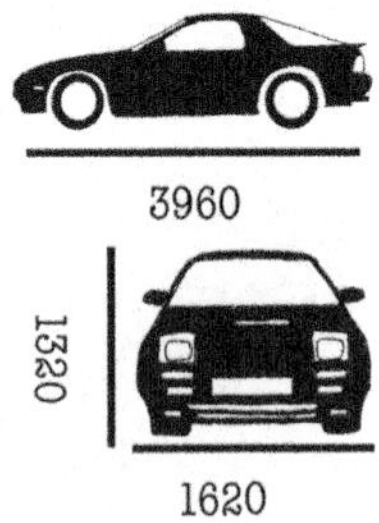

Datsun Cherry 1978 - 1982

You can argue whether this is really a coupe or just small hatch. However, underneath that pretty body is the wheelbase and strut suspension from the original model. That meant utter reliability, even if it wasn't that exciting. In 1981 overhead cam unit upped the bhp. All buyers bought this for the same reason they bought any old Cherry.

Engines: 1117•1270cc **BHP**: 52-60 **MPH**: 84 **MPG**:35
Gearbox: 5spd **Boot:** 310 **Weight:** 805

Nissan 200SX 1989 - 1994

Rear wheel drive, a turbo and pop up headlamps, all the required '90s tick boxes filled in there. Executive model had air and leather gear knob and steering wheel. Modded by Nissan over the years, ABS and LSD for '92, air con a year later with leather and a CD. Many never made it out of the decade without serious modification or damage.

Engines: 1809cc **BHP**:169 **MPH**: 137 **0-60**: 6.8
Gearbox: 5spd/ 4spd Auto **Boot:** 260

Nissan 300ZX 1984 - 1990

Technically still a Z Car but instead of a delicate and finessed this is a big, brutal optional turbo coupe/Targa 2 + 2. Weighty and not as pretty as it should be, but there is standard kit to enjoy. Slight revamp in '87 with colour coded bumpers and reposition of the door handles. Best ones owned by Burt Reynolds wannabes. Check for rust + crashes.

Engines: 2960cc **BHP**:170-228 **MPH**: 131-149 **0-60**: 10-6.7
Gearbox: 5spd/ 4spd Auto **Boot:** 235

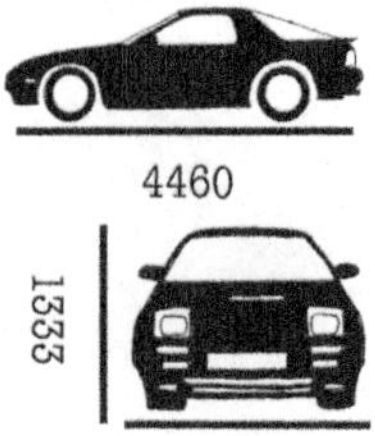

Nissan Silvia ZX 1984 - 1989

Almost infinite number of coupe variants, mostly aimed at mid-America with and without turbo assistance. 2.0 was discontinued in 1986. Very much a bargain bucket 924 which by '88 had a sunroof, air conditioning to go with the electric door mirrors, large bucket seats and remote fuel flap. The most important ingredient was reliability.

Engines: 1809 • 1990cc **BHP**: 135 • 144 **MPH:** 132 **0-60:** 7.9
Gearbox: 5spd/Auto **Boot:** 325 **Weight:** 1136-1195

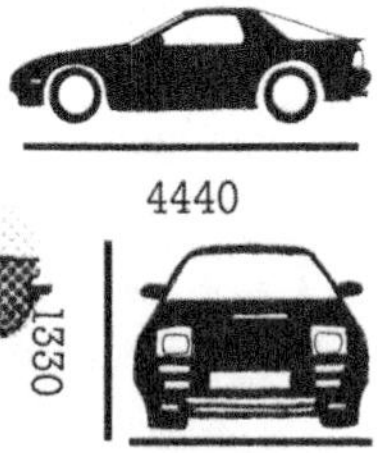

Opel Manta 1975 - 1988

Ascona wearing a pretty frock, just like the Cortina/Capri. By the '80s just a couple of engine options. Also two body styles, a hatchback and a two door coupe. Surviving beyond 1982 is the GTJ hatchback, the Berlinetta coupe and hatch and the best known GTE/Exclusive. Some said it became dated, never mind great to drive and easy to own Banger.

Engines: 1796 • 1979cc **BHP**: 90-110 **MPH:**121 **0-60**: 8.5
MPG: 31 **Weight**: 1000-1090 **Boot:** 380

Opel Monza 1978 - 1987

An Opel Commodore with just a couple of doors. Actually one hell of a Grand Turismo that by the '80s was simply powered by the 3.0 unit which got Bosch L-Jetronic in '83. Most ordered with 3spd Auto upped to a 4spd in '85. Good luxobarge kit for the time included electric windows and central locking. Always underrated.

Engines: 2969cc **BHP**: 180 **MPH:**128 **0-60**: 10.6 **MPG**: 24 **Weight**: 1430 **Boot:** 350

Porsche 924 1976 - 1985

The original Pork Banger. The VW/Audi group parts bin raid works in buyers favour. Bargain buyers always the standard and LUX models, Turbo and S less so unless there were issues. Multiple owners could not always kill them, but often inflicted abuse. Rust, bore wear, smoke. Pop up lights thou...

Engines: 1984cc BHP: 125 • 150 • 177 **MPH**: 127-134 **0-60:** 8.0-9.6 **Gearbox:** 5spd/3spd Auto **Boot:** 250

Porsche 944 1982 - 1992

Odd to think that these were once Bangers, but these middle order Porkers routinely fell into the wrong hands despite having the engine in the right place. S2 the most numerous and the turbo unless exploded maintained desirability. There is plenty to look out for, they will rust, belts, chain and tensioner all need recent replacement. Never relax.

Engines: 2.7•3.0 **BHP**: 163•190•220 **MPH** 149-161 **0-60:** 5.6-6.7 **MPG**: 28.9-29.2 **Gearbox:** 5spd/3spd Auto **Boot:** 250

Porsche 928 1977 - 1992

The market did not rate it as a substitute 911 so it lost value fast. That and multiple owner neglect, meant the early, quite pure cars fell to old Jag levels for a while. Tatty ones would always ruin your life. The fact that the air con does not work would be the least of your worries. Electrics always fun to sort out. Despite galvanisation, will rust. Nightmare.

Engines: 4.5•4.7•5.0 **BHP**: 240• 300•320 **MPH**: 168 0-60: 5.9 **MPG**: 25.9 **Gearbox:** 5sp/4spd Auto **Boot:** 200/400

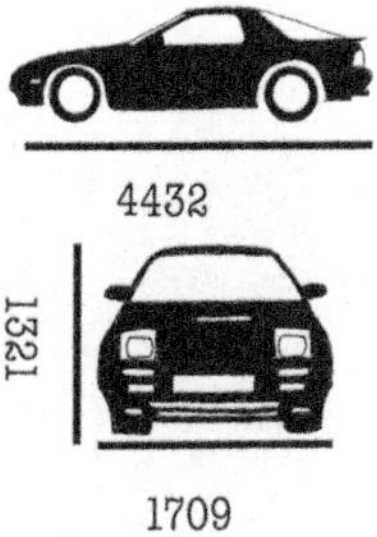

Reliant Scimitar GTE (SE6A) 1975 - 1982

The key to its second or third life as a Banger was the plastic body which reassured buyers that all was well if they didn't dig too deep. Certainly the Ford running should not be too frightening, but dropped down the ownership profile became more lairy and less caring. Consequently struggled as a practical classic, sf Plan SE6b. Rotten chassis, electrics. **Engines:** 2792cc **BHP**: 135 **MPH:**118 **0-60**: 8.56 **MPG**: 31 **Weight:** 1269 **Boot:** 566/1132

Reliant Scimitar GTE (SE6B) 1982 - 1986

SE6b from 1982 slightly lighter, stiffer, squarer and was better suited to the '80s, plus the latest Ford V6 but the competition from Europe and Japan was tougher than ever, so quite a dated old thing. It faded, the company stuttered and the Middlebridge was a short lived premium stop gap that never became a Banger, it just faded away. **Engine:** 2792cc **BHP**: 148 **MPH:**122 **0-60**: 8.8 **MPG**: 31 **Weight**: 1269 **Boot:** 566/1132

Renault Fuego 1980 - 1986

Based on the already dated 18 plus some 20 parts, the sum of all that was a unique looking coupe, just a shame it was made by Renault as they disintegrated fairly rapidly. Turbo had a residual of cool, but most would aim for a GTX with standard power steering, or TX with the 2.0 engine. Once it became a Banger then a 1.7 GTS would do.

Engines: 1.3 • 1.6 • 1.7 • 2.0 **BHP**: 64 • 96 • 110 • 132
MPH: 118 **0-60**: 8.8 **Weight**: 1010-1080 **Boot:** 337

Skoda Rapid 1982 - 1990

The prevailing gag was it's a 911, but cheaper. Banger money pretty much when brand new. Like a Porker with the engine mislocated. Available as a coupe and cabriolet. Vinyl roof alloy wheels and mud flaps. In 1988 bhp upped to 62 and Black Rapid as name suggests, was all black. Radio cassette standard. Low owner examples remained 'as new'.

Engines: 1289cc **BHP**: 58 • 62 **MPH:** 93 **0-60**: 14.2
Weight: 890 **Boot:** n/a

Subaru XT Coupe 1985 - 1990

It's the second oddest Subaru coupe, is a sort of SVX light, but looks like an '80s vision of the '90s near future. Can be switched to 4WD or simply engaged via kick-down. Permanent four wheel drive from '87 when automatic became and option. Quite an amount of gear to go wrong if neglected as most were, due to subsequent bemused owners.

Engine: 1781cc **BHP**: 134•136 **MPH**: 124 **0-60:** 8.7
MPG: 32 **Gearbox:** 5spd/4spd Auto **Boot:** 421

Toyota MR-2 1984 - 1989

Deconstruct the designation, Mid-Engine, Recreational, 2-Seater all wrapped up in a purposeful retro futro wedge bodywork. Sensational package, twin overhead cam, discs all round. Optional T-Bar roof from '86. Never a disposable Banger, but depreciated to real world affordability. Incredibly and rightfully popular and reliable when looked after.

Engine: 1587cc **BHP**: 122 **MPH**: 120 **0-60:** 7.6
MPG: 39 **Gearbox:** 5spd **Weight**: 975 **Boot:** 142

Toyota MR2 1989 - 1999

Bulked up, more hairdressy and softer as tin or targa top. Came with electric mirrors and alloy wheels, T-Bar had wipe down leather. For '92 cats, fresh alloys, new front and uprated suspension. From '94 high compression engine and side impact beams, better suspension and new rear lights. Toyota toughness helps some owners that neglect essentials.
Engine: 1998cc **BHP**:119 • 158 **MPH**: 124-135 **0-60:** 7.2-9.3 **MPG**: 35.8-35.9 **Weight:** 1275-1285 **Boot:** 219

Toyota Celica 1977 - 1982

Second generation model is the Carina with added sexiness as a two door coupe and a fast hatch. Several engine options but majority sold in the UK were the 2.0, choose the OHCs.. Roomy enough, but handling average. What was exceptional remained the reliability which is why it ended up as Banger of choice, rather than being picked for its dynamics.
Engines: 1.6• 2.0•2.6 **BHP**: 83-120 **MPH**: 111 **0-60**: 8.8 **Weight:** 1315 **Boot:** n/a

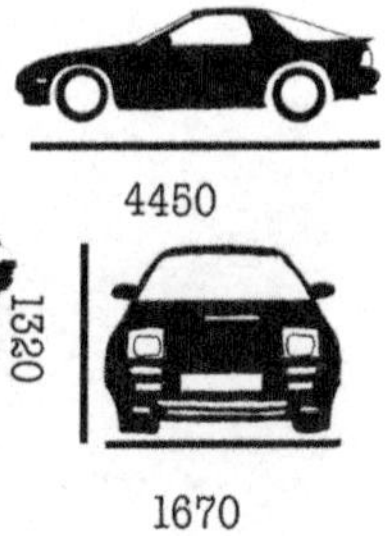

Toyota Celica ST/XT 1983 - 1985

Series 3 and that means a proper '80s right angle 2 + 2 coupe, no other formats for the UK market. More important was the responsive 16V engine. Redesignated XT in 1984 when power steering became standard and got a sharper nose. It wasn't long for the showrooms though but the few in circulation were sought after wedgies.

Engines: 1972cc **BHP**: 103 **MPH**: 109 **0-60**: 10.5
Weight: 1165 **Boot:** n/a

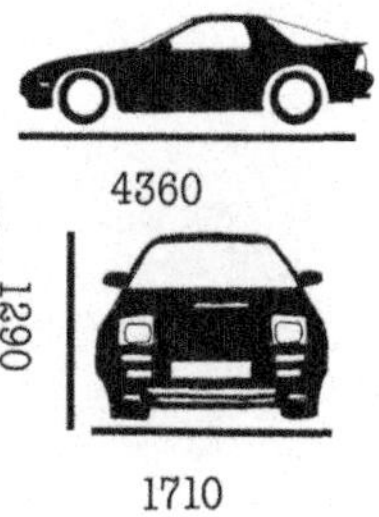

Toyota Celica GT 1985 - 1990

When four wheel drive was installed here's one of the most successful WRCs ever. For everyone else it was a soap bar shaped front wheel drive (Liftback) coupe that did not break down.1988 ABS became standard, but air con cancelled. The GT-Four was the cool one, but the GT in automatic and manual format remained the solid middle class coupe.

Engine: 1998cc **BHP:** 147 **MPH**: 130 **0-60**: 8.3
MPG: 30.1-35.6 **Weight**:1280 **Boot:** 320

Toyota Supra 1982 - 1985

Celica Supra officially and it looked uncannily like a big Japanese Capri, 3 litre. The UK got 100 a month and they all sold out, the big six cylinder brute had a lot of appeal. The independent suspension meant great handling and tailslides. 1986 optional 4 speed automatic. Older buyer appeal means that they lasted longer as Banger coupes for the masses
Engine: 2759cc **BHP:** 170 **MPH**: 126 **0-60**: 8.1
Weight:1265 **Gearbox:** 5spd/4spd Automatic + overdrive

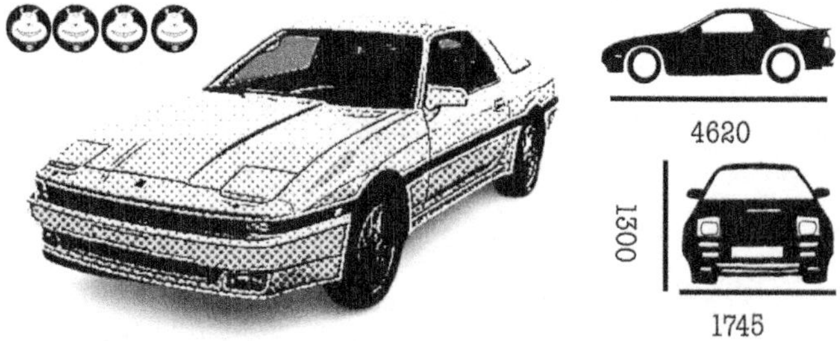

Toyota Supra 1986 - 1993

A70 generation Supra is more of a beefed up Capri and now with tailgate/liftback. More important is the fuel injected 24 valve which was optionally Turbo'd a bit outside the Banger brief. Overall this hard charging old thing was complicated but tough. The non turbo was much less complicated than the NSX and ZX rivals, so relative bargain.
Engine: 2954cc **BHP:** 201-234 **MPH**: 136-142 **0-60**: 6.1 - 7.5 **Weight**:1545 **Gearbox:** 5spd/4spd Auto **Boot:** 185/315

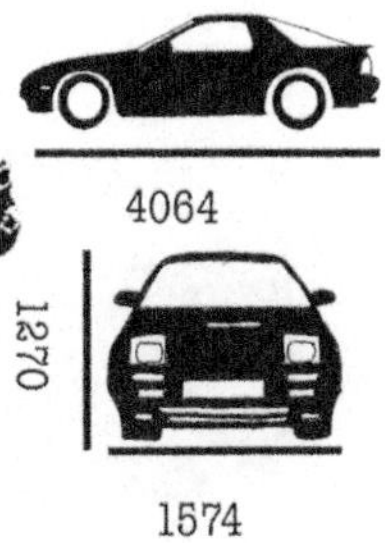

Triumph TR7 1975 - 1981

A little wedge of trouble throughout it's life. Never built proper in the first place, apart from the V8 (not covered) underpowered and underwhelming to look at never mind the marginal quality. Not much happened in the '80s just a sunroof, alloy wheels and radio in 1980 to give it a lift in the showroom. Proper Banger material thereafter.

Engines: 1998cc **BHP**: 105 **MPH**: 110 **0-60**: 9.1
Gearbox: 5spd/3spdAuto **Weight:** 1270 **Boot:** 184

Vauxhall Cavalier GLS/Sporthatch 1975 - 1981

Still an Ascona wearing a pretty frock, but now it has a little Griffin badge too. By the '80s just a couple of engine options, the two body styles, a hatchback and a two door coupe. For many it was a better proposition than a Capri, certainly tidy in the corners and practical to own. Out badged by the classy premium priced Opel one which outlived it.

Engines: 1796 • 1979cc **BHP**: 90-110 **MPH:** 121 **0-60**: 8.5
MPG: 31 **Weight**: 1000-1090 **Boot:** 380

Vauxhall Royale 1978 - 1982

It says Vauxhall on the tin, but it's really an Opel Commodore with fewer doors. Actually one hell of a Grand Turismo which just made it into the '80s with a bigger engine and electronic ignition in '81. Good luxocoupe kit for the time included electric windows and central locking. Always underrated. Great 4-seat Banger.

Engines: 2969cc **BHP**: 180 **MPH:**128 **0-60**: 10.6 **MPG**: 24
Weight: 1430 **Boot:** 350

Vauxhall Calibra 1989 - 1998

The most slippery car you could buy at the time here was the nearest thing to the '90s Capri. Basic 16V best, four wheel drive, turbo and leathered up V6. Proper 4 seater too. Galvanised shells from '95 help, Cavalier mechanicals can at least be cheap, broken 4×4 gearbox isn't. Suspension usually shot, red top 16V head gaskets go pop.

Engines: 2.0•2.5 **MPH**: 127-152 **0-60:** 6.4-9.8
MPG: 30.9-35.5 **Gearbox:** 5spd **Boot:** 300/980

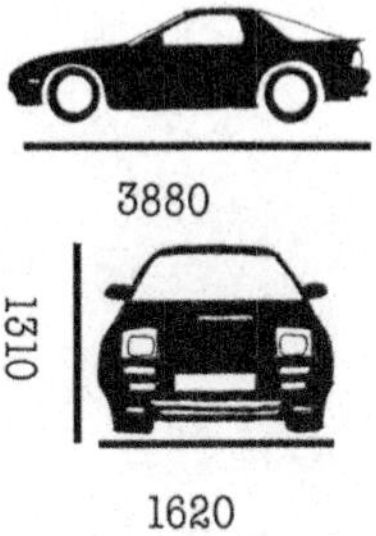

Volkswagen Scirocco 1974 - 1981

Technically a Golf was a less pretty Scirocco because it came first. Never mind, this is as good as small, affordable, high quality Euro coupes ever got. Like most bodies from the '70s rusted away. By the '80s just the GLS. GLI, GTI and Storm. 5-speed always preferable and because it was just a VW, ended up being neglected and a Banger as the rot set in.

Engine:1588cc **BHP**:85-110 **MPH**: 114 **0-60**: 8.9
Gearbox: 4spd/5spd **Boot:** 346/920

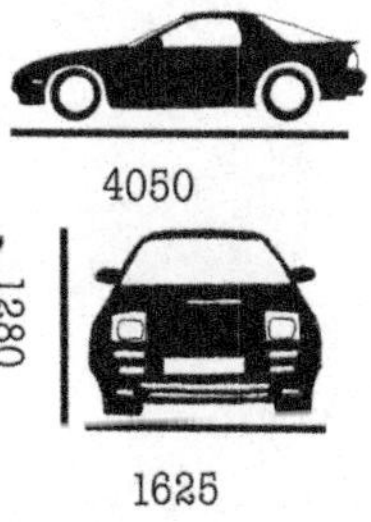

Volkswagen Scirocco 1982 - 1992

Underneath a Mark 1 with more rear headroom and luggage space. The Mk2 was not face lifted, but did gain body kits and various rear wings. Rot isn't so bad on these models, engines are tough and just get smokey and rattly with age. Gearbox linkage bushes go and become floppy. Electrics tend to be OK, this is solid Golf stuff and good value.

Engines: 1.5 • 1.6 • 1.8 **BHP**: 75-139 **MPH**: 118 0-**60**: 8.3
MPG: 34.7 **Boot:** 346/920

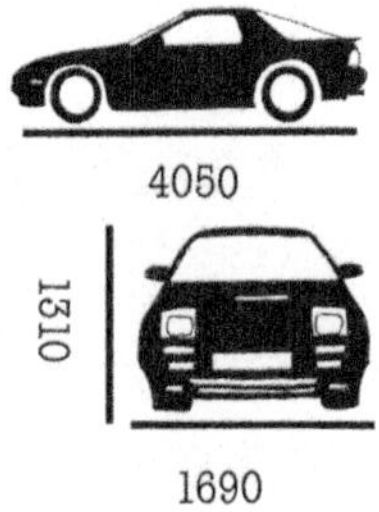

Volkswagen Corrado 1989 - 1995

A grown up Scirocco that contains plenty of Mark 2 Golf. Great to drive whatever the engine and there was a supercharged G60 and VR6. The Banger is the 2.0 8 valve, cheaper than Golf GTI. Decently rustproofed but some panels a problem now. Those engines are great provided not too tired and smokey. Suspension bushes, seized brake calipers.

Engines: 1.8•2.0•2.9 **MPG**: 28.3-35.5 **Top Speed:** 124-146 **0-60:** 6.7-10.6 **Boot:** 235/810

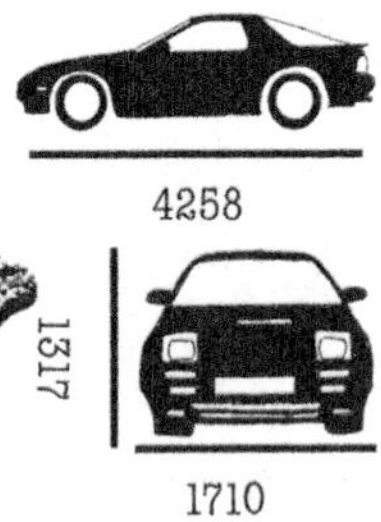

Volvo 480 1987 - 1995

Dodgy Dutch build quality at the time didn't help. It's a 440-460 with less doors and was galvanised, but this hasn't helped much. Side impact beams from '93 and some interesting special editions. Wedge shape and pop up lights are good, everything else is fairly grim, only made an average banger, but the fanbase luv 'em, so buy from them.

Engines: 1721cc **BHP**:109 **MPH**: 122 **0-60**: 9.6 **MPG**: 34.2- **Boot**:161 **Weight**: 1008 **Gearbox:** 5spd

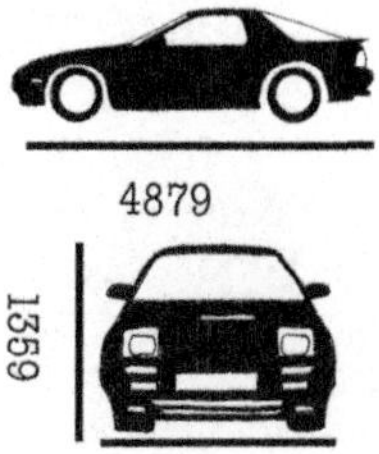

4879

1359

1707

Volvo 262 1977 - 1981

Cut and shut 260 saloon to make a Munster mobile. Bertone did their best, but this oddity was a rare sight. They only made 5622 of them, but at the time buyers only wanted ones they could fit a grandfather clock and occasional table inside. Cool in retrospect and a quick brick was not what anyone really wanted. Never broke down.

Engines: 2664cc **BHP**:148 **MPH**: 120 **0-60**: 10.1 **Boot**:395 **Weight**: 1450 **Gearbox:** Automatic

BangerConvertibles - Open Air Value

Incredibly the number of open top potential Bangers was starting to drop. We can blame the Americans for that. The Federal regulations not only glued on some big fat high rise rubber bumpers, but there were proposals that convertibles might be banned altogether. At the very least manufacturers were installing scaffolding to anticipate rollover requirements.

It is worth saying that there were numerous specialist coachbuilders willing to have a crack at taking the roof off any coupe, saloon or hatchback. Take Crayford, based in Kent, well known for tackling Ford Cortinas and Fiestas. They also lopped the pretty top off a Mercedes 200 when four seats were needed.

There was also a kit car industry which offered all sorts of fantastic creations and copies of old open topped cars. Indeed, Dutton was one of the largest suppliers. These mainly Ford based creations became Bangers in the way that a kit Caterham never would.

In the 1980s it was the BL leftovers which were the soft top Bangers of choice. Limited editions aside it was MGBs, TR7s and Spitfires that fell into disrepute before suddenly being redeemed as practical classics if you had a lock-up or some space in your front garden.

The new convertible order was now represented by the Mazda MX-5 which was of course a more than competent copy of the Brits that went before. The really safe and often worn out Banger buys remained the lopped hatchback models like the Escort, Astra and Golf. Can't go wrong with those.

For the grown ups with a flexible Banger budget and the need to get a couple of extra bodies on board would go for a value Saab 900, or possibly a Cavalier. Shockingly, Mercedes SLs drifted downwards to Bangerdom for a while before bouncing back into pre classic favour.

Alfa Romeo Spider 1970 - 1993

Graduated to a new decade and that meant it survived semi officially as a left hand drive only temptation in an Alfa showroom. Most buyers went the personal import route to get rusty ones from Europe or not rusty, but worn out ones from California. Reached its peak Banger existence in the '80s to '90s before settling into a comfy classic lifestyle.

Engines: 1962cc **MPH**: 118 **0-60**: 9.4 **MPG**: 30.7
Gearbox: Weight: 1120 **Boot:** 300 **Seats**: 2

BMW 3 Series by Baur 1981 - 1985

The German coachbuilders installed a bit of overhead scaffolding into the '02 and E21 3 Series the latter not official in the UK, but they still seemed to get through in decent numbers. It was the E30 generation that made it to the showrooms. Never the neatest solution and sitting in the rear felt claustrophobic with the roof up, or down.

Engines: 1.6 • 1.8 • 2.0 • 2.0 • 2.3 **BHP**: 89-141 **MPH**: 99-124
0-60: 13.8-8.7 **MPG**:23-30 **Boot:** 460 **Weight:** 1010-1110

BMW 3 Series Convertible 1986 - 1993

The open topped legend was born in the '80s and was an instant hit, buyers always prepared to pay for such epic build quality. Great 6 cylinder engines, the fours will plod on though. Electric hood and leather on the 6 cylinders. Killed by rot, head gaskets. Fairly long decent into Bangerdom though when it started to look a bit dated.

Engines: 1.8•2.0•2.5 **BHP:** 115-•129•171 **MPH**: 135 **0-60**:8.7 **MPG**: 30.1-35.3 **Boot:** 312 **Weight:** 1270

Fiat Strada Cabrio 1983 - 1985

Bertone took the two door installed a roll bar and a bijou boot area. Launch coincided with a serious spruce up in 1983 so a less challenging front end and improved fascia with electric windows and better seat trim. Rust was the big killer along with terrible overall build quality. Owner neglect meant these looked leaky and shabby on the used lots.

Engines: 1498cc **BHP**: 85 **MPH:** 103 **0-60**: 10.3 **MPG**: 31-38 **Gearbox:** 5spd/3spd Auto **Boot:** 330 **Turning:** 10.3

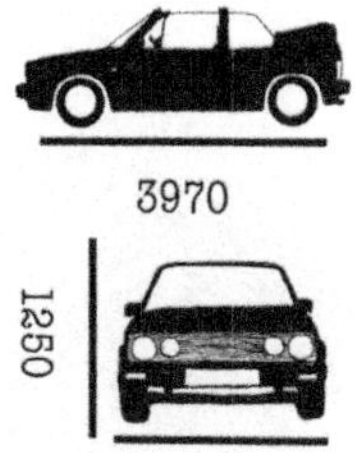

Fiat 124 1967 - 1982

Ancient old thing that dates from the '60s and is based on the versatile 124 that became a lot of other things. Revamp in '72 when officially a UK model, but always left hand drive with a new fascia and detail changes. Most came here as rusty Euro imports or sunblasted California Bangers. Specialist right hooker conversions in the UK.

Engines: 1592cc **BHP:** 108 **MPH**: 115 **0-60:** 9.8
Boot: 181 **Weight**: 960

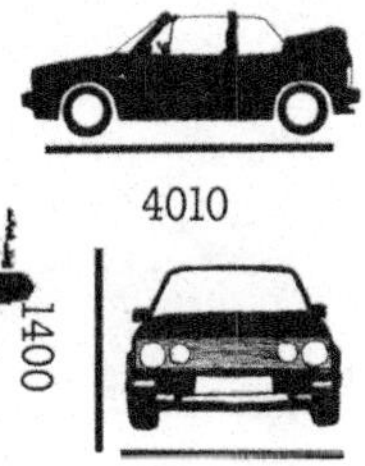

Ford Escort Cabriolet 1984 - 1990

Karmann did this neat job on the Escort and the roll hoop never looked out of place, but like a lot of '80s roof jobs, always a bit floppy. For a couple of months there was a 1.3, the core sales were the 1600 Ghia, the XR3/XR3i and random special editions. Depreciated to affordability pretty quickly and had standard Escort running gear. Brilliant.

Engines: 1296t • 1597cc **BHP**: 79 • 107 **MPH**: 107
0-60: 10.3 **Weight:** 970 **Gearbox:** 5spd **Boot**: 380

Jaguar XJS Cabriolet 1983 - 1987

3.6 AJ6 came first as the first open Jag for donkey's years. Targa style pop out roof panels and folding rear. Substantial roof bars which all looked a bit odd and that depressed values. V12 from '85. Low miles can be fatal, they need exercise, so smoke, coolant, oil leaks, worn suspension and radius arms are what will cost a fortune and upset buyers.
Engines: 3.6 • 5.3 **BHP**:225 • 299 **MPH**: 134-150 **0-60**: 7.3-8.0 **MPG**: 18.8-24.3 **Boot:** 393 **Seats**: 2+2

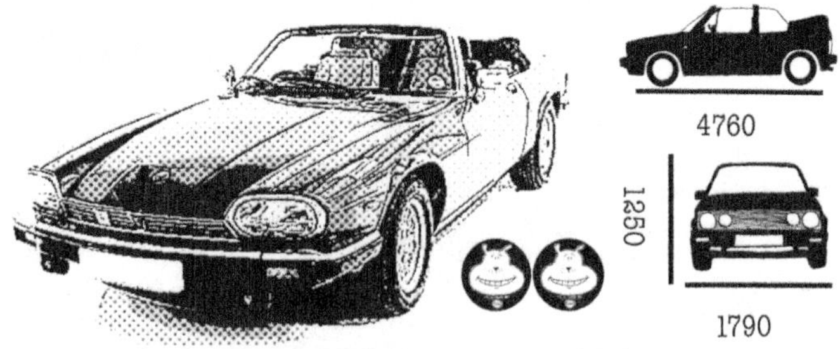

Jaguar XJS Convertible 1988 - 1991

At last a full off roof courtesy of some major structural work that included a new subframe. Came with a power hood, headlamp wash/wipe, Starfish alloys, leather, heated front seats, trip computer and cruise control. Digital ignition from 1988. That lecky roof breaks, never mind the ungalvanised body and any issues with the V12. Nightmare.
Engines: 5343cc **MPG**: 19 **MPH:** 150 **0-60:** 7.9
Gearbox: 3spd Auto **Boot:** 393 **Seats**: 2+2.

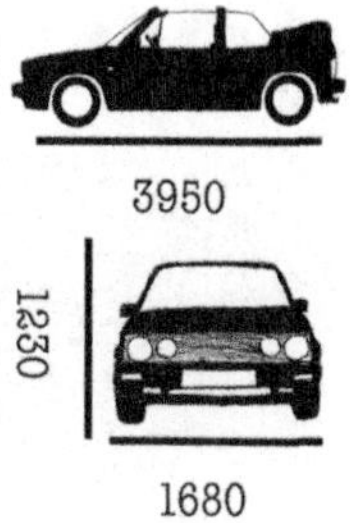

Mazda MX-5 1989 - 1998

Pop up lights and averagely perky 1.6 engine are all the ingredients you need for a fun time. Easy to live with and a very simple manual hood. There are Japanese imports with extra kit like air con and much less underseal. Overall, best Banger chop top in history. Rust, brakes, hood, nothing unfixable. Made Brit roadsters seem arthritic and grim.

Engines:1597cc BHP 114: **MPH:** 114 **0-60**:9.1
Gearbox: 5spd **Weight**: 955 **Boot:** 160 **Seats**: 2

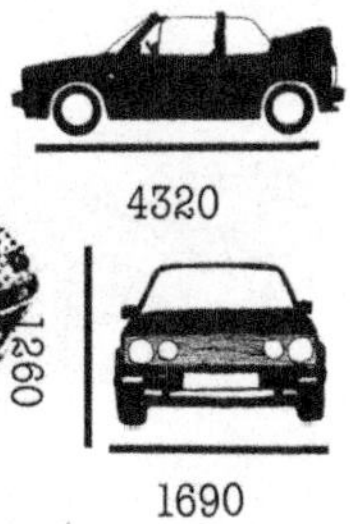

Mazda RX-7 Convertible 1989 - 1992

Largely forgotten, the Rotary was unique and perfectly suited to cruising about. Despite being well built, the Rotary engine is a harbinger of oil leaks and expensive doom sometimes with an added turbo. Excessively clever when compared to an XJS or SL, the massive depreciation helped but the spinning pistons ultimately didn't.

Engines: 2354cc **BHP**: 200 **MPH**: 148 **0-60:** 6.7
Gearbox: 5spd **Boot:** 200 **Weight**: 1205 **Seats**: 2

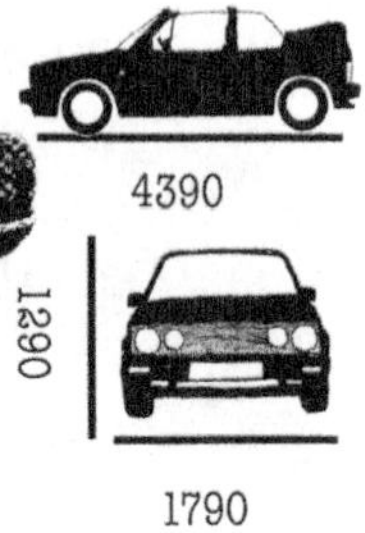

Mercedes SL 1980 - 1989

This classy convertible was built for the '80s and although it never really became a Banger, they still depreciated because the V8 was thirsty, or W107 dated. 24 and 32 valve engines from '89. 5spd always a no cost option, but the majority were 4spd Autos. Everything expensive to fix, best to buy from a deceased estate, or divorcee.

Engines: 2.8 • 3.0 • 4.0 • 4.2 • 5.0 • 5.6 **BHP**: 185-326
MPH: 124-140 **0-60:** 9.6-6.9 **Gearbox:** 4spd Auto **Boot:** n/a

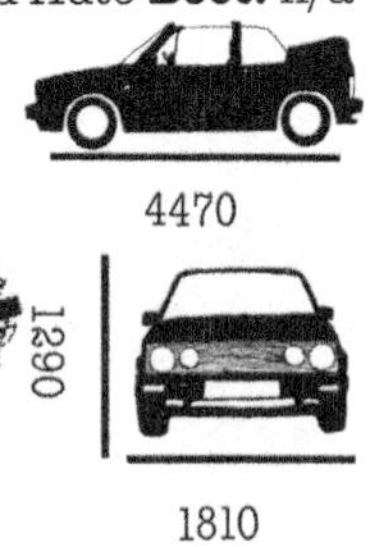

Mercedes SL 1989 - 2002

Nomenclature nerds know its an R129 and one the last truly great Merc. Electronically controlled 722.6 automatic gearbox in 1994 is rather complicated. Biggest facelift in 1998, 17" wheels, new taillights, bumpers, and seats, chromed dials. Under the bonnet less characterful V6 and revised V8. Fragile wiring looms, shabby ones terrifying.

Engine: 2.8 • 3.0 • 3.2 • 5.0 **BHP**:193-320 **MPG**: 22-25.1
MPH: 140-155 **0-60:** 7.2 **Gearbox:** 4-5spd Auto **Boot:** 260

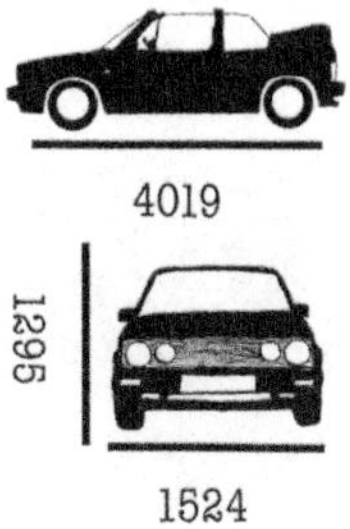

MGB Convertible 1974 - 1980

At the end of its life the MGB is bulked up with Federal bumpers and running on ancient underpinnings. That contributed to the rapid decent into modern Bangerdom. Arrival of the Limited Edition in '80 only meant buyers parked them in lock ups. Otherwise this was an outdated old open topped fossil, but flat caps loved them.

Engine: 1798cc **BHP:** 95 **MPH**: 105 **0-60**: 12.1 **Boot:** 262 cuft **Gearbox:** 4spd overdrive on 3rd/4th **Weight:** 920

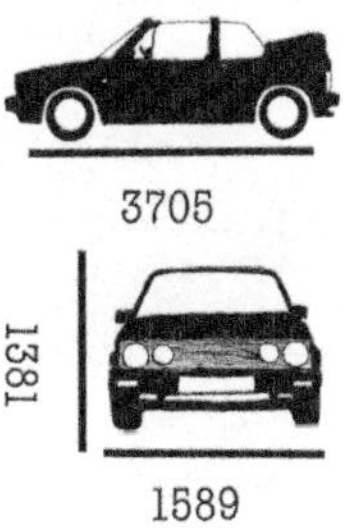

Peugeot 205 CJ-CTi 1983 - 1996

Pretty Pininfarina GTi came first, basic 1.4 CJ from '88. Very light, even flimsy at times but this was beefed up significantly, remained practical, economical and easy to get along with. Well known for oil leaks, smokey engines, noisy cams and blowing head gaskets. Still great to drive. Proper open air Banger after just a few years.

Engines: 1.4 • 1.6 **BHP**: 65-115 **MPH**: 115 **Gearbox:** 5spd **Boot:** 216 **Weight**: 936 **Turning:** 11

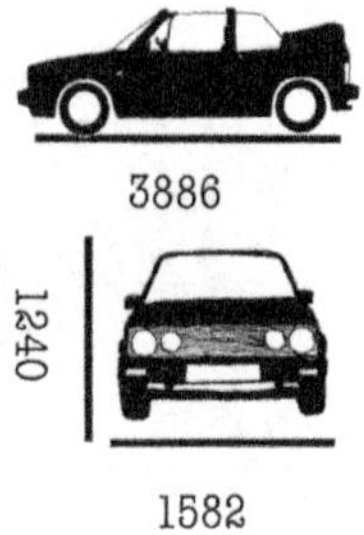

Reliant Scimitar SS1-SST 1984 - 1995

British roadster revival should have started here, but fit, finish and fugliness too terrible. SST Turbo might have fixed that in '90. Didn't. Ford and Nissan engines a good thing of course. Quite a Brit Bitza, with suspension from a Sierra and seats from a TR7. Oh yes and it became the Scimitar Sabre with 1.4 K-Series. Looked less scary but a lost cause. **Engines:** 1.3•1.4• 1.6•1.8 **MPG**: 33.2-34.9 **MPH:** 99 -111 **0-60:** 9.6-12.7 **Gearbox:** 5spd **Boot:** 190 **Weight:** 840+

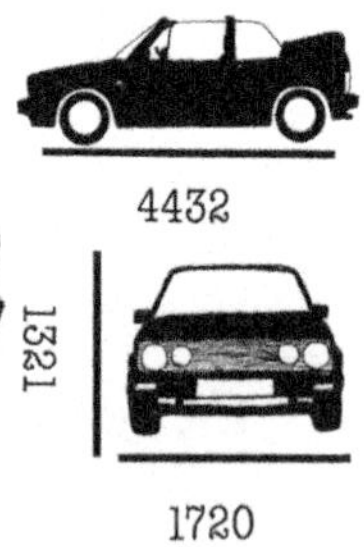

Reliant Scimitar GTC (SE6B) 1980 - 1986

SE6b version was slightly lighter, stiffer, squarer and better suited to the '80s, Ogle did the roof surgery, with substantial roll bar plus the latest Ford V6 made sense. Unfortunately it had limited appeal despite not being as gaff prone as a Stag. Reliant was a company in trouble so here's your open top Brit Banger. **Engines:** 2792cc **BHP**: 148 **MPH:**122 **0-60**: 8.8 **MPG**: 31 **Weight**: 1266 **Boot:** 7.2 cu ft

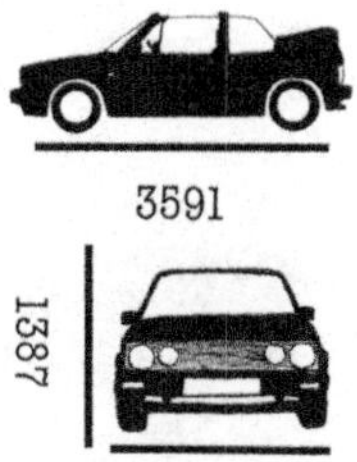

Renault 5 Convertible 1985 - 1989

Super rare Super Cinq but these were around in the '90s for not much. EBS was the company that did the chop. Great little transverse box. Always a budget buy and the 1.4 is probably the best all rounder. Build average, electrics, head gaskets, gearbox bearings, oil leaks and like everything from this era, rust is what kills them. Even a diesel was an option.

Engines: 1.0 • 1.1 • 1.3 • 1.4 • 1.7 • 1.6D **MPH:** 105
MPG: 41-51.6 **Turning**: 10.25 **BHP**: 47-90 **Boot:** 270

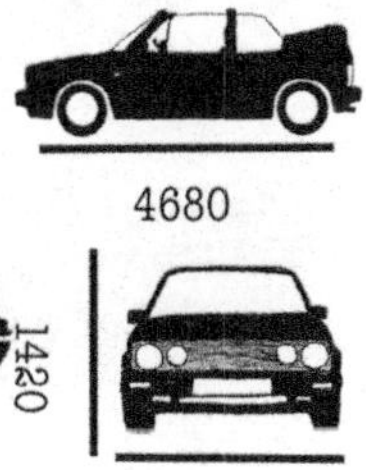

Saab 900 Cabriolet 1984 - 1993

Ancient underpinnings, but a rock solid Banger legend, that never needed a roll-bar. Light Pressure Turbos in 1990, Limited run models to '93 were SE and Turbos. 16 valvers are fun. Six figure mileages were a given with these. Non Turbo underwhelming, but less Banger bother. Rattling timing chains, noisy camshaft, blowing turbos. Brilliant.

Engines: 2.0 • 2.0 Turbo **BHP**: 133-175 **MPH**:126 **0-60:** 7.5
MPG: 27.9-28.8 **Weight**: 1370 **Boot:** 650

Skoda Rapid Cabriolet 1985 - 1990

What do you call an open top Skoda? A skip! according to the old gag, but there really was a cabriolet. Still had a rear spoiler, alloy wheels, whilst inside the reclining front seats had removable head restraints. Otherwise not a great deal happened except in 1988 when the bhp went up to 62. Never that many around, a pretty instant open Banger.

Engines: 1289cc **BHP**: 58 • 62 **MPH:** 93 **0-60**: 14.2
Weight: 890 **MPG**: 27.9-28.8 **Weight**: 1370 **Boot:** 650

Toyota Celica Cabriolet 1987 - 1988

Fairly grim looking conversion courtesy of the American Sunhood Co, especially with the botched two-part Boy Scout tent erected. Toyota is all about quality and this had less than zero as it wobbled down the road. 1988 ABS became standard, but air con cancelled. None of that mattered because no one wanted it. Banger from day one.

Engine: 1998cc **BHP:** 147 **MPH**: 130 **0-60**: 8.3 **MPG**: 30.1-35.6 **Weight**: 1285 **Boot:** 320

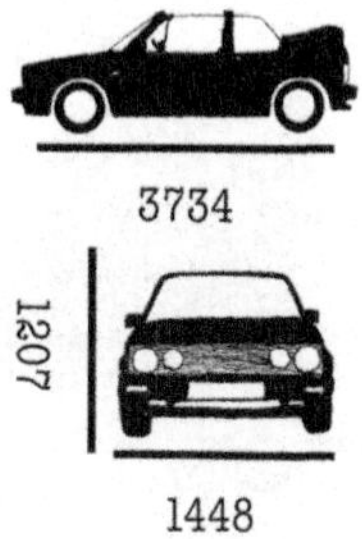

Triumph Spitfire 1970 - 1980

Piece of ancient British Car Industry history with a separate chassis and utterly awesome engine accessibility which you might just need. Ok to drive but outclassed by everything as no one really wanted a cramped, underwhelming sports car that you couldn't do proper shopping in. Irrelevance meant it became a classic faster than a Banger.

Engines: 1493cc **BHP**: 71 **MPH**: 101 **0-60**: 10.9
Gearbox: 4spd /Overdrive **Weight:** 712 **Boot:** 190

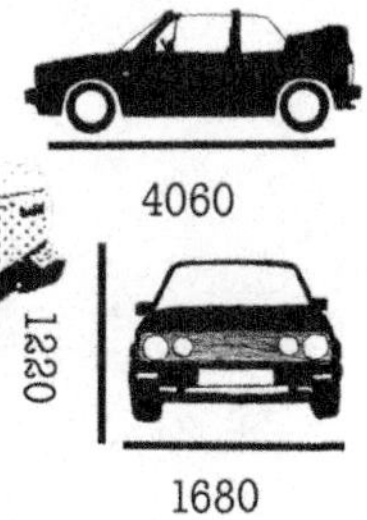

Triumph TR7 Convertible 1979 - 1981

A little wedge of trouble throughout it's life. Never built proper in the first place, underpowered (not V8) and underwhelming to look at never mind the marginal quality. Not much happened in the '80s just alloy wheels, plaid seat trim and radio in 1980 to give it a lift in the showroom. Proper open air Banger material thereafter.

Engines: 1998cc **BHP**: 105 **MPH**: 110 **0-60**: 9.1
Gearbox: 5spd/3spdAuto **Weight:** 1270 **Boot:** 184

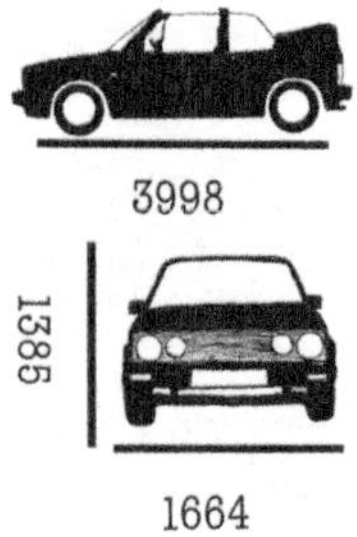

Vauxhall Astra Convertible 1987 - 1993

Quite a lot of ordinary enough Mark 1 underneath the Bertone-built convertible with its standard power-operated hood was excellent value for money. Dumpy to look at and drive, plus everyone wants and wanted a GTE, but the basic 1.6 does a decent open air job. Most have rusted away, smokey rattly and overdue for a cambelt change. **Engines:** 1.6•2.0 **MPG**:34.1-42.2 **Top Speed:** 106-121 **0-60:** 10.5-9 **Gearbox:** Man/Auto **Boot:** 289 **Seats**: 4

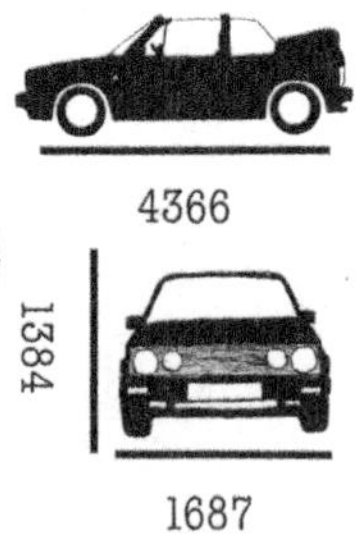

Vauxhall Cavalier 1981 - 1989

Looked like a convertible that belonged to loadsamunny Befordshire plasterer. Had the same specification as an SRi, but with an added coachline. Had flush GL wheel covers, wind down rear side windows but no headlamp wash/wipe. What gives long term owners grief is noisy camshafts and hard valve stems, so smoke and drama as the miles built up. **Engines:**1796cc **BHP**: 114 **MPH**: 116 **MPG**:30-38 **Gearbox:** 5spd/3spd Auto **Boot:** 510 **Weight**: 1085

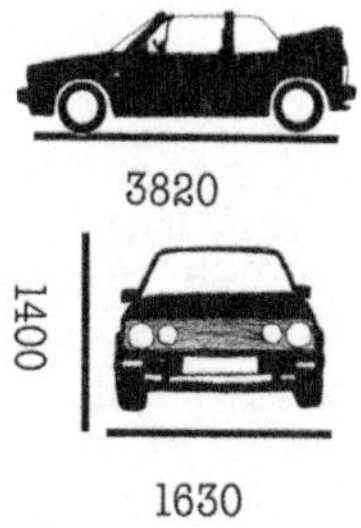

Volkswagen Golf Cabriolet 1980 - 1993

Fabulous cabriolet for the people, every bit as iconic as the hatch and put together initially by Karmann. Kept it's cool Mark 1 style and pram hood, based on the GLI and GTI.
From 1990 an electronic hood became standard all had colour coded body kit including basic cheery 1.5 Clipper. Same buying issues (bore wear) as Mark 1, plus roof leaks.
Engines: 1.5 • 1.6 • 1.8 **MPH**: 108-111 **0-60:** 9.4 **MPG**: 33.3-36.5 **Gearbox:** 5spd **Boot:** 220 **Weight:**805

LuxoBangers - ComfyLimoLife

Liberties have been taken here with what counts as a luxury car. There are the really obvious ones like Rollers, good old Banger Jags and S-Class Mercedes which eventually descended into affordability, because that's the way the used car market works. There is though room for some slightly quirky Europeans which technically might belong in the Ford Granada Ghia X class.

What we have is a few manufacturers who are no longer associated with luxury motoring and don't seem capable of getting that knack back, but let's give them some credit for trying. Alfa Romeo 6 was a long wheelbase failure, whereas the 164 was a rather exciting prospect related to the Saab 9000, which isn't in this section. Alfas though became Banger cheap, dead quick.

Audis are here because there is a suggestion of luxury courtesy of wood/plastic inserts. Admittedly a 200 is austere, delivering almost Scandinavian minimalism. They did feel special with the added benefit of an Audi badge was becoming credible because of World Rally wins and exceptional build quality.

Can't say the same for Renault, but the 30 was a really comfortable Gallic sofa. By contrast the Lancia Gamma was a big old rusty lump and could never be taken seriously as a fully functioning car, but here it is. What buyers at this level wanted, if they could not have the badge, was equipment.

Japan was ready to oblige, so wrapped up in the dullest, mostly rectangular shaped bodies was almost everything the Chairman of the Board would need. The Honda Legend, Toyota Crown and Datsun 280C/ 300C also delivered a level of build quality that a Jaguar/Daimler driver needed before parking on the hard shoulder.

Is luxury relative? Probably, whether it should include the Vauxhall Royale, Senator, Opel Commodore and the 260/760 Volvo or not is open to question. Actually the only question is, were they Banger affordable at the time? Yes, so they're in.

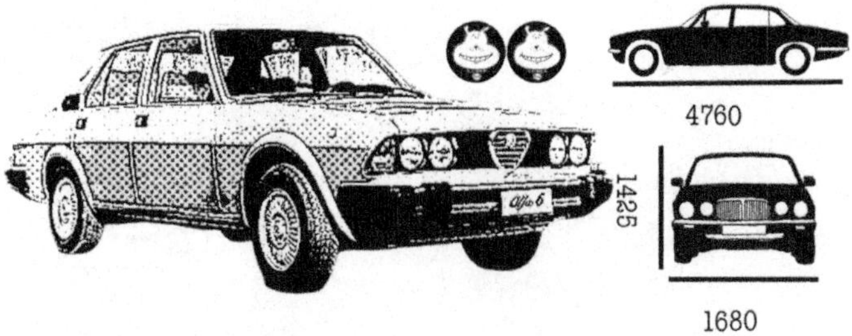

Alfa Romeo Alfa 6 1980 - 1985

Upmarket Alfetta proof that it wasn't just BL who could botch big cars despite some good ingredients like the 2.5 V6. Zero market for this dated lump in the UK. Unloved, it lost the quad headlamps in '83. Injection replaced three carbs in '85, but hardly any built, just over 12,000 so it was soon forgotten, neglected and once broken down would rot away.

Engines: 2492cc **BHP**: 158 **MPH:**:121 **0-60:** 9.5 **MPG**: 20 **Boot:** 500 **Weight**: 1470 **Seats**: 5 **Doors:** 4

Alfa Romeo 164 1988 - 1997

Surprisingly accomplished big Alfa. Reassuringly odd interior and controls. Easily the sexiest of the Type 4 cars (Croma/Thema/9000) which the Bangerpedia promotes to luxury status and although the FWD+V6 combo a handful, one of the best big saloons to drive hard. Always needed looking after, electrics, suspension and V6 need attention.

Engines: 2.0•3.0 **MPG**: 27.1-36.1 **Speed**:152 **0-60:** 9.9-7.7 **Boot:** 505 **Weight**: 1200 **Seats**: 5 **Doors:** 4

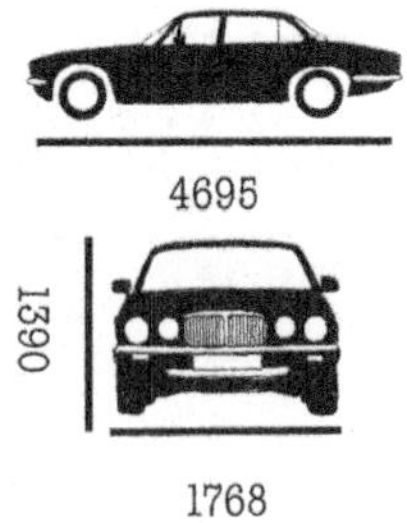

Audi 200/Turbo 1980 - 1984

A 100 with a different SE badge, quad headlamp, more spec and in some cases, a turbo bolted on. The extra spec was velour trim, cruise control, electric windows, central locking, electric sunroof, spoked alloys and metallic paint. Despite all that the SE and Turbo was nothing special, not least because it didn't deliver an executive experience.

Engines: 2144cc **BHP**: 136-182 **0-60:** 7.5 **MPH:** 139 **MPG**:23 **Boot:** 642 **Weight:** 1260 **Seats**: 5 **Doors:** 4

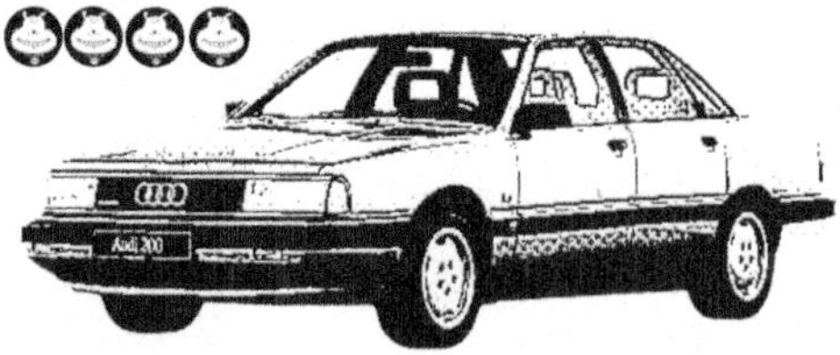

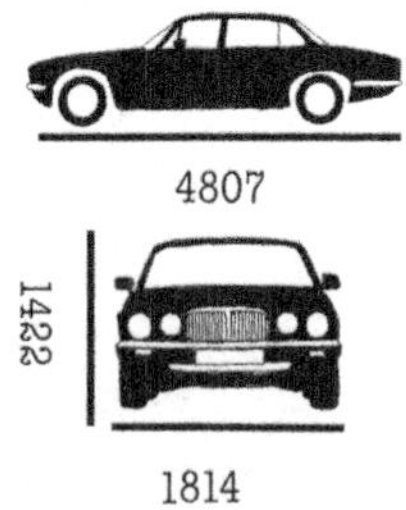

Audi 200 1984 - 1989

Still looks like a 100, this time the new one with some added Quattro. Spec includes Cruise control, air con unless you have the E model which did have a radio cassette, but not the Blaupunkt like the Turbos. Significantly galvanised bodywork from '85. Still nothing special and cancelled early. Big, Bargain, Baffling, Banger.

Engines: 2.2 • 2.3 **BHP:** 138-182 **MPG**: 23 **0-60:** 7.6 **MPH:** 124-144: **Weight:** 1260 **Boot:** 570 **Seats**: 5 **Doors:** 4

Audi 100 V8 1988 - 1993

Looks like a 100, but it shares only the doors with that model here is the blueprint for the great big, four wheel drive, hyper luxury uber saloon. Actually far too much tech for the time and not as dependable as it should have been. Historically important, but not worth the effort of tracking one down. A8 for effort, but C- for execution.

Engines: 3.6•4.2 **MPG**: 23 **0-60:** 6.8 -7.6 **MPH**: 152-155
Boot: 570 **Seats**: 5 **Doors:** 4

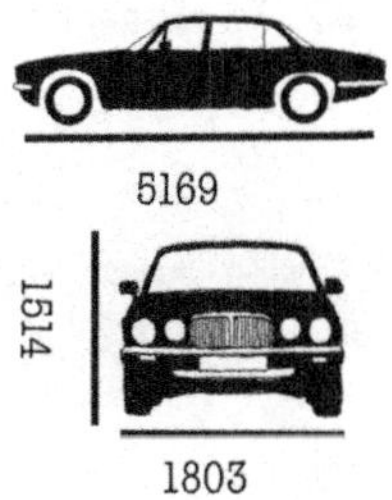

Bentley T2 1977 - 1980

A Roller Shadow II with a Bentley badge and grille from the modern monocoque era. The marque was fading fast by this point, so a surprisingly common Banger at the time unless doing matrimonial duties. Available in a long wheelbase format. Brakes and suspension, never mind the Rolls V8, is what finished off most when Bangerdom arrived.

Engines: 6750cc **MPG**:13.2 **0-60**: 10.9 **BHP**: 170 **MPH**:118
Boot: n/a **Weight**: 2116 **Seats**: 5 **Doors:** 4

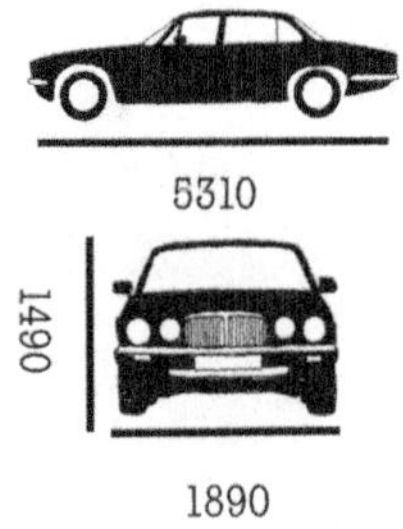

Bentley Mulsanne 1980 - 1992

Still a Shadow underneath despite looking a bit different on top with it's big old corporate breeze block body that had to work hard to represent all the premium marques and spin offs. Turbo model really did bring back the 'fastest lorry' Le Mans image. Standard Mulsanne became the S in '87 with uncredited 230bhp, fuel injection and optimistic 170mph speedo. A lot of Banger and trouble for not much money.

Engines: 6750cc **BHP**: 230 **MPH:** 123-135 **0-60**: 6.8-9.5 **MPG**: 11 **Boot:** 350 **Weight**: 2345 **Seats**: 5 **Doors:** 4

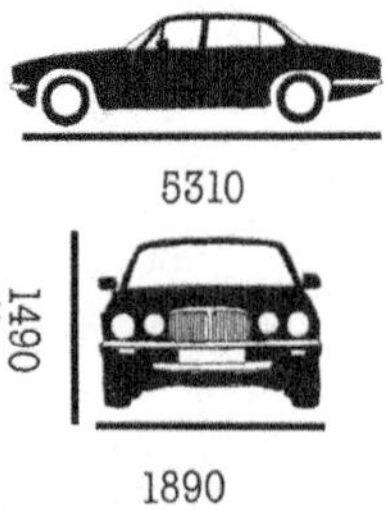

Bentley Eight 1984 - 1992

Here is the point at which Bentley got their 1930s groove back. Still an identikit Rolls but the wire mesh grille was more of a statement, it had a front spoiler rubber insert bumpers and was de-specced enough to be ten grand cheaper. Quicker to the banger bargain parking bays round the back of premium dealers. Still costs a fortune to fix.

Engines: 6750cc **BHP**: 260 **MPH:** 129 **0-60**: 9.5 **MPG**: 11 **Boot:** 350 **Weight**: 2245 **Seats**: 5 **Doors:** 4

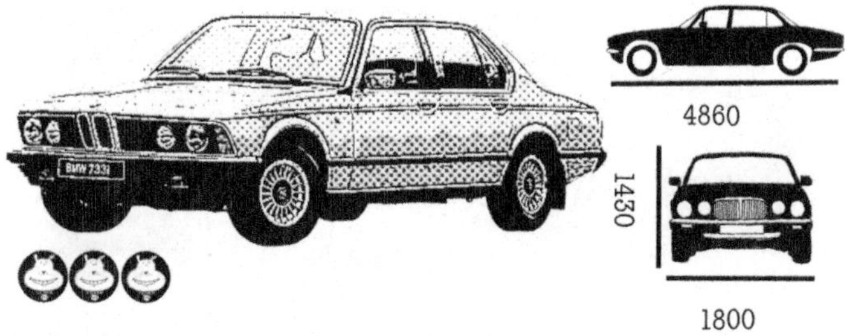

BMW 7 Series 1977 - 1986

Appeal was the sporty drive, quality build and tech tour de force including on-board computer, service interval indicator, a "control panel check" and climate control. This E23 generation was the first BMW with an anti-lock braking system (ABS), driver's airbag and double wishbone front suspension. Facelift in 1983. Neutered by it's epic dullness.
Engines: 2.8 • 3.0 • 3.2 • 3.5 **BHP**: 181 **MPG**: 21.7 **Boot:** 480 **MPH**:122 -135 **0-60:** 7.9-9.5 **Weight:** 1480

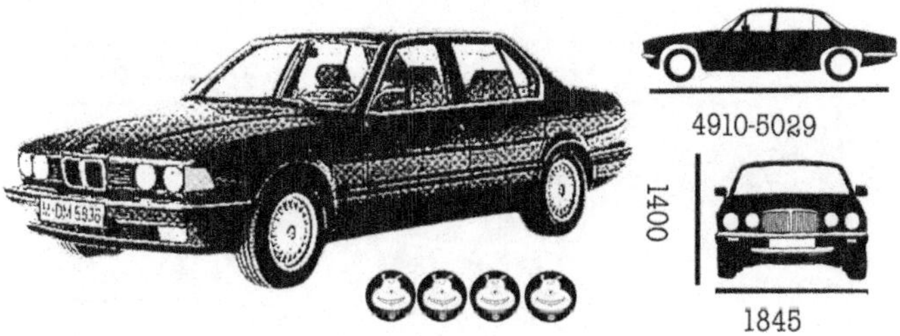

BMW 7 Series 1986 - 1994

BMLimoW comes of age with the E32. Great to drive, the 6 cylinder engines exceptional and the V12 overkill. Perfect from the off and no changes, SE spec upgraded over time, '88 remote locking and cross spokes. Overall pretty damn reliable and it would be the electronics which cause the most upsets, otherwise worn suspension, exhaust and brakes.
Engines: 2.8 • 3.0 • 3.5 • 4.0 **MPG**: 21.7-25.3 **Boot:** 500 **MPH**:140-155 **0-60:** 7.3-9.5 **Weight:** 1600 **Seats**: 5 **Doors:** 4

Daimler DS420 1968 - 1992

It's a posh people carrier for 7 passengers and their luggage. Beloved of Mayors, undertakers and royalty. It's a unique Daimler, built by Jaguar with an XK engine. It's got a great big bonnet, a chassis and is relatively straightforward to live with. Became and largely remains cheap as upmarket chips, used for Banger racing, or wedding duties in perpetuity.

Engines: 4325ccBHP: 164 **MPG**: 22.4-23.7 **Speed**: 110 **Weight:**2140 **Boot:** Not revealed... **Seats**: 6-8

Daimler Sovereign III 1979 - 1986

Refreshed XJ with injection, added fluted grille, extra trim and liberal extra chrome and walnut inlay. Basic Sovereign and over the top Vanden Plas but names dropped in '83 when it simply became the plain old 4.2. No more manual gearbox, but electric sunroof, metallic paint, trip computer. Bestest of trad Brit Bangers, but Breakdowns R them.

Engines: 4235cc **BHP**: 205 **MPH**: 126 **0-60:** 8.7 **MPG**: 18.4 **Weight**: 1780 **Boot:** 400 **Seats**: 5

Daimler Double Six 1981 - 1993

Sexy old shape retained for the big V12. A big and beautiful creation with a ruinously expensive drinking habits. Actually had a power cut in the '90s, down to 260bhp. Probably the best built of these beasts. Least loved for some time but properly rare and the very cheapest of any multi-cylinder saloon in captivity. Luxury belief it's a Banger.

Engines: 5343cc **BHP:** 295 **MPH**:150 **0-60:** 8.7 **MPG**: 18.4
Weight: 1926 **Boot:** 400 **Seats**: 5

Daimler 3.6/4.0 1986 - 1994

'80s slightly squarial Jag with fluted grilles and added walnut/chrome frippery. Not the most loved incarnation with irritatingly digital dashboard complicated and prone to failure. Late '88 aerodynamic mirrors, exterior trim changes, inside Boxwood inlays. New 4.0 engine from '89 and back to analogue instruments. Dispiriting electrics.

Engines: 3.6 • 4.0 **BHP**: 203-226- **MPG**: 18.4-27.2
MPH: 136-138 **0-60**: 8.5 **Boot:** 430 **Weight:** 1730 **Seats**: 5

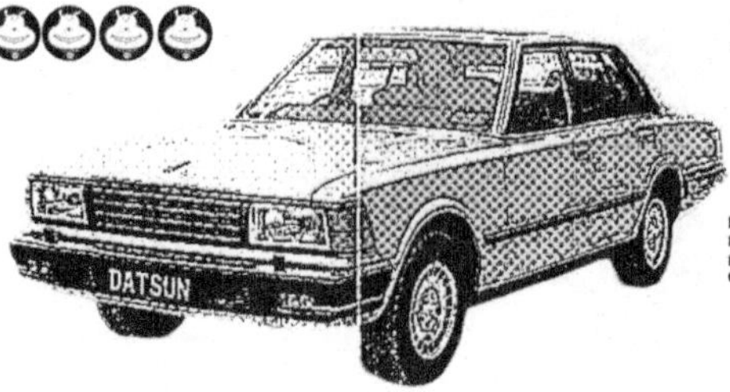

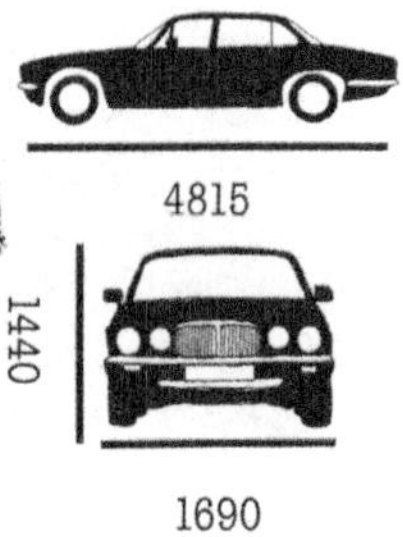

Datsun 280C 1980 - 1984

It's C for Cedric, (although that could stand for chrome) but you can't sell a car with the same name as your grandad. Here's a big slab of square Limonothingness that you can easily lose in the company car park. On the big upside it came with everything as standard and that included air conditioning. Never broke down.

Engines: 2753cc **BHP:** 90 **MPH**: 100 **0-60**: 13.8 **MPG**: 28 **Gearbox:** 5spd/Auto 3spd **Boot:**n/a **Seats**: 5 **Doors:** 4

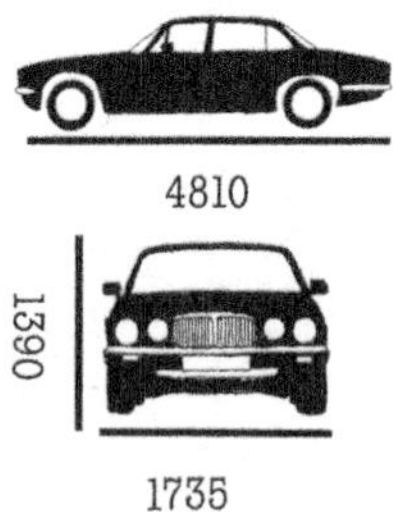

Honda Legend 1986 - 1991

Rover Sterling related, but as this is the company's first Limo, soon to become a Luxobanger. That excellent transversely mounted V6 was replaced in 1988 by larger 2.7, although it didn't feel that special. Electric sunroof, alloy wheels, leather and air conditioning. Utterly reliable even in old age when rust would inevitably bite.

Engines: 2.6•2.7 **BHP**: 171-167 **MPH**: 131-132- **0-60:** 8.0 **MPG**: 23-25- **Boot:** 470 **Weight:** 1350-1380

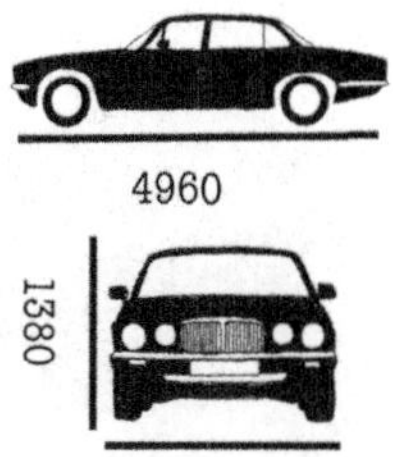

Jaguar XJ6 1979 - 1986

Italian subtle spin on a design classic that worked with only marginal improvements in build quality. Overall still a let down BL barge, with gradual trim upgrades over the next few years, but nothing important. Not as lovable as previous generations, but became Bangers just as quick. Electrics, engine bore wear and suspension degradation killed them.
Engines: 3.4 • 4.2 **BHP:** 162-205 **MPH**: 117-135 **0-60:** 8.9-11 **MPG**: 18.4-20 **Weight**: 1770-1780 **Boot:** 400 **Seats**: 5

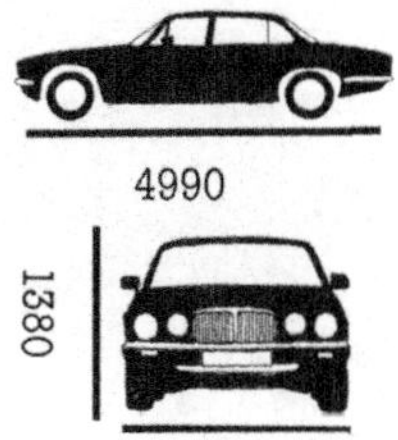

Jaguar XJ40 1986 - 1994

'80s slightly squarial Jag. Not the most loved incarnation with irritatingly digital dashboard complication and prone to failure. Got the Sovereign badge from Daimler with air con and central locking. Revamp in '89 plus the new 4.0 as well as a proper analogue dashboard, plus standard ABS. Not a great Banger most ended up at the breakers pretty quick.
Engines: 2.9 • 3.6 • 4.0 • **BHP**: 148-223 **MPH**: 122-136 **MPG**: 20-22 **0-60**: 9-9.6 **Boot:** 430 **Weight:** 1770 **Seats**: 5

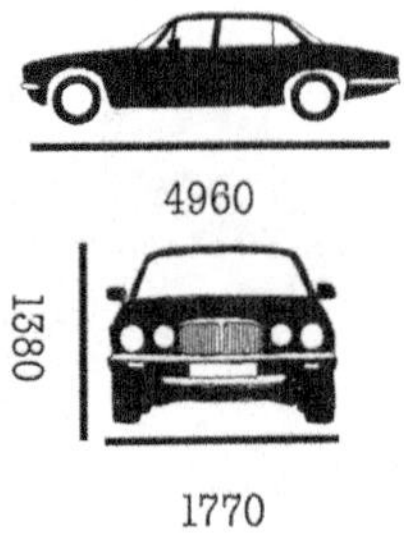

Jaguar XJ12 Series III 1979 - 1993

Sexy old shape retained for the big V12. A big and beautiful creation with ruinously expensive drinking habits. '90s ones downgraded to 264bhp, so stick with the old HEs for sheer guts. Probably the best built of these beasts. Least loved for some time but properly rare and the very cheapest of any multi-cylinder saloon in captivity.

Engines: 5343cc **BHP:** 295 **MPH**:150 **0-60:** 8.7 **MPG**: 18.4 **Weight**: 1926 **Boot:** 400 **Seats**: 5

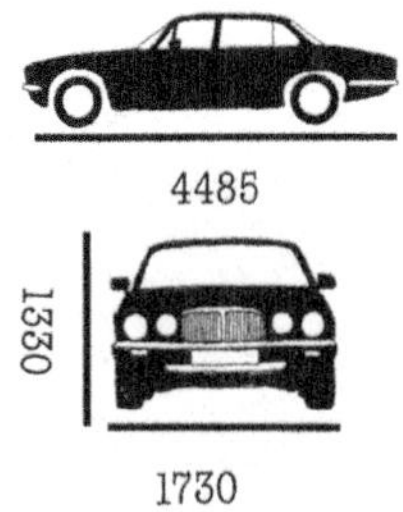

Lancia Gamma 1976 - 1984

Huge fastback looks, old series 1 still sold until '82 as UK market was stone dead. Revised engine and had Delta- style 'shield' grille and new 6Jx15 alloys with 15 holes. Most were Brit AP automatics and apparently many converted to manuals. Central locking and some had steel sunroofs. Rust and general flakey build killed the brand.

Engines: 2.0 • 2.5 **BHP**: 138 **MPH**: 121 0-60: 10.1 **MPG**:24 **Gearbox:** Auto **Boot:** 500 **Weight:** 1340 **Doors:** 4

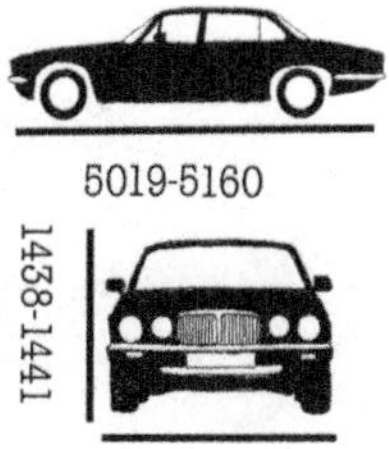

Mercedes S-Class 1979 - 1991

The greatest plutocrat shifter of all time bar none with the high tech kit as other makers lag behind. So airbags, ASR anti-slip and offset crash friendly bodywork. Those brilliant all-alloy V8 engines and ambience of utter solidity was a wonderful combination. Never really went wrong, even after being million mile posh hotel taxis. Best Banger S ever.

Engines: 2.8 • 3.0 • 3.9 • 4.2 • 5.0 • 5.6 **MPG**:17.8-22.5
Speed: 124 - 155 **0-60:** 7.1-10.9 **Boot:** 510 **Seats**: 5

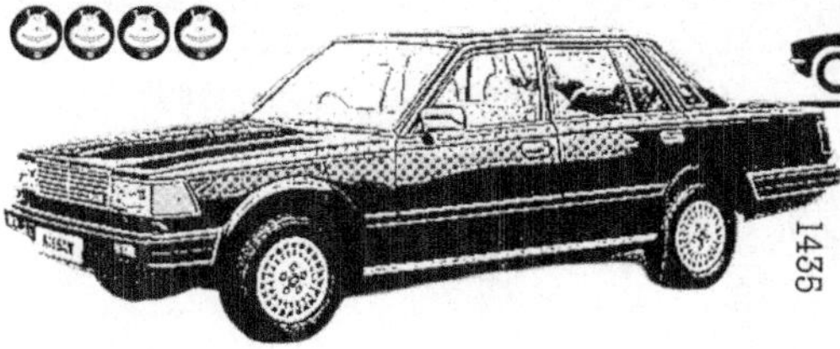

Nissan 300C 1984 - 1987

Same as the Datsun Cedric but with a fresh badge and revised engine and an automatic only option. Visible from space by the colossal amounts of Oriental chrome which either offends or charms you. Unlike the other directors who chose Jaguar XJ6s, this will run until the liquidators decide otherwise. Rapid Bangerdom awaited and rewarded buyers.

Engines: 2960cc **BHP**: 155 **MPH**:116 **MPG**: 28
Gearbox: Auto **Boot:** n/a **Seats**: 5 **Doors:** 4

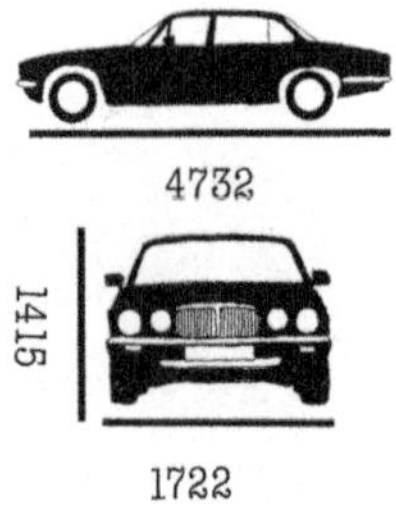

Opel Commodore 1980 - 1983

A Rekord with a slightly longer bonnet and some added chrome wheel trims. Under that bonnet was a six cylinder engine. Standard S model had velour, heated rear window and a clock. Big spec with the Berlina CD meant alloy wheels, sunroof, electric windows and central locking. Engine upgrade in '81. German build solid until rot arrived.
Engines: 2490cc **BHP**: 115-136 **MPH:** 118 **0-60**: 10.2
MPG: 25. **Gearbox:** 4-5spd Man/Auto

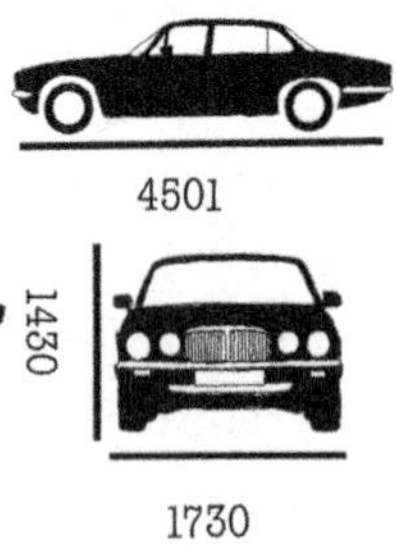

Renault 30 1975 - 1984

When big hatches were still regarded as potentially execucool, in reality a flashier 20 with a V6. Extremely comfy in the real world courtesy of all independent suspension and coils at the rear. TX trim is velour, wood fascia, electric windows and central locking. '83 revised switchgear and auto standard to make instant sofa Banger.
Engines: 2664cc **BHP:** 142 **MPH**:117 **0-60**: 9.8 **MPG**: 25
Gearbox: 5spd/Auto **Boot:**395 **Weight**: 1270

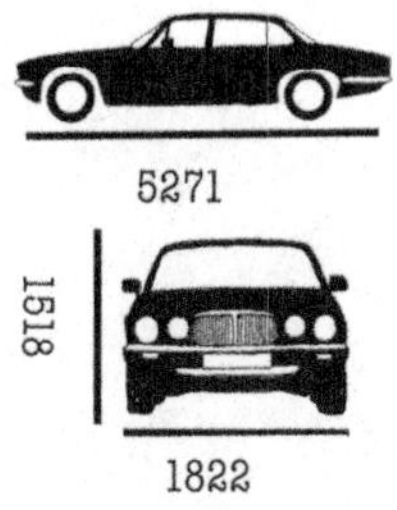

Rolls Royce Silver Shadow II 1977 - 1980

Monocoque Mark 2 with toned down chrome, subtle front air dam plus new fascia and air con. Rack and pinion steering made it a bit sharper when on matrimonial duties. Available in a long wheelbase format as the Wraith. Brakes and suspension, never mind the Rolls V8 is what finished off most when Bangerdom arrived with the wideboys.

Engines: 6750cc **MPG**:13.2 **0-60**: 10.9 **BHP**: 170 **MPH**:118
Boot: n/a **Weight**: 2116 **Seats**: Bride & Groom **Doors:** 4

Rolls Royce Silver Spirit & Spur 1980 - 1989

A Shadow underneath, but on top this is a clumsy if fabulously well finished wedding tackle. Lots more legroom for the bride and groom. Major modernist upgrades in '86, finally fuel injection, anti lock brakes and climate control air. Silver Spur is the long one. Followed Shadow to Bangerdom then it's suspension, brakes & rot that cost lots to fit.

Engine: 6750cc **BHP:** 260 **MPH:** 120 **0-60**: 12.6 **MPG**: 15
Boot: 400 **Seats**: 5 **Weight**: 2257 **Doors:** 4

Toyota Crown 1981 - 1983

Another rectangular barge from the east which was packed full of features that few properly appreciated. Zero image, but max kit that included velour, electric aerial, central locking, air conditioning, electric windows and power steering. Front and rear stereos meant this was a car to be driven about in. Best upmarket cab, velour a problem...

Engines: 2759cc **BHP**: 145 **MPH**: 113 **0-60:**10.4 **MPG**:21
Gearbox: 3spd Auto **Boot:** n/a **Weight:** 1442 **Doors:** 4

Vauxhall Royale 1980 - 1983

A Carlton (well an Opel Rekord) with a slightly longer bonnet and added chrome. Under that bonnet was a six 3.0 cylinder engine. Spec includes alloy wheels, tinted glass, steel sunroof, metallic paint, electric windows and central locking. Spec change in '81, revised seats, remote drivers door mirror. German build solid until rot arrived.

Engines: 2968cc **BHP**: 180 **MPH:** 127 **0-60**: 10.5 **MPG**: 22
Gearbox: 5spd Man/Auto **Boot:**391 **Weight:** 1519

Vauxhall Senator 1984 - 1987

The Royale slipped away and the Opel Senator existed for a while before the Griffin badges came in when the Senator was revamped. German built, like a Granada. Two engine options and top spec CD had LCD instruments, air con, electric windows, wood grain on the doors. What mattered was oil leaks, fuel injector seals, failing electricals.

Engines: 2.5 • 3.0 **BHP:** 140-177 **MPH:** 121-128 **0-60**: 8.8 **MPG**: 23 **Gearbox:** 5spd/Auto **Boot:** 500 **Weight:** 1385

Vauxhall Senator 1987 - 1994

Upmarket Carlton powered by sixes and topped off with the egg box grille, entering the '90 catalytic converters. Certainly smooth and lots of kit the CD had electronic ride control, alloys and cruise. 24 valve 3.0i was also the ultimate cop car at the time. Worn suspension bushes, oil leaks, fuel injector seals and electrical issues with age.

Engines: 2.6 • 3.0 **MPG**: 25.4-32.7 **Gearbox:** 5spd/Auto **Boot:** 530/930 **Seats**: 5 **Doors:** 4

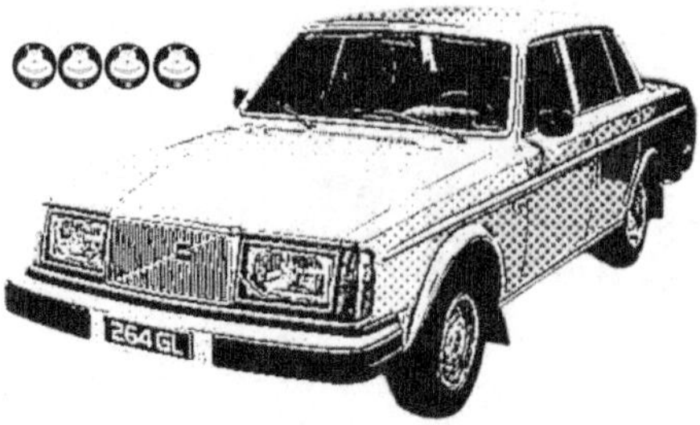

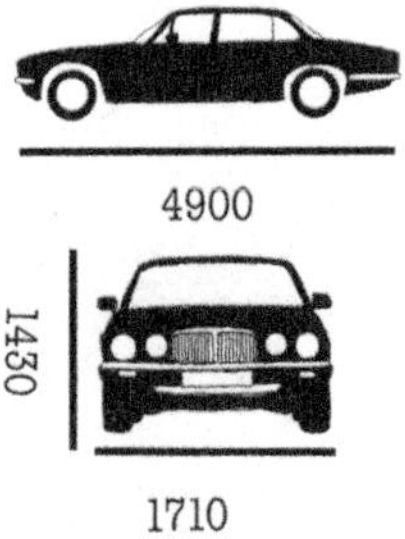

Volvo 260/264 1974 - 1985

New brick based on the 164 and wrapped around the joint venture Renault/Peugeot and eventually DeLorean V6. It was a revised unit for the 1980s and increased in size by Volvo to 2.9. 260 GL becomes the 264GLE in '81 with leather, air conditioning and headlamp wash/wipe. Big luxury square Bangernomics saloon, see also Crown/Gloria.

Engines: 2849cc **BHP**: 155 **MPH**: 111 **0-60:** 10.8 **MPG**: 20 **Gearbox:** 5spd/Auto **Boot:** 394 **Seats**: 5 **Doors:** 4

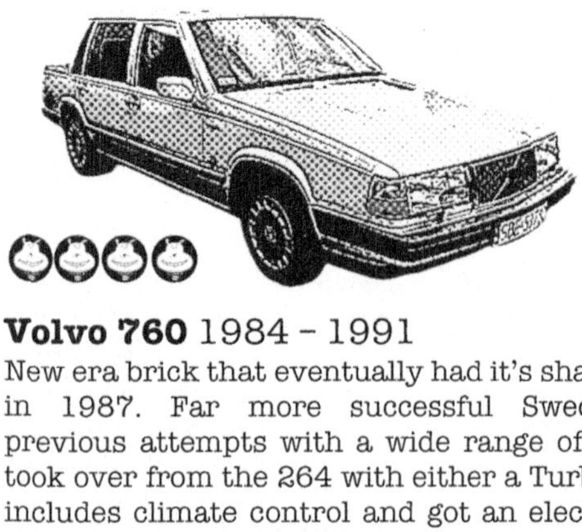

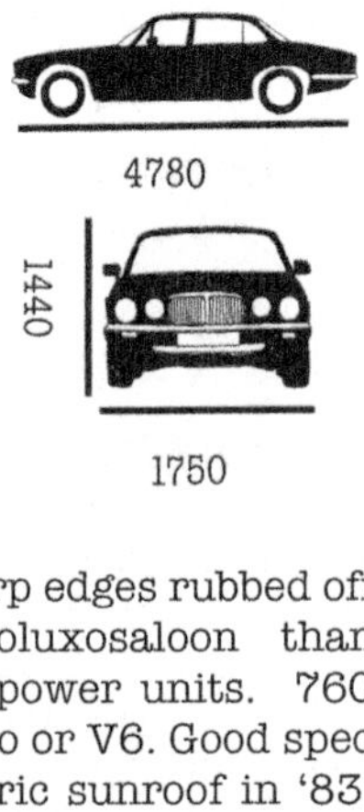

Volvo 760 1984 - 1991

New era brick that eventually had it's sharp edges rubbed off in 1987. Far more successful Swedoluxosaloon than previous attempts with a wide range of power units. 760 took over from the 264 with either a Turbo or V6. Good spec includes climate control and got an electric sunroof in '83. Prime Banger plus thirst and complication made it cheap.

Engines: 2..3 • 2.9 **BHP**: 180-156 **MPH**: 120 **0-60**: 9.5 **MPG**:23 **Gearbox:** 5spdMan/4spdAuto **Boot:**394

Banger Yank Tanks - V8s & V6s etc

What do we have here then? Well, this is an acknowledgement that if you wanted one of those full sized, full fat motors from Ammurrika, some manufacturers were only too happy to oblige.

By the '90s car makers tried to make more of an effort by putting the steering wheel on the correct, more familiar right hand side. Previously everything was resolutely a left hooker.

Technically it would always be possible to get absolutely anything into the UK by the personal import route. Indeed, if you look at the various official records they are in conflict as to what was actually available. Here then are the ones which represent the models and marques sold in the '80s which became Bangers once they had outlived their usefulness. Or simply the subsequent owners couild not come to financial terms with the ferocious fuel bills.

One route for these cars to be around in numbers would be tax free and diplomatic sales. There were a lot of showrooms in London which offered this service to the 'Diplomatic Immunity' Community' as well as airmen who wanted something familar to drive after they landed their McDonnell Douglas F-4 Phantom .

The Yank Tank featured were mainly from the big three Ford, Chrysler and General Motors covering most of the major model categories. Going to the bother of bringing in a huge saloon/coupe which was wildly out of scale to the toy town British A and B roads is impressive, if mad.

Otherwise bagging a Corvette or Camaro made some sense in value terms by the time it was a Banger. However, a Mustang would have been a huge dissapointment and didn't even look the part. It was probably the off road Blazers and Jeeps which made the most sense with their relative comfort and ability to tow and muck about in the mud.

The Banger bottom line always was that mechanically they were straightforward and the parts on a par with Euro cars, or cheaper plus postage. Otherwise it was just paying for fuel, probably worth it to be Yankee cool.

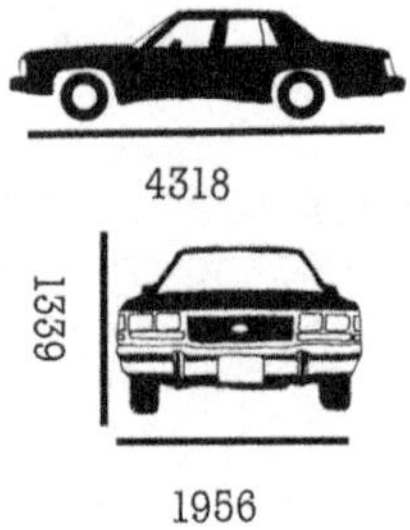

American Motors Pacer 1975 - 1980

The first 'small wide car' with the right hand door longer than the left hand, topped off with marginal 6 cylinder engines proved too weird for the UK raised on BL 's finest. Not just a bubble shaped hatch, also an even more awkward estate. Not economically viable for Brit buyers. Everyday cool by Wayne's World association. Banger for a bit then.

Engines: 3.8 • 4.3 • 5.0 **BHP**: 124 **MPH**:96 **0-60**: 11.2 **MPG**: 17 **Gearbox:** 3spd Auto **Boot:** 912 **Cost:** £5000

Buick Skylark 1979 - 1983

Compact in Yank terms, in reality a fairly large saloon and coupe with a cutting edge transverse engine layout which as usual had gutless outputs and marginal mpg. Hard to see why anyone would buy one especially with a standard four speed gearbox which explains why most were the 3 speed automatics. Majority of buyers went for the coupe.

Engines: 2.5•2.9 **BHP:** 90-115 **MPH**: 109 **0-60**: 12.5 **Gearbox:** 4spd manual/3spd Auto **Boot:** n/a

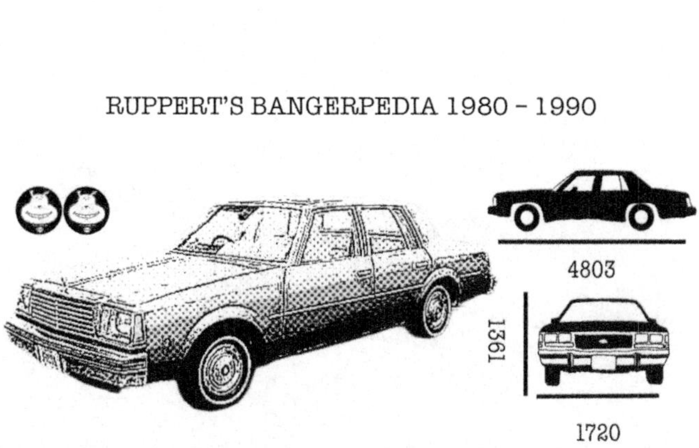

Buick Century/Regal 1981 - 1985

Workaday relatively compact Buick as saloon, and estate, sorry station wagon, badged as the Century. Plus there was the fancy coupe wearing a Regal badge. Incredibly the pathetic 110bhp produced by the V6 potentially could be boosted by a turbo to 170bhp in the Regal Sport. Typical '80s Yank and like most imports not especially cheap new.

Engines: 3.8 • 4.4 • 5.0 **BHP:** 110-140-170 **MPH**: 100
0-60: 10.5 **Gearbox:** Auto **Price:** £7500

Buick Rivera 1978 - 1984

Rather marvelous that it was possible to buy what is an absolute giant of coupe which was perfectly suited to the American Highways, but not the byways of the UK. Hardly a big seller the popular option was the V6 with an added optional turbo that delivered a substantial 180bhp. Old fashioned land yacht.

Engines: 3.8 • 4.2 • 5.1 **BHP**: 110-170 **MPH**: 112 **0-60**: 10.9
Gearbox: 3spd Auto **Weight:** 1760 **Boot:** n/a

Cadillac Seville 2 1979 - 1986

Caddy for a new generation meant that it was front wheel drive, but that bustle back styling was quite something (19th century) else. Here was a compact Caddy and the V8 diesel was meant to tackle the oil crisis. Trouble was that the barely adequate 105bhp didn't suit anything apart from an FX4 taxi at the time. The Seville would return. See below...

Engines: 4.2•6.0•5.8D **BHP**: 106-147-162 **MPH**: 116
0-60: 10.4 **Gearbox:** Auto **Weight:**1822-1898

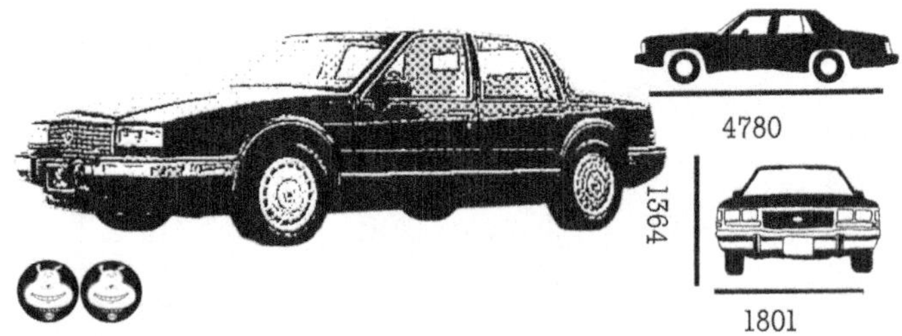

Cadillac Seville 1989 - 1992

In many ways this could be just about any right angle Yank from the '80s, only the Caddy badge gives it away. Sticking with the transverse front wheel drive rather than usual Euro RWD barge. V8 does its job and no soppy diesel or six cylinder to spoil the experience. The details and interior are dated. RHD might help, fast forward to 1998.

Engines: 4900cc **BHP:** 200 **MPH:** 125 **0-60:** 8 **Gearbox:** 4spd Auto **Boot:** 409 **Weight:** 1564 **Price:** £28,995

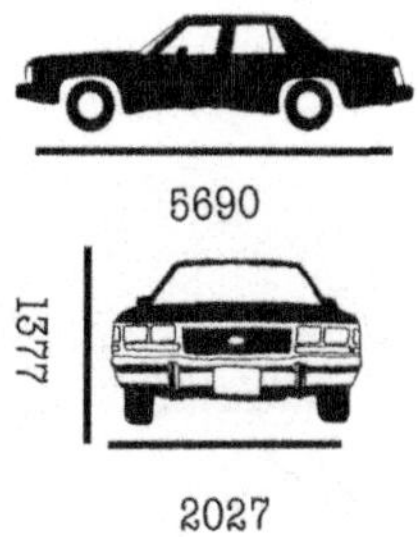

Cadillac Eldorado 1978 - 1985

What everyone really wanted, a great big sod off Luxo coupe, except this was the recession hit '70s. As a result a cut-back shadow of its former self, yet still a Torpedo boat rivaling 17 feet long. Technically a bitza with Oldsmobile running gear and Buick body panels, no longer the hand built preserve of the elite. No diesels just the huge V8 with marginal mpg.

Engine: 5737cc **BHP**: 170 **MPH**: 116 **0-60**: 9.8
Gearbox: 4sp Auto **Boot:** 460 **Seats**: 5 **Doors:** 4

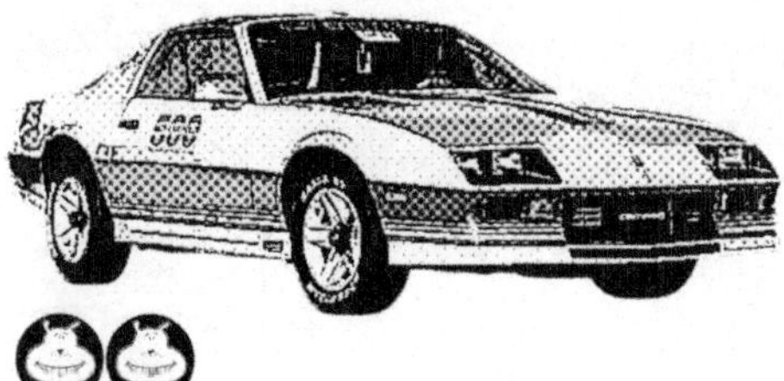

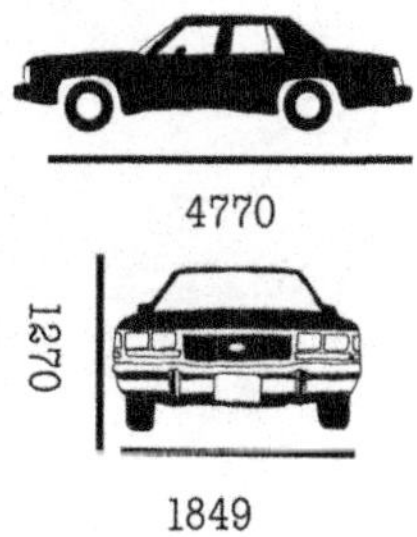

Chevrolet Camaro Z28 1981 - 1986

Everyone wanted a Z car because of Burt and the Smokey film. It looked great, well the '70s one did, but the reality was that beyond the V8 burble there wasn't a lot to it. A big automatic myth with a Phoenix on the bonnet. Might not get you a '79 Sally Field shaped girlfriend. Parts cheap, freight may not be. Unstressed, seized brakes and major rust.

Engine: 5733cc **BHP**:175 **MPH**: 112 **0-60**: 9.2 **MPG**: 20
Boot: 328 **Gearbox:** 4spd Auto **Weight**: 1490

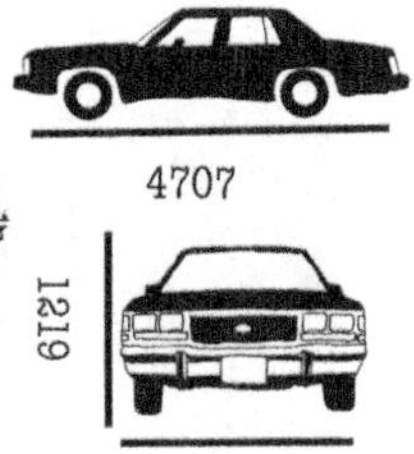

4707

1219

1753

Chevrolet Corvette 1981 - 1986

Third generation Corvette was pretty tired by this point and being strangled by the emissions regs, it still looked the part even if it was outclassed by everything. In theory manual available, C4 from '84 and the supercar performance ZR-1 would have been a private import. A Banger to the extent it was a lot of coupe and attention for not much money.

Engines: 5733cc **BHP:** 190 **MPH:** 142 **0-60:** 6.6
Weight: 1500 **Gearbox:** 3spd Auto/4spd Man

5390-5479

1433-1478

1915-2014

Chevrolet Caprice 1980 - 1985

Default big hire car for that coast to coast holiday in Reagan's America. Saloon was too big for Blighty at 17 feet and 8 inches in Imperial. Basic and cost saving engineering with a live rear axle and rear drums along with a three speed automatic. The very last of the Dinosaur Yank Tanks and at least GM didn't bother bringing the diesel lump.

Engines: 5002cc **BHP:**130 **MPH**: 100 **0-60:** 13.9
Gearbox: 3spd Auto **Weight**: 1660

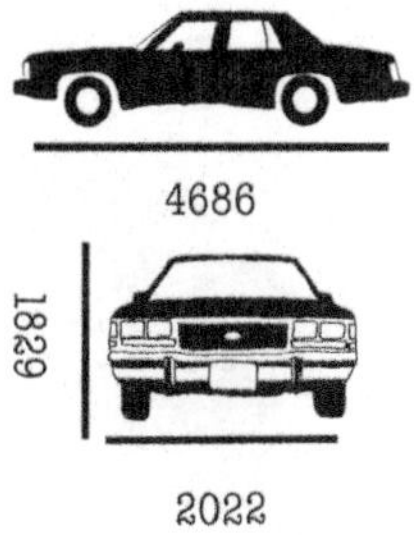

Chevrolet Blazer 1978 - 1985

Not much choice when it came to big SUVs which put this old thing in the frame. Second generation looked very cool. Behind the driver and passenger steel roof was a removable GRP one, so even cooler for rear seat passengers. Six cylinders or V8. The real choice was flakey Range Rover or a Blazer that was comfy on road and solid tow truck.

Engines: 4.0•5.0 **BHP**: 115-167 **MPH**: 90 **0-60**: 13.1
Gearbox: 3spd Auto/4sp Manual **Cost:** £9000

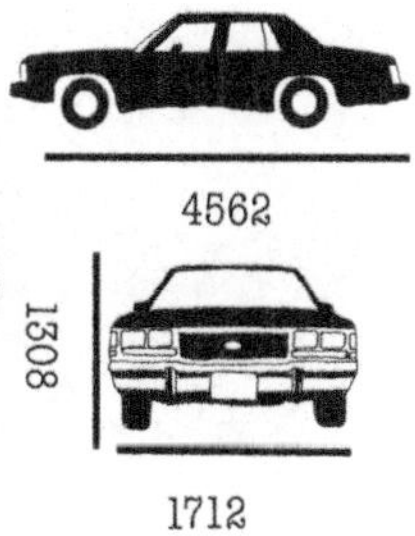

Ford Mustang 1978 - 1984

Abysmal late '70s Mustang 3 downsizing of the icon to make it slower, dumber and duller. This is a two door saloon for Florida pensioners with a choice of neutered engines (and a turbo) paired with a basic live rear axle and leaf springs struggling to keep the show on the road. Incredible they believed anyone would want this when the Capri was alive.

Engines: 2.3•3.3•4.2 **BHP**: 116-152 **MPH:** 99-109
0-60: 12.1 **Gearbox:** 4spd Man/Auto **Cost:** £7700

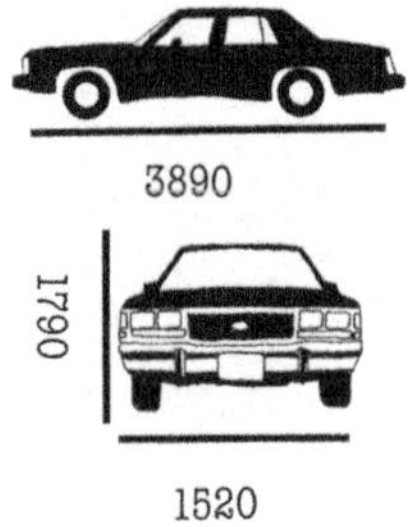

Jeep CJ-7 1978 - 1986

Still possible to draw a line from the WW2 hero to this one which meant it had live axles and semi elliptic springs even if front discs helped bring it all to a halt. The chassis was new with more outlying suspension which improved on road handling, mostly for idiots. Specify a diff lock and either a straight six or V8. Always a special order model.

Engines: 4235•4981cc **BHP:** 110-119 **MPH:** 93 0-60: 14.1
Weight: 1128 **Gearbox:** 3spd/4spd/Auto **Doors:** 2/3

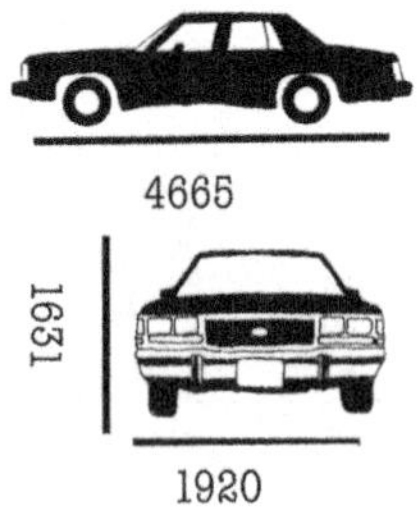

Jeep Wagoneer 1978 - 1986

In an age when the Range Rover was just a three door and quite likely to break down, here was a wonderfully rugged demonstration of how the whole family could go off road in some comfort. The underpinnings were basic and most buyers went for the six cylinder although the V8 had the full time 4×4. Faux wood panels wonderfully kitsch.

Engines: 4235•5896cc **BHP:** 110 **MPH**: 100 **0-60:** 12.6
Weight: 1920

Bangindex by Car Builder

RUPPERT'S BANGERPEDIA 1980 - 1990

www.bangernomics.com
www.bangernomics.com
www.foresightpublications.com

James Ruppert still regrets ever starting this Bangerpedia and committing to a whole series of these volumes. He has driven 484 of the 485+ models featured here. Always interested in motoring history (grade 1 CSE), he bought all sorts of MOT borderline Bangers that were prehistorically awful. Once sold cars then switched to writing about used ones. Spent many years driving around the country looking at car lots and talking to blokes who sold them. Wrote for newspapers including The Independent, The Sunday Times and Evening Standard. Best known as a writer for Car magazine, Autocar, Performance Car, Supercar Classics and many others. Dreamt up the word Bangernomics in 1990. Founded Free Car Mag the only consumer car magazine launched in the last decade. Believes we are being Demotorized. Currently banned from being in the mainstream motoring media. Banging on about marginal motoring only makes a marginal living. Please consider the following titles for inclusion on your bookshelves to help pay for food, fuel and automotive tat.

Order Books from www.bangernomics.com which takes you to flyscreenqueen.co.uk
Somewhere on Substack as Bangernomics

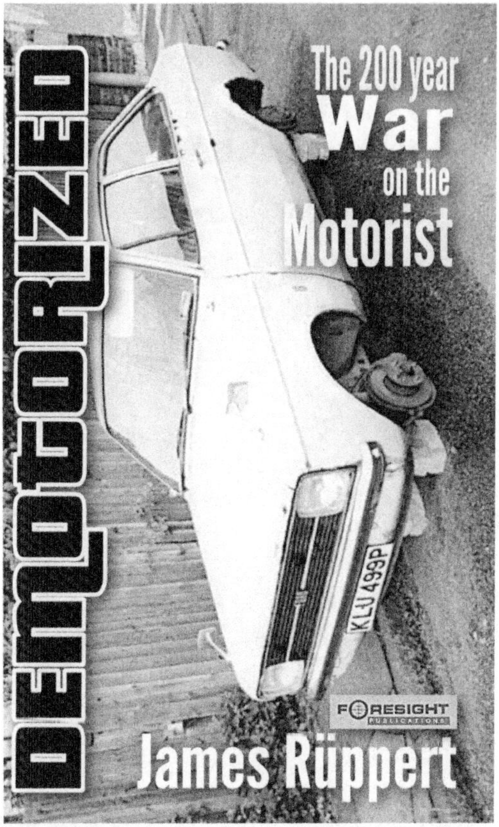

Demotorized. This is the not quite definitive history of how parking became an industry, governments overtaxed motorists, carmakers lied about how safe and environmentally friendly they were and tested their emissions on monkeys and humans. Also why robot cars are so dangerous and electric cars are not the answer. Also, who is behind the ongoing plan to Demotorize the world. Printed in 2020 it predicted the future with terrifying accuracy.
Buy it before it gets banned.

Rabbit Hole Underground Car Park Join the Conspiracy Rabbit as he goes deep, deep undercover to find out why fuels are not fossil, cars that run on water, how those Germans survived WW2, a Jeep that went to the moon, how evil the World Ecommunist Forum is, how to win a war with a pick up truck, why Commies can't build cars, but the Chinese can copy them, all that big trouble in Japan, them electricity cars being a gateway drug, why Castro could not ban cars, but then again who really owns your motor, while at the end of the day: Yuri Bezmenov was right.

The Award Winning and so good the BBC based a documentary (Das Auto) on it **The German Car Industry, My Part in its Victory.** Winner of the Mercedes-Benz Montagu of Beaulieu Trophy for the best motoring book of year. Contains Yuppies, BMW 3, 5, 6 & 7-Series (yes that's all there was back then) and references to contemporary 1980s music.

The Critically acclaimed and best selling **The British Car Industry Our Part in Its Downfall**, which has been described as "Beautifully written with considerable wit" by the Daily Telegraph and The Daily Express said, "It's informative, well-written and extremely funny" which was really nice of them. The story of the motor industry from 1945 to 2005, explaining just why you can't buy a British built family hatchback from a British owned company. Plus all the cars, James's Dad bought.

Channeling the absurdist spirit of Spike Milligan" said Classic Car, others just called it "Witty", that's **My Mini Cooper Its Part in My Breakdown** which has the full history of the world's favourite small car, plus the history of what came before but not after. Also details the on-off restoration of a Mini Cooper that cost £200 in 1979. The expense of restoring the bodywork and mechanicals ought to put off most sane people. Except that original minis are always worth far more than you could imagine.

Ruppert's Bangerpedia deals with the confusing line up of noughties models. The Bangerpedia does this with a fairly ridiculous rating system involving Slog the Bangernomic Dog. The briefest of guides to each of the 700+ models includes some fairly marginal buying advice, a sarcastic appraisal and an almost definitive indication as to whether it will fit into a garage, or not.

Ruppert's Bangerpedia Modern Classic covers the epic '90s decade which was a golden period for Bangers. The Bangerpedia does this with a fairly ridiculous rating system involving Slog the Bangernomic Dog. The briefest of guides to each of the 528+ models includes some fairly marginal buying advice, a sarcastic appraisal and an almost definitive indication as to whether it will fit into your garage, or not.

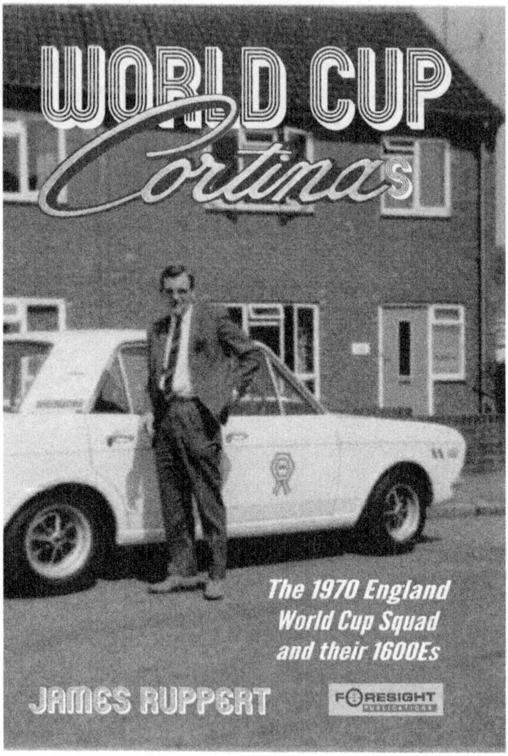

World Cup Cortinas In 1970 something very remarkable happened. Not only had England qualified for the World Cup in Mexico because they were defending champions, but most important of all Ford had loaned every squad member the greatest saloon car in the world. A book about what happened to those Ford Cortinas and how footballers bought better cars when they earned more money and no longer owned the same motors that your mum and dad drove.

Free Car Mag - 0-100 (issues) in 6.9 Years A very brief appreciation of the art of printing car magazines in the UK and a 'how to' guide of how not to do it. In many ways just an excuse to reprint all of our amazing covers in one place purely for reference purposes. It also chronicles how the Mag went from commercial to controversial.

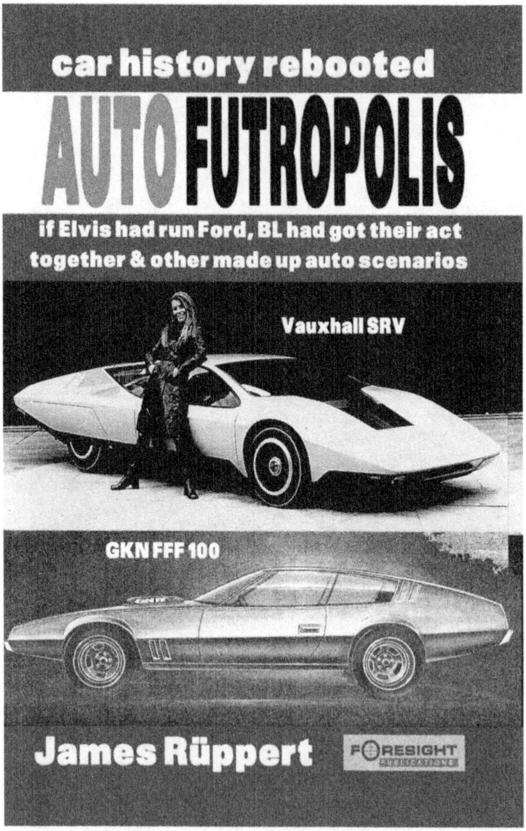

Just imagine if BMC had not been so terrible, that Elvis ran a car company, levitating motors were a reality along with steam powered gentleman's carriages and an electricity car designed by and for gentleladies...well, wonder no more. Here is a fully illustrated book which rewrites and redraws automotive history.

Bangernomics The Board Game Here is a book that thinks it is a board game. Well, you have to take it to bits, but the cover is the actual playing service. All you need to do is pinch a few Matchbox scale models from your toy box and a dice from a proper game like Monopoly. Then set about destroying the book which contains playing cards with Bangers on them. Simply chase your mates around the board)cover of the book and follow the daft instructions. The idea is to get the most Bangers and not to go bankrupt in the process. A bit like real marginal motoring. Fun for all the family. Probably. Contains a fake currency which is not exactly legal tender. You can download all the parts to play, apart from the model car and dice, from Bangernomics.com

Bangernomics Diet is a faux academic course designed to get you a Doctorate on the cheap. It is dead easy, just pay your money and fast forward to the end where you can tear out and frame the Proficiency Certificate, or print it off if you have the digital one. You can then call yourself a Doctor of Bangernomics. Lots of scanned articles from Bangernomics Mag and Free Car Mag, so buy the cheap digital one.

In the beginning, 1993, there was Bangernomics and now there is **Bangernomics Rebooted** which contrasts the absurd expense of buying a new car with the supreme good sense of buying well used. At a stroke depreciation no longer became an issue, running costs were slashed and there were no finance charges to be endured. Here is the original book, republished and effectively rebooted. So it is absolutely useless to any car buyer unless they have access to a time machine.

The world of motoring is in a desperate crisis. Demonised, despised and attacked by every wrong thinking government, local authority, pressure group and even car manufacturers themselves. Bangernomics is here to bring motoring back to the masses, saving time, money and automotive headaches. Squashing together the original Bangernomics, Bangernomics Bible and Bangernomics Diet into one easily digestible guide to buying and running an older cost efficient motor.

Only **Bangernomics can save the World.**

There is a new version of the **Bangernomics Bible**. Most of it is now in the Bangernomics Will Save the World so this has become the top 200 Bangernomic tips. Which may change from time to time.

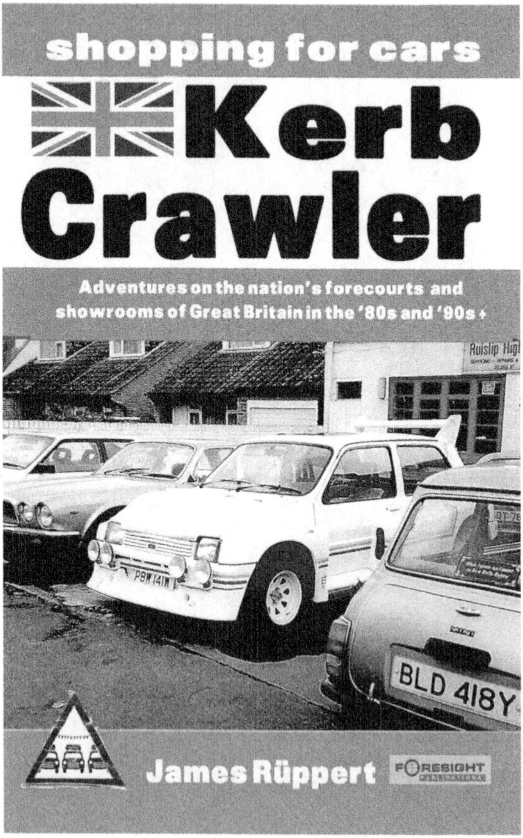

Shopping for cars can be a full time job, well it was for me so here's **Kerbcrawler** In the pre Interweb age it meant actually going to look at cars for sale. It meant talking to the blokes selling the cars face to face. Find out how I got sued by one of the 'stars' of the Italian Job, was told off by the Deputy Prime Minister, find out what the worst car Sir Ian Botham ever owned was, and that time I lent my car to Bjork. A book to dip in and out of...

He was a man running out of time and that time was 1973. **Spencer Haze** is a comic superhero who first hit the 21st century in the year 2000. First on the 4Car website, then later in national newspapers and car magazines. Some say he was even on the television and might well have been real. Here is just about every frame he ever squeezed into, plus a TV script and random pictures that have never been seen before. Here is everything possibly no one ever wanted to know about a fictional bloke called Spencer who loved cars, people and the absolute truth. Here's his **Comicarpocalypse**

The only pro-motorist car mag not in captivity*

It costs nothing, but contains everything you need to be a more anarchistic, bolshie and less co-operative car driver.

***www.freecarmag.com**

Printed in Great Britain
by Amazon

48313763R00175